Nightmares

Your Guide to Interpreting Your Darkest Dreams

J.M. DeBord

About the Author

J. M. DeBord, who is known as RadOwl the Reddit dream expert on the popular website reddit.com, is the author of *Dreams 1-2-3: Remember, Interpret, and Live Your Dreams*. He has appeared as a featured dream expert and dream interpreter on numerous media programs, including *Coast to Coast AM, Darkness Radio,* and *The Moore Show*. He has touched millions of lives with his insights and answers, gaining him international acclaim for his ability to demystify dreams and their interpretation. He has a Bachelor of Arts degree from the University of Cincinnati and lives in Tucson, Arizona.

Nightmares

Your Guide to Interpreting Your Darkest Dreams

J.M. DeBord

Also from Visible Ink Press

Ancient Gods: Lost Histories, Hidden Truths, and the Conspiracy of Silence
By Jim Willis
ISBN 978-1-57859-614-0

Angels A to Z, 2nd edition
By Evelyn Dorothy Oliver and James R. Lewis
ISBN 978-1-57859-212-8

Armageddon Now: The End of the World A to Z
By Jim Willis and Barbara Willis
ISBN 978-1-57859-168-8

The Astrology Book: The Encyclopedia of Heavenly Influences, 2nd edition
By James R. Lewis
ISBN 978-1-57859-144-2

The Dream Encyclopedia, 2nd edition
By James R. Lewis and Evelyn Dorothy Oliver
ISBN 978-1-57859-216-6

The Encyclopedia of Religious Phenomena
By J. Gordon Melton, Ph.D.
ISBN 978-1-57859-209-8

The Fortune-Telling Book: The Encyclopedia of Divination and Soothsaying
By Raymond Buckland
ISBN 978-1-57859-147-3

The Handy Bible Answer Book
By Jennifer R. Prince
ISBN 978-1-57859-478-8

The Handy Islam Answer Book
By John Renard, Ph.D.
ISBN 978-1-57859-510-5

The Handy Mythology Answer Book
By David Leeming, Ph.D.
ISBN 978-1-57859-475-7

The Handy Religion Answer Book, 2nd edition
By John Renard, Ph.D.
ISBN 978-1-57859-379-8

Real Miracles, Divine Intervention, and Feats of Incredible Survival
By Brad Steiger and Sherry Hansen Steiger
ISBN 978-1-57859-214-2

Real Visitors, Voices from Beyond, and Parallel Dimensions
By Brad Steiger and Sherry Hansen Steiger
ISBN 978-1-57859-541-9

The Religion Book: Places, Prophets, Saints, and Seers
By Jim Willis
ISBN 978-1-57859-151-0

The Spirit Book: The Encyclopedia of Clairvoyance, Channeling, and Spirit Communication
By Raymond Buckland
ISBN 978-1-57859-172-5

The Witch Book: The Encyclopedia of Witchcraft, Wicca, and Neo-Paganism
By Raymond Buckland
ISBN 978-1-57859-114-5

Please visit us at www.visibleinkpress.com.

Visible Ink Press®
43311 Joy Rd., #414
Canton, MI 48187-2075

Visible Ink Press is a registered trademark of Visible Ink Press LLC.

Most Visible Ink Press books are available at special quantity discounts when purchased in bulk by corporations, organizations, or groups. Customized printings, special imprints, messages, and excerpts can be produced to meet your needs. For more information, contact Special Markets Director, Visible Ink Press, www.visibleink.com, or 734-667-3211.

Managing Editor: Kevin S. Hile
Art Director: Cinelli Design
Cover Design: Graphikitchen, LLC
Typesetting: Marco Divita
Proofreaders: Larry Baker and Shoshana Hurwitz
Indexer: Larry Baker

Cover images: Shutterstock

ISBN: 978-1-57859-758-1
Library Hardback ISBN: 978-1-57859-809-0
eBook ISBN: 978-1-57859-808-3

Cataloging-in-Publication Data is on file at the Library of Congress.

10 9 8 7 6 5 4 3 2 1

Printed in the United States of America

Table of Contents

Photo Sources

Introduction

The nightmare isn't unusual for a nine-year old. It starts off with me biking around my hometown neighborhood in Dayton, Ohio. I loved riding my bike and dreamed about it frequently. It was just a normal day doing a normal thing. Then I notice a man following me in a black convertible car, maybe a Cadillac. It's 1979 and cars like that are steel and chrome beasts that belch smog and noise. The dream zooms in to his scarred face, evil grin, and feverish eyes burning with diabolical intent. He wants me—wants *my soul.*

My soul. That's a big idea for a nine-year-old. As a kid I didn't think much about it or even know what it was. My family attended church occasionally, and I said my prayers at bedtime. There was a God somewhere up there in the sky, but down here on Earth, on the asphalt streets of my neighborhood, it didn't help me much as I tried desperately to outrun the evil man with the crazy eyes and the icky skin of a cadaver. I heard his terrible laughter, the howl of the predator chasing its prey. Pure terror. If he catches me, I won't just die, I'll lose my soul!

I see a streetside store. People will be inside—they will protect me. Next thing I know, I'm inside the store. It's empty, and there's only one place to hide. In 1979, every convenience store in my town had a pinball machine. I dash behind it, crouch, and wait, cowering against a wood-paneled wall.

In my mind's eye, I see the front of the store. The black car pulls up. The bad man knows where I am. His shadow falls across the entrance. I feel his menace, and I'm trapped. It's the end of all I am and have ever known in my nine years of life. Fade to black.

The horror of the nightmare jolts me awake. *Where am I?* A moment ago, I was trapped in the back of a store waiting to die in a way that would be worse than any movie I'd watched. Not that I'd watched much of anything scary, anyway—our 13-inch television with its telescoping antenna picked up three channels, and Bugs Bunny was my favorite cartoon. I had no conscious memory of ever seeing a scary movie; my parents didn't allow it. The popular ones of the time were *The Amityville Horror* and *Alien*. The evil man's appearance and behavior fit the archetype of the supernatural movie bad guy, but I know that now as an adult. Back then, I lived in a bubble. The world was a safe place. Adults protected me. But no one could protect me from the terrible man who wanted my soul, and nothing could stop him … except by waking from the nightmare in my bed, scared and shaking and realizing where I am.

Introduction

The man was gone. I was safe. For now.

Standard nightmare, right? Sure, it was terrifying, but that's why we call a scary dream a nightmare—we have a special word for the experience. And usually, the nightmare ends and that's it. Wake up, everything's fine, life goes on.

But here's where my story detours into *Black Mirror* territory. A few years later, a dream analyst spoke to my seventh grade enrichment class and asked for volunteers to explore a nightmare that really stuck with them. *Oh yeah, I got one for ya!* During the intervening years, the memory of the undead man who wanted my soul popped up randomly like stepping on a snake, a living thing lying in wait to strike when my eyes were elsewhere. Unforgettable. The analyst used a hypnotic regression process to help me reenter the dream and trace its roots.

There, in my classroom, with my classmates standing in a circle around me, their hands touching my body to anchor me in physical reality, I step back in time to see two families in a feud. Bad blood between them. The analyst asks me to question them about the feud, and all I know is that they hate each other beyond reason. He directs me to speak with them and try to end the feud. Find a compelling reason. I think about it and say, "Fighting is wrong; please stop hurting each other."

Silence. They stare at me. Then all hell breaks loose. Dark words muttered. Murder in their eyes. They close in on me. Danger, danger!

The analyst pulled me out of the hypnosis, and thereafter I was a wounded animal fleeing into my teenage years with that nightmare hunting me. The gash in my psyche left a blood trail. Easy to follow. I had plenty more nightmares—they're common at that age—but the evil man blended into the background. I guess I had new problems to deal with.

Then, during my twenties, he appeared again in my nightmares with the same agenda: hunt me down and claim my soul. I'd be dreaming something ordinary and suddenly a black funnel cloud would bear down like the evil man. Run, run! But never able to get away, just pray and hope that death passes over. I'd wake up screaming, feeling cursed. I gave my soul to Jesus, took it back, gave it again, took it back.

By then I was a wreck. Most nights I went to sleep so intoxicated it's a wonder I dreamed at all.

Then I sobered up and used dreamwork to help me heal. It saved my life but didn't give it back. Not fully, anyway; just enough to keep me going. *Something* still haunted me. I'd encounter people in waking life who had the same diabolical eyes as the evil man, the same lust for fear and ability to appear at just the right time to sidetrack me. I also encountered beings of light and love. They intervened before I could fall into complete despair and never return to this reality.

Soon afterward, though, the encounters would slip from my mind, and I'd question what really happened. Albert Einstein said, "A coincidence is a small miracle when God chooses to remain anonymous." Believing that a supernatural experience is a coincidence or imaginary puts us back to sleep, back under the spell until the next encounter shocks us out of the stupor and we remember with a terrified cry that we fell asleep on the battlefield and the battle still rages. The battle was inside me. Author Nikos Kazantzakis knows what I mean when he says in the opening to his novel *The Last Temptation of Christ*:

> The dual substance of Christ—the yearning, so human, so superhuman, of man to attain God, has always been an inscrutable mystery to me. My principal anguish and source of all my joys and sorrows from my youth onward has been the incessant, merciless battle between the spirit and the flesh, and my soul is the arena where the two armies have clashed and met.

I'd lived long enough to get really angry about being the evil man's plaything. Through dreamwork, meditation, and prayer, I gained the power to fight back, and when his minions came one night in a dream to kidnap me off a dark street and take me to him, I said no, tell me where he is and I'll go to him. I appeared inside a steel office tower with black reflective windows. Top floor. Master suite. His fortress. Dead of night, the witching hour. I see a clear glass coffin in the middle of the spacious room. Inside it lay the evil man, a vampire in his moment of vulnerability.

A trap....

Now I'm standing over the open coffin and seeing him lying there, motionless. He could have walked onto the set of *Star Wars* and played the role of Darth Sidious, the Dark Lord. The face covered in craggy burn scars; the eyes overflowing with sickly power and malevolence; the embodiment of my pain and hate. I grab his neck and choke him, fingers sinking into his rubbery flesh, a dead fish. He just looks me in the eyes, delighted by my skyrocketing rage. I hear his slithery voice in my mind. *Yes! Feed your anger—BE your anger!*

I can't beat him that way. I'll only become him. The nightmare flutters away and dissolves. I'm in my bed. Tears. Anguish. Despair. The battle is hopeless. Death is my only way out. I ask God to take me; I'm ready to go home. Silence is the reply.

The evil man vanished from my dreams for a while. Oddly, the better I handled myself in daily life, the more he appeared in my dreams. And when I was really in a groove, his dark presence congealed behind the scenes, an evil wizard who conjured black magic and sent his minions to work against me. When I was in the gutter, he mostly let me be, and after the encounter with him in his fortress I lost my mojo and slipped back into my old ways.

Introduction

Now I know why. He's a counterforce that's activated by my goodness, and his role is to neutralize me, or better yet, convert me to the Dark Side. It's a role he's played going back countless generations. My nightmares gave him a name: the Dark Master.

Now I ask you: Do you think the Dark Master is just a nightmare figure with no connection to ordinary reality? The nightmare ends, and he no longer exists. The personal encounters I had with him or because of him, some seemingly supernatural, are not proof of his existence outside my nightmares but instead could be what I surmised because of their good vs. evil theme and how it reflected the battle for my soul. After all, he is archetypal, and the definition of archetype is "original form." Archetypes originate from beyond physical reality. Encounters with them stretch the mind to its limits. Some minds break.

As a nine-year old, when the Dark Master first announced his presence in a nightmare that haunted me for the next 30 years, I was a noob when it came to encounters with archetypes, but that makes no difference. The *collective unconscious*, a term coined by Swiss psychiatrist Dr. Carl Jung, is a repository for them and it is most readily accessed while dreaming. It's why we can dream about things we have no experience with or even an inkling of their existence. Dragons, for example, appear as mythological images in all major cultures throughout history, and you can dream about them even if you've never heard of such a thing. Perhaps the Dark Master is like a dragon, dormant down in the mind's deepest cave until awakened. Then it swoops in to protect its treasure: you and me. Our souls.

After all, archetypes assume personalized forms for each of us but exist as countless forms in all of us. You may have encountered the Dark Master, too, and know what it's like to be hunted by what we call *evil*.

I was a good kid overflowing with love and kindness, and my life's trajectory pointed toward great possibilities until something evil tried to destroy me. The fight for my soul compelled me to find answers and learn the truth about nightmares and dark dreams. At the conclusion of this book, I'll give you my answer to whether the Dark Master exists in objective reality and share the explosive finale to a 30-year struggle. The experience changed my life, and that was the point. It may have saved me from a worse fate.

***

There are reasons for nightmares. Some are as simple as bad digestion and illness. Some reasons relate to a person's psychology and emotions, to shocking events and chronic situations, and to trauma, abuse, angst, loss, and death. And some are existential, challenging a person to break a pattern or habitual response or to break out of their shell and claim their greater power. Some cultures perceive living through a nightmare and coming out on top—or just surviving it—as a great accomplishment. It raises the status of the person to the level of a hero who wins the battle and saves their people. In those cultures, nightmares are a calling to greatness.

A calling to greatness. That's a very different way of viewing nightmares than psychology and medicine offer. Trauma may seem like a strange path to greatness but it's how we create our heroes. Boot camp is controlled trauma to the body and mind that produces soldiers who can win wars, for example. Special Forces training is brutal, and the small percentage of recruits who pass the test join an elite club of super-soldiers. Saints often endure terrible ordeals that make them the elite among the clergy and the holy; and shamans find their calling through life-and-death illness of body, mind, and spirit. If they survive, they become heroes entrusted with special knowledge and power. And if they die, well, the next recruit steps up to do battle.

The initiatory ordeals that shamans, saints, soldiers, and other heroes go through are a tacit agreement to be subjected to conditions that make a person become greater than they would be if they were not pushed to their limit and beyond. Some nightmares, especially existential ones, serve the same purpose. It may seem ridiculous that a person would *agree* to have nightmares, even subconsciously, but here's a simple fact about dreams that makes my case: They are self-created experiences. We create them in the subterranean regions of the mind—experiences we perceive and respond to as if they were happening right now.

We give ourselves dreams because of what the experiences offer. It's contrary to the popular belief that dreams happen *to* us, not *for* us, but the logic is undeniable. We create our dreams. We create our nightmares. But why? And what purpose does it serve? The answers to those questions lend guidance for interpreting dark dreams and nightmares and understanding not only their meaning but also the self-created experience of them.

My personal experience with nightmares and decades of experience at dream interpretation give me a special ability to teach you not only how to interpret the content of nightmares but to answer why you have them in the first place and to help you stop having them.

***

Before we launch this ship and sail away into discussion of common symbols and themes in nightmares and dark dreams, you need to be aware of another strange dream phenomenon. Yeah, I already told you about the Dark Master and that's pretty damn strange, but the odyssey we are undertaking presents other mysteries, and as your captain, there's only so much I can do to prepare you before you find out for yourself. I'm referring to a special type of nightmare that defies conventional interpretation techniques: the generational nightmare.

Heads up! You may never encounter this beast in the wild, and dream analysts in the comfort of their office may encounter it only a few times in their careers. They may not recognize the thing that confronts them, that swats away their attempts to penetrate its secrets and scrutinize its origins. Search every book about the psychology of dreams and the techniques for interpreting them, and you may find a hint or two. Most people, even the most learned in the ways of dreams, do not know much about generational nightmares.

The gist is that the extremes of trauma, violence, and brutality create memories that pass down to the next generations. It may be trauma experienced by individuals, families, communities, races, or nations. DNA is a wonderful storage system, and inside each of us are the encoded memories of our ancestors. We may even be aware that their experiences shape our instincts, affecting us from within, and are presented to us as if those memories are *one's own*—to my knowledge, that part is not yet proven, but I've run across tantalizing evidence. But few of us know that generational memories can take form as nightmares and whack us from out of nowhere with the full force of what our ancestors experienced.

For one man, the generational nightmares recurred as the imagery of a black wave of death sweeping across the landscape. Seeing through the eyes of someone who is not him but who feels familiar, he and the other people with him in the nightmares look to the horizon and know what's coming. They can't escape the black wave—there's nowhere to run or hide—and they will all die when it reaches them. You can look up the entry "Tidal Waves/Tsunamis/Floods" in this book and get great ideas about the various ways of interpreting it as a dream symbol. You can use techniques of dream interpretation to try to understand what the black wave symbolizes. But it'll do you no good in this case because it symbolizes the Nazi war machine sweeping across Poland in 1939, and the eyes out of which the man sees it are an ancestor's who lived and died there.

The man had tried everything to understand his nightmares and couldn't put his finger on their source. None of the standard ways of interpreting them rang his bell of recognition. Then a simple question did the trick. Did your ancestors experience a black wave of terror? The Nazi death machine was as black as it gets. He immediately recognized the monster devouring the landscape that he saw through the eyes of his ancestor. Or maybe it wasn't one ancestor but several of them who experienced that tragedy together and passed on the memory to him.

You may ask, if they all died, how did their DNA pass on to him? The answer is found in a hypothesis that memory is ubiquitous, stored not only in brain cells and DNA, and the ability to access memories that don't originate with oneself is like tuning a radio to a station. Generational nightmares tap the memories of people who are close to one's personal wavelength. Naturally, ancestors resonate personally, but other factors like mutual circumstances, conditions, and interests resonate, too.

Carl Jung experienced something similar before the Nazi wave swept over the world. During the 1920s and '30s, from his office in Switzerland, he encountered Wotan, the German god of war, in the dreams of his German patients, and it baffled him. He could find no psychological source in his patients to explain the blood lust that manifested in their dreams. For the most part, they were psychologically healthy, urbane people—not savage killers. Sure, they had their problems and that's why they sought

Dr. Jung's help, but they weren't psychotic. He knew well that dream imagery of the Wotan variety could be a dramatization of inner conflicts and personal issues, but the learned Swiss physician tested and probed and analyzed his patients and came up empty. Only after the fact did he fully realize the archetypal source of the imagery and the unique manifestation of it as Wotan in the German psyche. Talk about a harbinger!

Generational nightmares may replay the memories verbatim, and as a descendant you may vividly experience the terror and pain of your ancestors as your own. But the few cases of generational nightmares with which I danced presented the memories wrapped in symbolic imagery like revelers at a costume ball, and the cushion it provides from the true horror lurking behind the mask may be a blessing because once you see into the eyes of that Medusa, you may never be able to look away.

* * *

Past lives are another phenomenon that may instigate nightmares. Bad things happen, and like with generational nightmares, their energetic power carves a groove into the record of time and carries it forward to be remembered by dreaming through the eyes of the people you were in past lives. You may see the joys you experienced, the loved ones you were close to, the places you lived, the roles you played, and the things that interested you. And you may see and *re-experience* the tragedies and terrors.

One man re-experienced a terrible event that happened during the U.S. Civil War. In the recurring nightmare, he's a Confederate soldier fighting on the front lines near his home. The Union army breaks through the lines and overruns the area. He deserts his post and runs home in the dead of night, but he's too late. Union soldiers have set fire to his plantation home. He hears screams and terrified cries as he hides in the bushes and watches his family members flee the burning home and be slaughtered. He's ashamed of himself for hiding instead of running out and dying, but he knows that his death won't accomplish anything.

The nightmare repeated exactly night after night, and with each retelling it left out more of the opening scene and focused more on the scene at the house. Blood and guts and pain. The slaughter is super-vivid, and his feelings of anguish and despair are beyond words.

I'm well-acquainted with the reasons behind recurring nightmares, and I'm an expert at decoding symbolism and analyzing dreams. But in the above case, it only helped me rule out the obvious possible causes, such as a terrible family life or powerlessness or a raging sense of injustice. See, when I began discussing those nightmares with the man who experienced them, I didn't know that they all happened *before he turned four years old.* Roughly half of children between ages three and six experience frequent nightmares. There's much about the world they are starting to experience that frightens them. But the extraordinary content and adult themes of his nightmares are way beyond what most young children experience, giving their dreaming mind nothing to build such a complex story around. Past-life memories are the most likely source. I can't say for sure—what I know for sure is that the past life phenomenon is real, that bad things happen, that the memories are ubiquitous, and that they can enter our dreams. We can even dream about scenes from the past lives of other people.

I've encountered dreams that put you in the scene of real murders; dreams that foresee coming natural and man-made disasters; dreams that probe the black heart of psychopaths; dreams that create shared spaces for multiple people to come together while dreaming; and dreams that open doorways for contact with inhuman entities with awesome intelligence and power. I would say that I've seen it all, but I know better than to make that claim—I'm sure more surprises are ahead. I'll teach you as much as I can while keeping the discussion grounded in the proven techniques of dream interpretation and conventional dream theory. A fascinating voyage awaits you.

All right, shipmates, let's set sail!

Prologue

The nightmare isn't unusual for a nine-year-old kid. It starts off with me biking around my hometown neighborhood in Dayton, Ohio—I loved riding my bike and dreamed about it frequently—just a normal day doing a normal thing when I notice a man following me in a black car, maybe a Cadillac. The year is 1979, and the car is a beast made of steel and chrome. The dream zooms in to the man's scarred face, evil grin, and eyes burning with diabolical intent. He wants me—wants *my soul*.

My soul. That's a big idea for a nine-year-old. As a kid, I didn't think much about it or even know what it was. I said my prayers at bedtime, thinking a god was somewhere up in the sky, but it didn't help me much down here on Earth, on the asphalt streets of my neighborhood, while trying desperately to outrun the evil man. I hear his terrible laughter, the howl of the predator closing in on its prey. Pure terror. If he catches me, I won't just die, I'll lose my soul!

I see a streetside store. People will be inside—they will protect me. Now, I'm inside the store, but it's empty, and I see only one place to hide. In 1979, every convenience store in my town had a pinball machine. I dash behind it and cower against a wood-paneled wall.

In my mind's eye, I see the storefront. The shiny Cadillac pulls up. The bad man knows where I am. His shadow falls across the entrance. I'm trapped. It's the end of all that I am and have ever known in my nine years of life. Fade to black.

The horror of the nightmare slaps me awake. *Where am I?* A moment ago, I was about to die in a way that would be much worse than any movie I'd ever watched—not that I'd seen much of anything scary, anyway. Bugs Bunny was my favorite cartoon, and my parents didn't let me watch scary movies. The popular ones of the time were *The Amityville Horror* and *Alien*. The behavior and appearance of the man in my nightmare fit the archetypal mold of a movie bad guy with supernatural powers, but that's only something I know now as an adult. As a kid, I lived in a bubble. The world was a safe place. Adults protected me. But no one could protect me from the evil man who wanted my soul, and only by waking up from the nightmare safe in my bed was I saved.

Standard nightmare, right? Sure, it was terrifying, but usually, a nightmare ends, you wake up, and everything's fine. Life goes on. End of story. But here's where my story detours into *Black Mirror* territory. A few years later, a dream analyst spoke to my seventh-grade enrichment class and asked for volunteers to explore a nightmare that really stuck with them. *Oh, yeah, I've got one for ya!* During the intervening years, the memory of the undead man who tried to take my soul popped up randomly like a snake hidden in the grass of time. Unforgettable. The analyst used a hypnotic regression process to help me re-enter the dream and trace its roots.

There, in the classroom, with my classmates around me, I stepped back in time to see two families in a feud. Bad blood between them. The analyst asked me to question them about the feud, and all I could find out was that they hated each other. He directed me to speak with them and try to end the feud, to find a compelling reason for it. I thought about it and said, "Fighting is wrong; please stop hurting each other."

They stared at me. I felt hopeful. Then, all hell broke loose. Dark words were muttered. Murder showed in their eyes. They closed in. *Danger, danger!*

The analyst eased me out of the hypnosis, and thereafter, I was a wounded animal fleeing into my teenage years with that nightmare hot on my tail. The gash in my psyche left a blood trail. Easy to follow. I had plenty more nightmares—they're common at that age—but the evil man blended into the background. I had new problems to deal with.

Then, during my twenties, he appeared again in my nightmares with the same agenda to hunt me down and claim my soul. Sometimes, I'd be having an ordinary dream when suddenly, a black funnel cloud would bear down like the evil man. *Run, run!* But I was never able to get away and only managed to pray and hope that death passed over. I'd wake up screaming, feeling cursed. I gave my soul to Jesus, took it back, gave it again, took it back.

By then, I was a wreck. Most nights, I went to sleep so intoxicated, it's a wonder I dreamed at all.

Then, I sobered up and used dreamwork to help me heal. It saved my life but didn't give it back. Not fully, just enough to keep me going. *Something* still haunted me. I'd encounter people in my waking life who had the same diabolical eyes as the evil man, the same lust for fear and ability to enter the scene at just the right moment to sidetrack me. I also encountered beings of light and love. They intervened before I could fall into total despair and never return to this reality.

Soon afterward, though, the encounters would slip from my mind, and I'd question what really happened. Albert Einstein once said, "A coincidence is a small miracle when God chooses to remain anonymous." Believing that a supernatural experience is coincidental or imaginary lulls us back to sleep and under a spell until the next encounter shocks away the stupor and we remember with a terrified cry that we fell asleep on the battlefield and the battle still rages. The battle was inside of me for my soul. Author Nikos Kazantzakis knows what I mean when he says in the opening to his novel *The Last Temptation of Christ*:

"The dual substance of Christ—the yearning, so human, so superhuman, of man to attain God ... has always been an inscrutable mystery to me. My principal anguish and source of all my joys and sorrows from my youth onward has been the incessant, merciless battle between the spirit and the flesh ... and my soul is the arena where the two armies have clashed and met."

> **Sometimes, I'd be having an ordinary dream when suddenly, a black funnel cloud would bear down like the evil man. *Run, run!* But I was never able to get away....**

I'd lived long enough to get pissed off about being the evil man's plaything, and through dreamwork, meditation, and prayer, I gained the power to fight back. When his minions came one night in a dream to kidnap me off a dark street and take me to him, I said no, tell me where he is. I'll go to him. Time to end this.

Now, I'm inside a steel office tower with black, reflective windows. Top floor. Master suite. His fortress. I see a clear, glass coffin in the middle of the sterile, spacious room. Inside it lay the evil man, a vampire in a moment of vulnerability.

A trap?

I'm standing over the open coffin and seeing him lying there motionless. He could have walked onto the set of *Star Wars* and played the role of Darth Sidious, the Dark Lord. His face was covered in craggy burn scars; his eyes were overflowing with sickly power and malevolence. He embodied all my pain and hate. I grabbed his neck and choked him, my fingers sinking into his rubbery flesh. A dead fish. He just looked at me, delighted by my skyrocketing rage. I hear his slithery voice in my mind. *Yes! Feed your anger—BE your anger!*

But I can't beat him that way. I realize while dreaming that I'll only become him. The nightmare flutters away and dissolves. I'm in my bed. Tears. Anguish. Despair. The battle is hopeless. Death is my only way out. I ask God to take me; I'm ready to go home. Silence is the reply.

The evil man vanished from my dreams for a while. Oddly, the better I handled myself in daily life, the more he appeared in my dreams. And when I was really in a groove, his dark presence congealed behind the scenes, an evil wizard who conjured black magic and sent his minions to work against me. When I was in the gutter, he mostly let me be, and after the encounter with him in his fortress, I lost my mojo and slipped back into my old ways.

Now I know why. He's a counterforce that's activated by my goodness, and his role is to neutralize me or, better yet, to convert me to the Dark Side. It's a role he's played going back countless generations. My nightmares gave him a name: the Dark Master.

Now, I ask you, do you think the Dark Master is just a nightmare figure with no connection to physical reality? The nightmare ends, and he no longer exists. The encounters I had with him, or because of him, are not proof of his existence outside my nightmares, but the "good versus evil" theme sure made me think so. After all, he is archetypal, and archetypes have one foot in ordinary reality and one in a reality beyond it. Encounters with them stretch the mind to its limits. Some minds break.

As a nine-year-old when the Dark Master first announced his presence in a nightmare that haunted me for the next 30 years, I was a noob when it came to encounters with archetypes, but that makes no difference. The collective unconscious, a term coined by Swiss psychiatrist Dr. Carl Jung, is a repository for them that's most readily accessed while dreaming. It's why we can dream about things we have no experience with or have even an inkling of their existence. Dragons, for example, appear as mythological images in all major cultures throughout history, and you can dream about them even if you've never heard of such a thing. Perhaps the Dark Master is like a dragon, dormant down in the mind's deepest cave until awakened. Then, it swoops in to protect its treasure: you and me. Our souls. Archetypes assume personalized forms for each of us but exist as countless forms in all of us. You may have encountered the Dark Master, too, and know what it's like to be hunted by what we call *evil*.

The famous psychiatrist Dr. Carl Jung gave us the concept of "archetype imagery," universal symbols from mythology, literature, art, fairy tales, and religion that we all understand to imbue distinctive meanings.

I was a good kid, and my life's trajectory pointed toward great possibilities until something evil tried to destroy me. The fight for my soul compelled me to find answers and learn the truth about nightmares and dark dreams. In the epilogue of this book, I'll give you my answer to whether the Dark Master exists in objective reality and share the explosive finale to a 30-year struggle. The experience changed my life, and that was the point. It may have saved me from a worse fate.

***

Nightmares occur for several reasons, some as simple as bad digestion or illness. Some reasons relate to a person's psychology or emotions, some as a response to shocking events or chronic situations, and some resulting from trauma, abuse, angst, loss, or death. Others are existential, challenging a person to break a pattern or habitual response or to break out of their shell and claim their greater power. Some cultures perceive living through a nightmare and coming out on top—or just surviving it—as a great accomplishment. It raises the status of the person to the level of a hero. In those cultures, nightmares are a calling to greatness.

A calling to greatness. That's a very different way of viewing nightmares than psychology and medicine offer. Trauma may seem like a strange path to greatness, but it's how we create our heroes. Boot camp is controlled trauma to the body and mind that produces soldiers who can win wars, for example. Special Forces training is brutal, and the small percentage of recruits who pass the test join an elite club of supersoldiers. Saints often endure terrible ordeals that make them the elite among the clergy and the holy, and shamans find their calling through life-and-death illnesses of the body, mind, and spirit. If they survive, they become heroes entrusted with special knowledge and power. And if they die, well, the next recruit steps up to do battle.

The initiatory ordeals that shamans, saints, soldiers, and other heroes go through are tacit agreements to be subjected to challenges that drive a person to become greater than they would be if they were not pushed beyond their limits. Some nightmares, especially the existential ones, serve the same purpose. It may seem ridiculous that a person would *agree* to have nightmares, even subconsciously, but a simple fact about dreams that makes my case is that they are self-created experiences. We create them in the subterranean regions of the mind—experiences we perceive and respond to as if real. We give ourselves dreams because of what the experiences offer. It's contrary to the popular belief that dreams happen *to* us, not *for* us, but the logic is undeniable. We create our dreams. We create our nightmares. But why? What purpose does it serve? The answers to those questions lend guidance to interpreting dark dreams and nightmares and understanding not only their meaning but the self-created experience of them.

My personal experience with nightmares and how to interpret them give me a special ability to teach you not only how to understand their content but to answer why you have them in the first place. Understand the message of a nightmare, and it will stop haunting you.

***

Before we launch this ship and sail away into a discussion of common symbols and themes in nightmares and dark dreams, you need to be aware of another strange dream phenomenon. Yeah, I already told you about the Dark Master, and that's pretty damn strange, but the odyssey we are undertaking presents other mysteries. I'm referring to a special type of nightmare that defies conventional interpretation techniques: the generational nightmare.

Heads up! You may never encounter this beast in the wild, and dream analysts may encounter it only a few times in their careers and not recognize the thing that confronts them, that swats away their attempts to penetrate its secrets and scrutinize its origins. Search any book about the psychology of dreams, and you may find a hint or two. Most people, even the most learned in the ways of dreams, do not know much about generational nightmares.

The gist is that the extremes of trauma, violence, and brutality create memories that pass down to the following generations. It may be trauma experienced by individuals, families, communities, races, or nations. Inside of each of us are the encoded memories of our ancestors. We may be aware that their experiences shape and affect us and are presented to us as if the memories are *our own* but not know that *their* memories can take form as *our* nightmares and whack us out of nowhere with the full force of what they experienced.

For one man, the generational nightmares recurred as the imagery of a black wave of death sweeping across a rural landscape. Seeing through the eyes of someone who feels familiar but is unknown to him, he looks to the horizon and knows that he can't escape the black wave. It's a symbol for the Nazi war machine sweeping across Poland in 1939, and the eyes from which he sees it are an ancestor's who lived and died there. He'd tried everything to understand his recurring nightmares but couldn't put his finger on their source. None of the standard ways of interpreting them rang his bell of recognition. Then, a simple question did the trick: Did your ancestors experience a black wave of terror? The Nazi death machine was as black as it got. He immediately recognized the monster in his nightmares, and the realization hit him full force.

You may ask, if his ancestor died, how did the memory pass on to him? The answer is found in a hypothesis that memory is ubiquitous, not just stored in brain cells and DNA. Accessing memories that don't originate with oneself is like tuning a radio to a station. Generational nightmares tap the memories of people who are close to one's personal wavelength. Naturally, ancestors resonate personally, but other factors, like mutual circumstances, conditions, and interests, resonate, too.

Dr. Carl Jung experienced something similar before the Nazi wave swept over the world. During the 1920s and '30s, from his office in Switzerland, he encountered Wotan, the German god of war, in the dreams of his German patients, and it baffled him. He could find no psychological source in his patients to explain the bloodlust that manifested in their dreams. For the most part, they were psychologically healthy, urbane people—not savage killers. Sure, they had their problems, and that's why they sought Dr. Jung's help, but they weren't psychotic. He knew well that dream imagery of the Wotan variety could be a dramatization of inner conflicts and personal issues, but the learned Swiss physician tested, probed, and analyzed his patients and came up empty. Only after the fact did he fully realize the archetypal source of the imagery and the unique manifestation of it as Wotan in the German psyche. Talk about a harbinger!

Generational nightmares may replay the memories verbatim, and as a descendant, you may vividly experience the terror and pain of your ancestors as your own, but the few cases of generational nightmares I danced with presented the memories wrapped in symbolic imagery, and the cushion the costume provides from the true horror lurking behind the mask is a blessing because you may never be able to look away after staring into the eyes of that Medusa.

Past lives are another phenomenon that may instigate nightmares. Bad things happen, and similar to generational nightmares, their energetic power carves a groove in the record of time and carries forward. You may dream about the joys you experienced, the loved ones you were close to, the places you lived in, the roles you played, and the things that interested you, but you may also see, and *reexperience*, the tragedies and terrors.

> **Generational nightmares may replay the memories verbatim, and as a descendant, you may vividly experience the terror and pain of your ancestors as your own....**

One man reexperienced a terrible event that happened during the U.S. Civil War. In the recurring nightmare, he's a Confederate soldier fighting on the front lines near his home. The Union army breaks through the lines and overruns the area. He deserts his post and runs home in the dead of night, but he's too late. Union soldiers have set fire to his plantation home. Hiding in the bushes, he hears terrified screams and watches the slaughter of his family as they flee the burning home. He's ashamed of himself for hiding instead of running out and dying, but he knows that his death won't accomplish anything.

The nightmare repeated exactly night after night, and with each retelling, it left out more of the opening scene and focused more on the scene at the house. Blood, guts, and pain. His feelings of anguish and despair were beyond words.

I'm well acquainted with the reasons behind recurring nightmares, and I'm an expert at decoding symbolism and analyzing dreams, but in the above case, it only helped me rule out the obvious possible causes, such as a terrible family life or a raging sense of injustice. See, when I began discussing those nightmares with the man who experienced them, I didn't know that they all happened *before he turned 4 years old*. Roughly half of children between the ages of three and six experience frequent nightmares because they are starting to experience much about the world that frightens them, but the extraordinary content and adult themes of this man's childhood nightmares are way beyond what most young children experience. His dreaming mind possessed nothing from personal experience and memory to build such a complex story around. Past-life memories are the most likely source. I can't say for sure. What I do know for sure, though, is that the past-life phenomenon is real, that bad things happen, that their memories are ubiquitous, and that they can enter our dreams. We can even dream about scenes from the past lives of other people.

I've encountered dreams that put people into the scenes of real murders; dreams that foresee coming disasters; dreams that probe the black hearts of psychopaths; dreams that create shared spaces for multiple people to come together while dreaming; and dreams that open doorways for contact with non-human entities with awesome intelligence and power. I would say that I've seen it all, but I know better than to make that claim—I'm sure more surprises are ahead. I'll teach you as much as I can while keeping the discussion grounded in the proven techniques of dream interpretation and conventional dream theory. A fascinating voyage awaits you.

All right, shipmates, let's set sail!

Monsters and Creatures

Surprisingly, while scary movies, novels, and video games are full of monsters, nightmares are not—at least, not the classic monsters we all know best. A nightmare could involve a small mouse pursuing you, and it makes no sense why you would run away in terror, but you do anyway, and the reason is because you know subconsciously what the mouse symbolizes. It could symbolize a small problem or defect in your character, and you run away because you refuse to face it; what makes dreaming about it a nightmare is your reaction to it—you react to what it symbolizes. As you are dreaming, you sense and react more to what you know subconsciously and less so to what you see. For that reason, nightmares don't need monsters—they can pack their terror in the form of symbols.

Then again, plenty of nightmares feature monsters. Dreams are deliberate about their choice of imagery and how they construct stories. Think of it as like the author of a novel making choices specifically to fit the story and touch the reader. After all, the author of dreams knows you better than you know yourself. It sees not only what is conscious about you but also what's subconscious—below the threshold of conscious awareness—and unconscious, buried even deeper in your psyche. You can bet that a monster or creature in a nightmare is chosen deliberately for what it means symbolically, what it means to you personally, and how you react to it.

If my dreams tried to scare me with an image of Frankenstein, for example, it may not be the best choice for the role because I feel sympathy for "the monster" and its plight. Plus, anyone who's seen the "Puttin' on the Ritz" scene in the movie *Young Frankenstein* may find it hard to ever fear a tap-dancing, lovable hulk. It's not to say that those personal associations will automatically come to mind if I see Frankenstein in a dream, but the author of my dreams has better options if it wants to scare me. It doesn't need a monster—just put a dangerous snake in the scene with me. Instant nightmare!

When interpreting the meaning of monsters and creatures, look first at their symbolism. Begin with the simple idea and analyze how it fits into the story. For instance, something in your life or in yourself is "a monster to deal with," and the author of the dream expresses the idea by telling a story about dealing with a monster. Unstoppable addiction is a monster. Serious illness is a monster. Terrible stress is a monster. The monster in your nightmare is a symbol, and the meaning is embedded within it. It's only a monster in the figurative sense.

Dreams help us digest emotions, and difficult emotions are a common source of nightmares. Undigested emotions are a common source of recurring nightmares, so as you analyze a dream, focus on the emotions. Let them speak to you. Search your memory for recent instances of experiencing them. Look for patterns of when and why you experience them. *All* dream symbols have an emotional component, and for some people, dream analysis works best by simply looking closely at their emotions; by digesting them, they find resolution to their nightmares. It really can be that simple.

A monster in your dream can be a symbol for many things, including life challenges, people who are being aggressive towards you, fears about unknowns in the future, or physical or emotional difficulties.

ALIENS

The first monster on our list is common in dark dreams, but it's not always nightmare material because one person's fear-inducing, cattle-mutilating alien is another person's cosmic friend and savior from space. Plus, by aliens, do we mean the inhuman greys with large, black eyes; the tall Nordics who can pass as humans; the xenomorphs from the *Alien* movies; or the Klingons from *Star Trek*? Each carries specific associations popularized by media and culture, and their meaning varies from benign to deadly in dreams.

Associations are where you begin with any dream symbol. They are the thoughts, memories, emotions, feelings, impressions, and perceptions that come to mind as you think about the symbol. If you associate aliens or a certain type of alien with something monstrous, scary, dark, and so forth, it gives your dream author the perfect type of character for expressing the idea symbolically.

Aliens may play the role of monsters when the meaning relates to powerlessness. It's a common role for aliens in dark dreams because humans are powerless against creatures from civilizations that possess abilities and technology way beyond ours. *Struggle all you want, Earthling, you are powerless against us!* When a dream presents such a scenario, you ask yourself, what am I up against that seems more powerful than me? A faceless bureaucracy that's out to get you, for example. A bureaucracy is distant, unfeeling, and even inhuman in how it can treat people, and you may perceive aliens that way, too. Now, you are dreaming about a bureaucracy or similar sort of powerful, distant group, and aliens symbolize it.

Aliens are perfect for the role when you are powerless against an addiction or compulsion that makes you unrecognizable to yourself. Your personality has a dark side that's so disconnected from your self-image, it's best described as *alien* to you. Aliens are also perfect symbols for overwhelming emotions that seem to come out of nowhere, like aliens teleporting into your bedroom. Aliens teleport into your dreams when something about them matches well with a situation or your personal psychology.

The following dream demonstrates a variation of the idea. It starts off with a scene where the dreamer is a member an army that uses advanced technology to fight against wave after wave of aliens. They battle until the end of time, then time starts over at the beginning, a new wave of aliens appears, and the battle continues. Her role in the story is logistical, and both her role and the story itself are really about her job in the front office of a school. The never-ending battle against the aliens dramatizes her battle against an onslaught of work. Battling the aliens until time starts over relates to how the end of one grading period leads to the start of the next one. Her job requires her to be logistical, which is the same as her role in the dream, and she utilizes advanced technology—computers, smartphones, software—to her advantage for a mission that feels overwhelming at times, the same as in the dream.

Fear is a common meaning for aliens in dreams. For some people, aliens represent their greatest fear because they have no base of reference. They can understand a violent animal or a deranged person. They can even understand most types of monsters, but aliens are from other worlds and don't behave according to human rationality, and fear can also be irrational, providing the dream author with a symbol whenever it wants to speak to incomprehensible and irrational fear.

> **Aliens are also perfect symbols for overwhelming emotions that seem to come out of nowhere, like aliens teleporting into your bedroom.**

In that sense, aliens in dreams can symbolize ideas found in phrases like *failure to communicate* and *meet eye to eye*. We may think or say, "Are you from another planet or something?" to express the ideas of incomprehension and irrationality. The alien says in reply, "Why, yes—yes, I am from another planet."

Aliens can drop in suddenly and radically change a person's life, and they are believed to abduct people from their homes. Now, imagine how the author of a dream can use those associations to symbolize situations in life. A big change comes out of nowhere, or someone unexpected shows up at your door and turns your life upside down. The news is full of ominous warnings about things that have or could have a big impact, or something beyond your control takes you away from your place of comfort and familiarity, like in the dream a young adult had about aliens in a spaceship appearing outside his bedroom window and taking him away from his family home. In his waking life, he's facing a situation where he wants employment but can't find it in the rural area where he lives. He can move to a city where it would be easier to find a job, and it feels like he has no other choice. The dream captures the situation's dynamics by presenting a scenario where aliens abduct him and take him away. It expresses the idea like a metaphor by making a comparison between alien abduction and feeling forced to leave his home.

Dreams play with language to connect ideas together, and the word "alien" also means foreign in the sense of "the concept is foreign." You encounter something in your life or in yourself that you don't understand, relate to, or feel part of—it is foreign to you. It's alien, and what better way for a dream to say "alien" than by using an actual alien? Dreams can use the same play on words to mean alienated, estranged, or isolated. The member of a team

The qualities of aliens that we hear from various stories involve creatures that come out of nowhere and impose their will upon us. In this way, they can symbolize something or someone who comes into your life unexpectedly and affects your life in undesirable ways.

that doesn't fit in; the black sheep of the family; the shut-in who never goes out in public. They are said to be alienated.

A person can be alienated or estranged from themselves, too—a situation ripe for nightmares involving aliens. Dreams want to reunite a person with the parts of themselves that are split off and alienated from the ego, but the psychology behind such internal splits can spell trouble if the ego resists or rejects something about itself that's unwanted or suppressed. Antagonism and hostility between parts of oneself are often behind powerful nightmares that involve aliens and monsters.

In a dream that plays on that idea, aliens perform surgery on the dreamer's brain. She hasn't been feeling like her usual self lately, and her thoughts have been going to strange places. The dream turns the situation into a story featuring aliens, meaning "alien to me," and brain surgery, meaning "alterations to thought processes."

Aliens can even represent something such as an ability, talent, or gift that's unintegrated with your personality. It's a lost child returning nightly to find its way home, and the longer it remains alienated from the personality, the more desperate it becomes and the more amplified and powerful are the dreams. When aliens look like children in dreams, a strong possibility is that they symbolize long-lost aspects of oneself.

Dr. Carl Jung theorized that the explosion of UFO sightings post–World War II resulted in part due to our mass alienation from the roots of authentic human experience. Plus, humanity faced the new threat of global annihilation from nuclear weapons—high-tech bombs that drop from the sky like alien spacecraft. We can march forward in life for only so long while under existential threat and disconnected from our psychological roots before instigating a strong pushback from the unconscious mind. When we can't step away under our own power to prioritize a life of meaning, the unconscious does it for us—forcefully. For some people, it means a midlife crisis, initiation ordeal, or psychological breakdown, and for others, it means manifesting the paranormal into their reality and the creation of initiation experiences that crack open the ego so it can know a greater reality.

> **Dr. Carl Jung theorized that the explosion of UFO sightings post–World War II resulted in part due to our mass alienation from the roots of authentic human experience.**

For dark dreams about alien abduction, the roots may be found in psychological possession, covered in the Possession entry.

A method of interpreting dreams is to restate them simply. When aliens invade your dreams, you restate the scenario as "something foreign or unknown can't be stopped or is unwelcome." Then, you search for the parallel with what's happening in your life. For example, unusual thoughts or emotions invade your mind. Germs invade your body. A virus invades your computer. A person or problem invades your life.

Dreams about an alien invasion increase when the news is full of reports about one country invading or threatening to invade another. It's an easy connection to make considering that alien also means "foreign," and foreigners are invading or threatening to invade.

A curious phenomenon is found in the prevalence of aliens and related imagery (flying saucers, Men in Black) in the dreams of people experiencing spiritual and psychic awakenings. They say that they interact with an alien intelligence teaching them advanced spiritual lessons and mental abilities and that they are being prepared for a mass change in humanity, a raising of the collective consciousness, or an apocalypse. The dreams recur, sometimes over years or decades, and may be better described as a dreamlike state of consciousness.

The experiences can result from sleep paralysis, mental illness, or drugs that cause mental dissociation from the body, but when those possibilities are ruled out, it leaves us with the possibility that they're real! Either way, analyze them as real; that's our approach to all dreams. They are experiences—occurrences—things that happen—not hallucinations or figments of imagination. Revelations from experimental science and disclosures from secret government programs have *proven* the existence of layers to physical reality that are far different from what we know. Unbeknownst to the public, and according to whistleblowers, contact between humans and aliens is treated as fact, not fiction, in some of the darkest corners of the covert world.

Another reason why aliens appear in dreams—the worst sorts of nightmares in some cases—relates to sleep paralysis, a condition of the body while experiencing vivid dreams. The medical literature refers to it as atonia, which means "muscle slackness." To prevent you from physically reacting to dreams, your brain sends signals to the spinal cord to paralyze your arms and legs. It's normal, but people can wake up and still be dreaming and paralyzed, and it scares the bejesus out of them. Since they are still dreaming and dream imagery responds to what they sense and feel, their dreaming mind translates their fear into imagery based on their worst fears: cue aliens in their bedroom.

And here's a twist: you open your eyes and become aware of what's going on, but you are still dreaming, and the dream imagery *augments* your waking reality. You don't know what's real and what's not. According to Dr. Carl Jung, dreaming is a function of the mind that never stops—it recedes into the background while a person is awake and may intrude into consciousness when boundaries are thin or while sleep deprived or mentally ill. Research has correlated it with near-death experience, out-of-body experience, time distortions, and other trippiness. And it so happens that many reports of alien abduction begin with statements such as "I was in my bed asleep and suddenly woke up paralyzed and terrified, then I saw the aliens." Those are REM intrusions or sleep-paralysis episodes—probably. Ask rock star Sammy Hagar about his alien contact experience, and he'll tell you that it's real.

Use the list below to look up discussions in this book that may give you more ideas about how to understand dreams about aliens.

See also: Apocalypses, Black-eyed People, Demons, Paralysis, Possession, Shadow People

BLACK-EYED PEOPLE

Here we have another type of monster that's easily misunderstood as encounters with actual beings. The experiences feel so real, it's natural to think that something supernatural visited you in your dream, but black-eyed people are dream characters and thought of as walking, talking symbols. The black eyes are part of the symbolism of the character, and they hint at the answer to the first question you should ask about any dream character: What do I see about myself in it? Eyes are said to be the windows to the soul, showing what's inside of a person. If a dream character has black eyes, it's hard to see much. It's not to say that nothing is inside of you; instead, it suggests something unknown about you.

The psychology of the subject is deep, but in a nutshell, while dreaming, you interact with emerging contents of the unconscious mind. By nature, it's new to the ego—the "you" in the dream space. You are seeing what's new in yourself, and because it's new, it's mysterious and unknown consciously, but it arises from the unconscious mind, and the unconscious knows everything about you. It creates not only your dream content but plays a co-creative role with the ego in creating the person—you—and when it wants you to see something new about yourself, it creates a humanlike dream character. The unconscious then may add features to the character to symbolically show you something about yourself that it knows but your ego doesn't, and black eyes are the number-one way that dreams say symbolically, "You can't *see* this part of yourself … yet."

We use our eyes to see, and in dream-speak, to "see" means to know, to comprehend. Like when you say, "A-ha, I see it now!," you mean that the light

Black eyes in a dream may be saying that you are being prevented from seeing something or that you are suffering from grief or loss.

bulb of comprehension switches on. You comprehend, and you are no longer "in the dark." Other possibilities of its meaning branch off that main idea. Black eyes can symbolize what you don't know about yourself and what you don't *want* to know—it's suppressed or new and mysterious. A subject of study is new to you, and you dream about a teacher of that subject with black eyes. You try to get to know a mysterious person and dream about a character with black eyes. You avoid looking at yourself in the mirror, then dream that your eyes are black and inhuman.

Black eyes can symbolize sadness, grief, and loss. They can symbolize dark emotions or no emotions. It's a metaphor for feeling dead inside. An example is given by the dream a college student experienced after a long bout with depression. In the dream, she wakes up in her dorm room, gets ready, leaves to go to class, and sees crowds of people walking around emotionlessly. She tries to talk with someone she knows, and suddenly, everyone stares at her with completely black eyes. Terrified, she runs back to her dorm and sees in the mirror that she, too, has black eyes. She then opens her computer. Its screen is black, and in the reflection, she sees somebody standing behind her. She then wakes up for real, screaming bloody murder.

To analyze the dream, begin with the guideline that dream characters are like actors playing roles, and those roles express ideas about you, the dreamer. The emotionless behavior of the characters in her dream dramatizes how she feels, especially when she's in public and trying to interact socially. She's depressed and can't connect emotionally. The black eyes are a symbol for her depression and lack of social connection. She feels that way even with familiar people, shown in the dream as wanting to talk with someone she knows and everyone's eyes turning black. In the dream, she flees to her dorm room, and the depression follows her there. It's in her eyes, too—she sees it reflected in the mirror and the computer screen. It's the dream's way of pointing her inward to find the source of the problem. The symbolism of seeing herself with black eyes expresses urgency—it says, "You need to *see* this; it's important." The scene is a play on the idea in the phrase "bring my troubles home with me." A bad depression is like a dark presence following you everywhere. Her dream is a wake-up call to deal with her depression.

In dream-speak, the color black can mean hated, sinister, diabolical, evil, or malevolent. Black eyes can symbolize possession by dark thoughts, feelings, ideas, or moods, as if a dark force takes over the person. We can tell when something isn't right about a person by the look in their eyes, and dreams can use black eyes to indicate feelings and perceptions not just about people but also about situations and circumstances when something feels dark or black about them.

Eyes turning black expresses the idea of an outside force taking over from within. For example, in a nightmare, the eyes of a group of people turn black after they look at a black-eyed little girl on an altar, then the same thing happens to the dreamer's family members when they look into the eyes of the group members. People begin behaving like monsters, cannibalizing themselves and each other. Then, someone reads from a Bible, and a group of people try to perform an exorcism on a second young girl.

The girl on the altar symbolizes a religious ideology that seems innocent, but it's actually sinister. It gets into people's minds, takes over, and spreads. The dream expresses the idea of psychological possession in the symbolism of people's eyes turning black after looking into the eyes of other black-eyed people, showing that the dreamer is witnessing the ideology possess her family members. The dream scripts their behavior to act like monsters as an exaggerated but truthful depiction of the ideology's sinister influence. It eats them from within—that's what the dream means by cannibalism.

> **Dreaming about black eyes can indicate issues related to sleep apnea, sleep paralysis, and sleep deprivation—when a person isn't sleeping well, it shows in their eyes.**

The exorcism scene symbolically enacts the dreamer's struggle against the ideology and its influence on her family. She wishes to be free of it. Exorcism frees a person from a sinister spiritual force, and her dream uses the symbolism of it to imply the idea of possession. In dream-speak, possession means that something exerts a magnetic hold. Like a sorcerer's spell, it binds and blinds people and changes their personality.

Nothing says "fear" like black eyes—especially fear of serious illness and death—because black eyes have long been associated with disease, but rarely does dreaming about it presage what's coming literally. Usually, it's figurative and connects with fear. For one woman, her nightmare about seeing her father with black eyes brought up heavy fear that he was about to die. His health was declining, and she knew what was coming, but her dream was an expression of her fear, not a prediction.

Dreaming about black eyes can indicate issues related to sleep apnea, sleep paralysis, and sleep deprivation—when a person isn't sleeping well, it shows in their eyes. Something's not right. Chronic sleep deprivation goes hand in hand with more frequent episodes of sleep paralysis, during which it's common to see people and other creatures with black eyes, oftentimes with a creepy or evil vibe.

Black-eyed people in dreams can symbolize the idea of seeing through something, especially something illusory or misunderstood. For example, a man dreams that people he knows have black eyes. He looks closer and sees their eyes turn completely white. Instead of reacting fearfully, he's sympathetic and wants to help. The dream reflects his sense that he can help people who appear out of reach emotionally, socially, and psychologically. He is drawn to those who are overlooked and shunned.

Finally, dreams can create visual puns and other sorts of imagery that play with words and mix ideas. It opens the possibility that black eyes symbolize an injury to the eye or the figurative meaning of a black eye as a blow to one's image or pride.

See also: Aliens, Evil, Ghosts/Poltergeists/Spirits, Possession, Shadow People, Vampires, Zombies

CENTAURS

The centaur, a creature that's half human and half animal, is the image of the duality of mankind as human and civilized on one hand and animal and wild on the other. Myths about centaurs are allegories for this duality. People can be civilized one moment, and with a flip of the switch, they are driven by animal passions. Their emotions and opinions swing wildly. A centaur is the very image of the battle between reason and instinct.

As a dream symbol, the centaur embodies those ideas, and as a symbol in nightmares, it's the image of inner conflict driven by doubt, discord, and contradiction. It's the conflict of opposites summed up in one picture, and that meaning is also found in other zoomorphic dream imagery such as a sea witch (a human–octopus hybrid), a minotaur (a human–bull hybrid), and a mermaid.

A familiar figure from mythology, the centaur can represent various forms of duality in your life, the balance—or conflict—between the animalistic and the human sides of a person.

The centaur is unique from them because its union of human and horse is also a picture of grace in motion and galloping desires. The centaur is a picture of balance, too, and when a person is out of balance, they're likely to dream powerfully. Conflict with a centaur in a dream can mean that a person is trying to find their balance. Dr. Carl Jung says that the psyche is self-regulating, and dreams are its number-one mechanism for balancing the system. The more out of balance the psyche is, the stronger the force the unconscious uses in dreams to regulate itself.

Nightmares can be thought of as a strong force of compensation to correct an imbalance in the psyche. It's strong medicine. The imbalance is probably in the relationship between the conscious mind and the unconscious mind—their viewpoints and priorities are far apart—which Dr. Jung says is the most common cause of nightmares. The centaur is a fusion of what is conscious about a person (their human half) and what is unconscious (their animal half). Its presence in a dream suggests the need for integration of unconscious content and the mediation of opposites within a person.

In that sense, the centaur is an ideal image to use for correcting issues in the psyche. Nightmares that use the centaur as a strong corrective force often involve combat between it and the dreamer, or it pursues the dreamer. The centaur is a symbol of whatever the dreamer is struggling against.

Take, for instance, one man's recurring dreams about a centaur pursuing him in his place of work, a shipping warehouse. The first dreams involve him being aware of the centaur and wishing it would go away—it's interfering with his ability to work. In later dreams, he hides from the centaur as it tracks him. The story evolves and climaxes with a dramatic confrontation where the centaur pins him to the ground, and the last thing he sees is its hooves descending toward his face.

The dreams reflect a growing imbalance related to his work situation. He thinks of himself as a workhorse—a centaur is half horse—who can take on the most demanding tasks and work the longest hours, but he is pursued by a growing realization that he can't keep up the pace forever. He's feeling the wear and tear and ignoring the warning signs, and it pursues him in his dreams in the form of a centaur that gets closer and closer to him. He is pursuing a goal of being an exceptional worker and won't slow down because he's proud and stubborn, but in the centaur, a symbol of the corrective force within him, he's up against something more stubborn.

A similar idea plays out in one woman's dream about a centaur pursuing her and her boyfriend. The centaur is a projection of her perception that her boyfriend never slows down; he's driven and passionate, but she wants to settle down and start a family. She fears that his inner nature will keep him away from home. In mythology, the centaur is a hunter that lives in the wild. It's never at home.

> **In the centaur, a person can see their inner nature and its needs for freedom, unbridled passion, and the expression of powerful feelings and desires.**

In the centaur, a person can see their inner nature and its needs for freedom, unbridled passion, and the expression of powerful feelings and desires. A dream about a centaur may reveal that a person is denying their needs and true nature. Take, for instance, a young man's dream about being a detective and investigating a crime. His investigation leads him to a large structure in the middle of nowhere. It's empty and dark. The back wall leads out to an open field, and there, he sees a female centaur. He questions her, and she asks him if he wants to have sex. Sure, he says, and they have wild sex out in the open.

The dream would appear to be perverse if not understood as a story about wanting to live closer to one's inner nature. The telltale sign is his role as a detective investigating a crime. The crime is against himself by living within self-imposed limits, symbolized as the dark and empty interior of the large structure. He desires to live with more freedom, open air, and a connection to nature, ideas captured by the picture of the open field populated by a horny centaur. The sex is, well, sex and all it symbolizes: passion, living in the moment, pursuit of pleasure. That's how he wants to live.

The body is a means of experiencing pleasure, and it literally has a mind of its own. Our most basic programming from birth onward is to maximize pleasure and minimize pain. The centaur as a symbol is fantastic for speaking to the needs, desires, and pleasures of the body and the personal experience of life within it.

The image of a centaur has many parallels with situations in life where the symbolism of legs comes into play. The four legs of a horse are an image of stability—four legs are more stable than two. Four is a balanced number with interesting numerological connotations. Dr. Jung referred to dream images made of fours as a quaternio, a symbol of a person's archetypal self. It appears in dreams that are the most powerful and impactful.

Combine horse legs with a powerful human torso, and the symbolism can mean that a person is immovable; they won't be swayed or budged. It can mean that they are materially stable and deeply rooted in the physical experience of life, common associations with the astrological sign of Sagittarius. It can mean that they possess great strength in their bodies and strength of will. The four legs propel the centaur quickly, and swiftness as an action or feature of a dream can mean "thinking on your feet" and "covering ground." The human upper half is made for thinking, and the animal lower half is made for speed. And because legs connect with the ground, the centaur can be a symbol of groundedness.

While the ideas above cover much of the ground for what a centaur can represent in a dream, uncovered territory relates to its use in fantasy fiction and video games. Dreams pick up on the use of characters in fiction and games, then insert them into stories that are like modern myths of the hero's journey, an archetypal tale about facing the challenges of maturity and accessing one's personal power. The centaur represents the forces of life, society, and oneself that are barriers to maturity and growth and, conversely, aids to them, depending on the context. In game-speak, it's a "boss character" of great strength and cunning that must be overcome for the dreamer (or gamer) to "level up." Defeating such a character in a dream can symbolize overcoming an obstacle to growth, and dreaming of being a centaur or having one as an ally can mean that the person is tapping into their inner resources to meet their challenges.

See also: Charon, Medusa, Minotaurs, Werewolves

CHARON

In Greek mythology, Charon is the ferryman who carries the souls of the recently deceased across the River Styx to the Land of the Dead. A dream can base the symbolic meaning of the character on its role in myth as a connector between the worlds of the living and dead. In this capacity, one of its roles is to help the dreamer find answers to why someone important in their life is gone. They have lingering questions or issues related to the person's passing. Charon takes them to where they can find answers.

A woman dreams that she's on a boat piloted by Charon on the River Styx. She reaches land and sees a childhood friend who died mysteriously as an adult. She runs up, embraces him, and tells him that she always loved him. He doesn't say much, but she can feel that he's not suffering and that he returns her love. She asks him how he died—she suspects that his wife murdered him—and he says that he killed himself. She feels relieved that he's okay in the afterlife.

Her dream helped her find answers to a troubling situation, but it's hard to say whether they are subjective or objective. Did she create the dream to tell herself what she needed to hear in order to put the matter to rest, did the dream open a supernatural channel to her friend, or was it something else entirely? The dreamer's sense of it is that she really did find her friend in the afterlife and that what he told her is the truth, and in the end, that's what matters most; it's her dream, and she can decide how to understand it.

Charon is a figure from Greek mythology who is responsible for taking the deceased to the Land of the Dead, so seeing Charon in a dream has an obvious meaning.

Dreams can reveal hidden information in ways that challenge skeptics to explain, and a common means of getting that information in "ESP dreams" is through visitations from deceased loved ones. Take, for instance, the woman who found out from her deceased aunt in a dream that her deceased father had a secret marriage that produced a child. The woman then combed through her father's financial records and found payments to the other family. In another fascinating case, a man's recently deceased father came to him in a dream to tell him where a gun was hidden inside his old house. The man found it there, in a place he'd never know otherwise to look. To skeptics, information obtained in such a way must be already known subconsciously by the dreamer, and in some cases, that's true, but it's a stretch to say that it explains all cases, especially considering the convincing body of evidence showing that more is going on than coincidence or subconscious mentation.

Charon's connection to the Underworld makes him an ideal sort of character in dreams with themes that connect with ideas such as "going within" and "finding oneself." They include a surface world of people and activity and an underworld, or inner world, where we encounter parts of ourselves that don't fit into the picture of ordinary life. It's the world of depth and soul. It's the unconscious mind.

Discovering the world within oneself through dreams can be revelatory. Charon acts as a guide—after all, the Underworld is his world, making him an ideal character to play the role. The dreamers tend to feel like they're in a sacred place, and Charon's presence is their permission to be there. Conversely, Charon can be a warning. You can't bullshit the Ferryman, and you don't have any wiggle room. Charon acts as a guide to discover what you're really made of and what life's all about, but he's also a test of one's character and giving up your illusions is the fare you must pay. It can free you from fear of death to live more fully, but the journey is often painful and perilous before reaching the destination.

> **Charon acts as a guide to discover what you're really made of and what life's all about, but he's also a test of one's character....**

Charon is associated with death, and death as a dream theme stretches from literal usages to figurative ones. On the literal side, Charon is a great character to use in stories related to mortality, and on the figurative side, nothing says "dead on your feet" or "bored to death" like death incarnate. Charon delivers the message that it's time to live again, to be active, to break the pattern or routine that's deadening or limiting you.

The dream author chooses Charon for the role because it can layer meaning on to such a character like coats of paint, and not a word has to be spoken to get across the message. It symbolizes the problem *and* the solution, the question *and* the answer, all of which the dream embeds as information in the symbol. Those dreams can be quite dramatic and powerful when the message behind them is especially important and urgent. We only get so much time in this life, and the takeaway from encountering death in a dream may be to enjoy the ride while it lasts.

Charon is also used as a character in a story that illustrates the person's psychology and current issues in life. In one such dream, the dreamer is on a boat with Charon. He sees dead bodies in the water and wants to dive in. Charon advises against it, but the dreamer does it anyway and regrets it. Following his impulse was a bad idea, and he wants to climb back into the boat. Charon sends him a mental picture of the boat toppling and the Ferryman tumbling out of it. It's the dreamer's choice; Charon doesn't tell him what to do, just what the result will be. The dreamer decides to swim to shore instead. The dream is a story about the wisdom of heeding advice and thinking about the likely outcome of actions before following impulses. Charon is a wisdom figure in this dream, with another layer of meaning related to being a guide for the dreamer to understand himself better.

See also: Ghosts/Poltergeists/Spirits, The Grim Reaper, Hell, Imprisonment/Entrapment

CLOWNS
See: Pennywise the Clown

CREATURES

Some monsters in dreams are difficult to classify. They are simply creatures, and their meaning is wide open. Their nondescript appearance may stem from the nonspecific source material; for example, the dream wants to tell a story about fear, and it's not a specific fear but fear in general. It then creates a creature that's fearsome and inserts it into a story for the dreamer to interact with their fear. Dreaming about something scary can reduce the intensity of response in the brain's fear centers by instigation, the creation of neural pathways that detour around them.

The undefined nature of a creature is a blank slate, providing the opportunity for a dream to show a person what they don't know about themself. Recently spawned content of the unconscious mind tends to take form in dreams as an amalgamation of legs and arms sticking out here and there, heads with odd-fitting features and pieces out of place, or just a blob with few discernible features. The imagery looks like a puree of features because the conscious mind cannot define it any better. In subsequent dreams, as the person gets to know what's newly emerging in them, the creature gains definition.

The same idea applies also to situations and circumstances that are outside of the dreamer's scope of experience. Their dreams translate their lack of comprehension as the creature's lack of definition. Dread and fear are common reactions to such imagery and are understandable as typical responses when people encounter the unknown. It stirs them in the dark places inside.

Then again, a dream can tie a scary creature to a specific situation and provide details that aid in its interpretation. One such example comes from the terrifying nightmare a woman had that opens by showing her folding laundry in her home when a skinless creature attacks her with a knife. An epic

In some nightmares, a threatening presence might not take a distinct form but, rather, be something amorphous—menacing but not really identifiable.

battle ensues. She throws salt on the creature, and it howls in agony, then she escapes outside, where the battle continues. A city bus runs over the creature. Bystanders who witness the scene detain her as if she's to blame. The dream ends with the creature getting up from the street and the dreamer knowing that the battle will continue.

The creature is skinless. The dreamer sees raw muscle and oozing blood all over it. Picture that image; what does it mean? To lack skin implies the idea of lacking protection—skin is protective. It also suggests the terms "raw wound" and "rubbed raw." Knowing that most dream characters are reflections of the dreamer, the natural question to ask is, does the dreamer feel unprotected, wounded, and raw? Then, consider the knife the creature wields as a weapon. Knives are for fighting that's up close and personal, suggesting the idea of something that's closely personal for the dreamer.

Those observations help her connect the dream imagery to her legal battle with a former employer over getting injured at work. The creature represents not only the situation but her raw and wounded feelings. The battle with it symbolizes her legal battle and more. Just prior to the dream, she found out that her former manager was spreading rumors that she's a bad person and a bad employee, and it's preventing her from getting a new job. Talk about rubbing salt in a wound! That meaning is enacted in the dream as her throwing salt onto the exposed flesh of the creature. The action of folding laundry in the opening scene symbolizes her efforts to get her life in order and find a new job—efforts that are sabotaged by the battle with the creature.

Then, the setting shifts from inside her home to outside in public, dramatizing the public nature of the lawsuit and the rumors flying. The symbolism of the city bus reinforces the idea of a public matter because it's public transportation. The dreamer thought that the lawsuit would vindicate her and solve her troubles, and the dream shows this idea through the symbolism of the bus flattening the creature. And through the symbolism of her being detained, it shows that she feels like she's being blamed for getting hurt while doing her job. When the creature rises at the end of the dream, it's a prediction that the battle with her former employer will continue.

Simplifying a dream helps you figure out what it really means. For example, avoiding a creature raises the question, what are you avoiding: memories, thoughts, feelings, realizations, your conscience? Battling a creature raises the question, what's the battle about? In the above example, it's a legal battle, but most battles in dreams represent battles within yourself and in your closest relationships. The creature could represent a battle of the head versus the heart, rationality versus emotion, or the ego versus the unconscious.

> **A person's creations are extensions of who they are and can have a life of their own.**

The dream author loves to play with the ideas we use in our figures of speech, and a creature can symbolize a habit or pattern, as in the term "creature of habit." The words "creature" and "creation" are similar enough for the author to use one to symbolize the other, and that idea leads to associations with Frankenstein and similar monsters. The creature is a creation of the person, and their dream wants them to own it. A person says "this situation is a real monster" but doesn't recognize their role in creating it.

Also, think of the ego and the personality as creations—your creations. How does the dream author show you something about yourself that you've created? It shows you a creature.

Creation links with creativity. A person's creations are extensions of who they are and can have a life of their own. Take, for instance, a woman's dream where she wakes up, goes to the bathroom, and sees small, freshly made, animated clay creations trying to escape from a box. She doesn't want them to escape, so she smashes them with a hammer. She then goes back to bed and wakes up again in a surreal environment of bright light and swirling color, and the clay figures are crawling around everywhere, directionless. She senses a creature in the bed with her and sees an expressionless girl from previous dreams standing at the foot of the bed staring at her. She then wakes up for real.

The clay figures are creations, and their animated movement suggests the ideas of "a life of their own" and "breathe life into your creation." In this case, the creatures are better thought of as creative ideas in an early stage of development. The dream shows them in a box, meaning "contained within certain parameters of acceptability and usefulness" imposed on her by her job in a creative profession. By smashing the clay figures before they can escape, she symbolically enacts her relationship with her creativity, taking the hammer of self-criticism to her creative ideas that don't meet her high standards. She discards them like waste flushed down the toilet, an idea suggested by the dream's bathroom setting. But she doesn't realize that her self-criticism is deeply offensive to the source of her creativity, the young girl who appears at the foot of the bed staring at her.

Can you hear the girl's unspoken question? "What did you do to my creations?" As children, we freely engage our imagination, and those play activities can form the basis of creative life as an adult. But as an adult whose creativity becomes their job, criticism is brought into the process. Some creative ideas don't pass muster, but the ideas must be generated, and the source of them comes from the inner child who learned to create before criticism came into the picture and who experienced their creations as *living parts of themselves*. The creature in bed with her is her creativity, which is firstly very close and intimate, like a bedmate, and is secondly most active in her dreams. The second time, she wakes up in the dream and finds herself in her bedroom—it's bright, colorful, and disorienting, and the clay figures crawl around everywhere—which is a picture of creative imagination doing its thing while the person sleeps and dreams. It freely blends and mixes.

The dream shows the progression of her creativity, beginning with the simple, clay figures, progressing to the creature in bed with her, and culminating with the young girl. They are various expressions of the same idea: creativity and the internal dynamics of it for the dreamer.

See also: Entities, Evil, Frankenstein, Ghosts/Poltergeists/Spirits, Mummies, Slenderman

DARK MAGICIANS

Magic in dreams is a great symbol for happenings that we can't explain conventionally or wrap the mind around. When bad things happen, it can seem like the work of black magic or a dark force. A relationship suddenly turns sour; a client changes their mind; luck runs out; illness and misfortune strike. It's like a Dark Magician is working against you.

To have a dream with a dark magician in it could be a reflection of yourself, but a bad side of yourself that can work against you.

A magician within you can work against you, known as the shadow side of the Magician archetype. It's a destructive pattern of thought and behavior, like when you're too smart or clever for your own good. It's the trickster that gets you to act against your own best interests and intentions. It's the trap of your own making. It's the lies, illusions, and falsehoods you spin or believe. The Dark Magician is you, but most people don't see themselves in their dream characters, particularly the darker ones, and consequently, they look outside of themselves for the cause of their troubles instead of inside for the true source.

The Magician archetype in us wields our intelligence, intuition, persuasiveness, cunning, and skill, and the dark side of it uses that power against us—and against those close to us and the planet—if we let it. It's too easy to believe that it comes from an external source or force, and that tendency to project is what gives outside forces power over us. Even when it appears that the Dark Magician is an external spiritual or energetic source, the dream character somehow originates within us. We are complicit in allowing it, attracting it, or even creating it. Usually, the source is found in a person's emotional life.

However, as a dream symbol, the Dark Magician is ready to play the role of someone or something in your life that uses lies, tricks, enticements, beliefs, head games, and psychological force against you. In this case, the Dark Magician really does originate externally of you, but it takes two to tango, and the character could be in your dream to show you what makes you susceptible to manipulation or culpable in inviting it into your life. A person who plays the victim or falsely claims innocence *begs* for a smackdown from the dark side of the Magician because the archetype desires you to assume responsibility for yourself.

Dreams show you what you don't know (especially about yourself) by comparing it with and symbolizing it as what you do know. You don't know what's causing your troubles but do know that Dark Magicians are known for causing trouble. Substitute labels such as voodoo priest, occultist, Satanist, warlock, and sorcerer, and now you have a name for this type of character, who appears in cultures and dreams worldwide.

The Dark Magician is the type of dream character who has much to show you about yourself. The true gold lay hidden in the dark places within us and the dark things about us, and the only way to the dark places and, subsequently, the gold within oneself is through the characters that inhabit them. When those characters are archetypal, the battle is with forces that are timeless and autonomous of the ego, in which case you are truly up against something with the power to destroy you physically, mentally, and spiritually. Tread carefully, and when you look within yourself for the source, focus on the parts that feel denied, wounded, and unwanted and on the emotions of anger, arrogance, grief, and fear.

See also: Aliens, Dragons, Evil, Ghosts/Poltergeists/Spirits, Pennywise the Clown, Slenderman

DRAGONS

Talk about nightmare material! Dragons are unstoppable, cunning predators that breathe fire, spit acid, and lay waste to whatever stands in their way. Does that sound like someone you know? Someone who spouts vitriol, won't take no for an answer, aims their fire at physical and psychological soft spots, and leaves a trail of destruction? The logical mind says, "The person is mean but not *that* mean; bad but not *that* bad; dark but not *that* dark!" But the metaphorical mind sees the connection. A metaphor compares two unlike things to create a meaningful connection between them, and that's how dreams create symbols. The comparison between a type of personality and a dragon is exaggerated, dramatized, and *true*.

See the hidden meaning—that's how you discover what a dragon symbolizes in a dream. If you only see the dragon, you don't see the meaning hidden behind the image. The dreaming mind is a translator, turning everything that runs through it while sleeping into symbolic imagery, and it follows the examples that we use in colorful language. We say that a person "breathes fire" because they spout angry words; that they have an "acid tongue" because of their corrosive use of language; that they are a "force of nature" because of their relentless energy and power of will. The dreaming mind translates those qualities into a picture that says 1,000 words. In other words, a dragon.

Most dream characters are personifications of aspects of the dreamer's personality and psychology, but people try to interpret their dreams by looking outward instead of inward. They look into the eyes of the dragon and fail to see what it reflects about them personally. Even when a dream points outward, it usually portrays dream characters subjectively based on the dreamer's thoughts, feelings, and perceptions. Let's say that two students dream about the same teacher, who has a ferocious temper. It scares the daylights out of one student, and they dream about the teacher as a

Like centaurs, dragons are another mythological beast that can find their way into dreams. Powerful and dangerous. The flames could represent harsh and hurtful words aimed at you by a negative person in your life, especially one who has power over you.

dragon, but the other student dreams about a porcupine because they perceive the teacher as "prickly." Both are dreaming about how they perceive their teacher's temper.

Personality is a construct built atop unconscious structures of the psyche. The base layer is what Dr. Carl Jung calls the archetypal layer, and it's the foundation of the psyche, aka the collective unconscious. It's tricky territory for anyone trying to interpret a dream because by nature, it's largely unknown to the conscious mind. When the conscious mind gets a whiff of what's emanating from deep down in the psyche, it perceives something much more vast and powerful than itself. Something ancient, archaic, beyond comprehension— which probably shouldn't be aroused from its slumber!

Mythology is largely an allegorical means for describing what humans encounter in the collective unconscious. Dragon mythology builds atop the experience of people who look long and hard within themselves with stupendous courage to keep going deeper despite the fearsome things they encounter in their own minds, and there, at the back of the darkest cave, atop the world's biggest pile of treasure, they find the dragon. And it's not a mere image; it's a force, a living thing. Dragon mythology reaches back to the beginning of recorded history. It's universal, and anything universal in mythology is very likely to be universal to the psyche of all people.

> **Mythology is largely an allegorical means for describing what humans encounter in the collective unconscious.**

You could say that a dragon lives in the heart of us all.

We all have a dark side, too, and in dreams, it can present itself as a dragon. The dark side of a person, often referred to as their shadow side, is, or at least *can be*, autonomous of the ego. It may have turf of its own within the psyche, and when you go there in a dream, you are an interloper. A powerful dark side can take any form in a dream that it wants to, tapping an innate and unlimited ability to create imaginatively. It's a capacity that everyone has but few people fully utilize.

Now, imagine that your dark side sees you coming in a dream. It wants to scare you away before you start realizing that the little kingdom it's built for itself inside of your mind is rightfully yours—it's usurped you as the ruler of your inner world. It takes the form of a dragon, and its problem is solved if you turn tail and run but not if you muster the courage to face it. The mythology of the hero who slays the dragon is an archetypal story about conquering one's dark side. The reward for doing so is the ability to claim a treasure of personal power beyond measure.

The use of a dragon as a dream symbol ranges from terrifying to amusing. For all the talk of the dark side of dragon symbolism, its other symbolic usages are more common in everyday sorts of dreams. For example, a woman dreams that she's in her bedroom, and her boyfriend turns into a dragon that flies around the room and performs tricks for her. The dragon then transforms back into her boyfriend and lies next to her in bed. Sexual tension smolders. Some powerful lovemaking is about to ensue, but he tells her that she must pay for his time. Pay for his time? She wonders if she can get a discount.

> **For both males and females, the dragon can symbolize the dark side of sexuality that devours and consumes.**

The dream is a story that encapsulates a situation with her boyfriend. He is very sensual and passionate, and she loves how he "performs" for her. The dream makes a clear connection between the dragon and him by transforming one into the other, but what is meant by his statement about paying for his time? Well, she's paying for their living expenses while he's unemployed. She gets more time with time at home (and in her bedroom!), but in a sense, she's paying for it. Her thought during the dream about getting a discount reflects her hope that her investment in the relationship will pay off when he gets a job.

That dream uses the common association between dragons and passionate sexuality as a basis for the symbolism. It certainly describes the qualities she loves about her boyfriend. In myth, the knight that rescues the virgin from the dragon tames the wildness of his sexuality—he tames the dragon within himself. For both males and females, the dragon can symbolize the dark side of sexuality that devours and consumes.

Dragons are also great symbols for fiery temperament. It's an association that one woman's dream used to symbolize her mother but with a twist: the dragon is made of glass. It's the dream's way of saying that her mother is both fiery and fragile.

The association between dragons and cold, calculating intellect comes into play in a dream set in the Arctic where the dreamer and a party of explorers try to enter a fortress protected by a dragon that outsmarts them. The dream dramatizes a situation in which one of the dreamer's coworkers, symbolized by the dragon, fiercely protects his turf, symbolized by the fortress, by refusing to share valuable information and knowledge. The Arctic setting reflects the coldness of the atmosphere, and the action of outsmarting the dreamer and his party reflects the coworker's manipulative tactics to avoid being forced to share. The person will not "open up."

Dragons are associated with strong materialism, hedonism, and possessiveness—they defend their treasure hoard. The idea branches out to include associations with jealousy, greed, pleasure, and envy.

A sleeping dragon can symbolize great power lying dormant in the psyche, but the imagery also implies ideas like "bloated" and "overburdened."

Another way of looking at it is that a sleeping dragon is best avoided due to the potential for danger or conflict. It can symbolize someone or something that's handled delicately, is nothing to mess with, or shouldn't be aroused.

A simple idea about the symbolism of a dragon and its use in a dream's story is that it's a reality check or gut check with no way to avoid it. You're just going about life as usual when the dragon appears—what are you going to do about it? Do you have the fortitude to face it? Another simple idea is that the dragon represents the idea of being set in your ways. Dragons are ancient creatures that do what they want with no way to change them.

See also: Fire, Snakes, War

FRANKENSTEIN

This classic golem of the movie world is also a regular type of character in the dream world, and it comes attached to its creator: you. In this case, it's an outgrowth of your ego, the offspring of your personality that knocks on the door and wants to be acknowledged because you, Dr. Frankenstein, have disowned something about yourself, and the longer it remains out in the cold, the angrier and more dangerous it becomes. The key to decoding the meaning is to see yourself in the character. After all, Frankenstein is your creation.

Frankenstein's monster appearing in a dream could represent something that you yourself created and then, like Dr. Frankenstein, disowned.

Frankenstein and creatures like it pursue relentlessly. It's a symbol for something you can't avoid or shake off, such as the regret over a big mistake or acting shamefully, especially if your hubris causes it; after all, hubris was Dr. Frankenstein's downfall. Also, Frankenstein's pursuit is painful to watch, and the parallels with ordinary life include watching the death of a relationship, hope, or personal dream. It's especially true of situations involving the death of the person you want to be or even a decline in your health and vigor.

Frankenstein is a big presence, making it a good symbol for big thoughts and big people but also big obstacles and problems. Take, for example, the dream where a man opens a door inside a house and up pops a ghostly, Frankenstein-type monster like an inflatable doll. It quickly grows to 10 feet tall, and he can go no further until dealing with it. The Frankenstein that blocks his path has no substance, and it's the dream's way of saying that he's making a big deal out of nothing. The inflatable Frankenstein contains nothing but air inside, right? His inflated ego is the obstacle because it takes offense to things and stirs him up, and that's what his dream means by making the inflatable Frankenstein an obstacle. He is his own obstacle!

This book offers more illumination for Frankenstein as a type of dream character. The discussions in the entries on Zombies and Mummies delve into the meaning of slow-moving and reanimated characters. Haunting is covered in the discussion in the entry on Haunted Dolls. The discussions in the entries on Creatures and Dark Magicians offer insight about dream characters that symbolize disowned creations. If a dream uses Frankenstein as something that's summoned or possessed, read the entries on Slenderman and Possession.

GENIES
See: Slenderman

THE GIRL FROM *THE RING*

Of all the scary imagery produced by modern horror movies, the girl from the movie franchise *The Ring* resonates the most deeply when measured by how often it appears in dreams. It's the image of a grimy, young girl dressed in white, her face covered by long, black hair that's dramatically revealed as demonic. In the movie, she crawls out of a television and into physical reality to kill people who watch a cursed video. She also crawls into people's nightmares!

The dream author may weave stories around the media we consume. A common misconception, though, is that the dream imagery is merely day residue, memories that seep into dreams, and it lacks meaning. But when it's part of a story and packs a punch, it's almost certainly meaningful, not day residue, and the stronger the punch, the more meaningful and memorable it is.

Some dream symbols carry meanings that are similar regardless of who dreams it, but most symbols and their meanings are highly personal. With a symbol such as the girl from *The Ring*, the fact that it's from a horror movie gives us a place to begin. It's a symbol of fear, but is it a general fear or a spe-

People who watch horror movies can sometimes experience characters from these films entering their dreams. The terriying girl from *The Ring* is one example.

cific fear, and does it relate to the movies' storylines or something else it triggers in the dreamer? Among the legion of possibilities are a fear of death because the girl in the movie is a killer; a fear of the dark because the movies use dark settings and other imagery for dramatic effect; and a fear of the dark side of the feminine because the character is female and dark.

A fear of the feminine is a common usage of the symbolism in the dreams of young men frightened by their encounters with mysterious, dark, feminine-oriented behavior and personality traits. For example, a young man dreams about encountering the girl from *The Ring* while searching a dark mansion. He screams, and the girl attacks. He then jolts awake. He's having difficulty with his girlfriend, and at times, especially during their fights, he sees her aggressive side, and it frightens him. In the movies, the girl doesn't look dangerous until her face is revealed, and his girlfriend doesn't seem dangerous until she shows her "other face." The dream puts him in a dark, unfamiliar place during the encounter, a symbolic way of saying that it's a new experience for him and he's feeling his way in the dark. Plus, it's frightening. That's how his dream began with movie imagery and wove a personally meaningful story around it.

On one level, the girl in the dream symbolizes his girlfriend, but it's only a starting point for getting to the next level by analyzing how she affects him internally. It's not so much his girlfriend that he fears, it's what he sees in her when she's mad or in a mood. That's why we say "fear of the feminine" rather than "fear of females" when discussing the psychology of it. The dark side of the feminine is a pattern of behavior that's unreasoning, manipulative, and exploitative. The behavior is a power play, and it's like encountering a supernatural force for the young man on the receiving end for the first time. The girl from *The Ring* is how the dreaming mind symbolically translates the subjective experience, and to some men, and women too, *all* females fall into that category because they are *all* mysterious and threatening. Plus, males and females alike can display the behavior.

A vengeful spirit possesses the girl in the movie, creating a strong association for use in dreams. Possession in dreams can mean that a person behaves abnormally or is possessed by a mood, feeling, thought, or idea. We ask in response, "What's gotten into you?," and a dream tells the story as something *getting into* the person. It's great symbolism for the idea of a sudden, dark change.

Possession is also a way of saying that a person allows something dark or scary in their personality to take over. *Hello, Mrs. Hyde!* That use of the symbolism features in a young woman's dream about having a threesome with her boyfriend and another young woman in an abandoned house. Turns out that the home belongs to her boyfriend's grandmother, and in the morning she's there, sitting in a pentagram surrounded by candles and possessed by demons, and the dreamer senses that she plans to take away her boyfriend. The spirit of the girl from *The Ring* then possesses the dreamer, giving her superhuman strength to lift the grandmother up by the neck and kill her. She then tracks down her boyfriend and gives him a big hug.

> **Possession by the girl from *The Ring* means that something dark takes over her personality when she uses sexuality to manipulate.**

The dream dramatizes the dynamics of how the young woman keeps possession of her boyfriend by manipulating him with sexuality. The other young woman who participates in the threesome is a projection of the dreamer, and it expresses the idea that her manipulative behavior comes from an unknown side of herself—like she becomes someone else. The grandmother represents the idea of traditional values, and the dream creates a scene where Grandma is possessed and surrounded by occult imagery to symbolize the young woman acting contrary to traditional values. Possession by the girl from *The Ring* means that something dark takes over her personality when she uses sexuality to manipulate. In the opening scene, the abandoned house means "abandoned my values," and emptiness means "empty inside."

She senses that Grandma is there to take away her boyfriend, and that detail is the crux of the personal context behind the behavior. In her mind, sex is what keeps him interested in her. Girls with traditional values don't have boyfriends or don't keep them for long. In that sense, Grandma, a symbol for traditional values, is a threat. The young woman uses sexuality as power, and in an exaggerated way, it's like gaining supernatural strength when she's possessed by the girl from *The Ring*. Hugging her boyfriend in the final scene appears sweet and innocent until you realize it's actually a way of saying "he's mine." She "possesses" him.

The girl from *The Ring* can symbolize thinking, feeling, and behaving in ways that are unusual, compulsive, and mysterious or the feeling that something is wrong about a situation, circumstance, or oneself. The character is a particularly good symbol for something that's wrong, but you can't put your finger on it. The dream imagery must be understood as figurative, not literal, but unfortunately, the tendency is to think too literally about dreams that feature such dark imagery.

The girl from the movie *The Grudge* is another dream character that fits the mold. The noir extends back much further in the history of movies and stories of this type. It's archetypal to the human experience—humans have always had imagery and stories on which to project the dark side of the feminine: witches, Medusa, and so forth. They are archetypal, and the supernatural, young girl is a type of figure that appears in dreams regardless of one's exposure to it in media and stories. Archetypal images are inborn, and myth, culture, media, and life itself make up the costume department where the dream author picks what works best with particular dreams. Archetypal images tend to appear in our most powerful dreams, so it's no wonder that dreams about a supernatural girl are often reported as nightmares.

> **Archetypal images are inborn, and myth, culture, media, and life itself make up the costume department where the dream author picks what works best with particular dreams.**

The girl with scraggly hair and unnaturally white skin began appearing in one boy's nightmares when he was five years old. She hunted him down and killed him every time he went to sleep. It taught him how to tell that he was dreaming—when the girl appeared, he was dreaming—and he responded by killing himself before she could. After two years of this dream recurring, he decided to fight back by projecting a hologram of himself for her to attack while taking aim from a sniper position and shooting her dead. Satisfied, he wakes up and feels great for the next week.

For a seven-year-old to devise a plan like that and carry it out ... he's a clever boy! And brave. It shows what we are capable of when driven by necessity. His severe eczema made his face dry and bloody from scratching, and kids would call him "monster" and "animal." Plus, his long hair made him look like a girl. The girl in the dream is really him, the "eczema boy" who looks like a girl, and his interaction with her is really a dramatization of his struggle. Around the time of the final battle with the nightmare girl, something shifted inside of him and enabled him to fight back against the taunts and bullying, giving him the power to fight back in his dream. As he grew older, he continued to develop his powers of dream lucidity. The nightmares were a terrible initiation, but he passed the test and came away stronger.

We can say the same of the reason why this type of character and others, like dragons and sorcerers, populate our dreams. They are the challenges that come from inside of us and push us to become more of what we can be, to rise to the occasion and face our fears.

The imagery of the girl from *The Ring* emerging from a television has an obvious possible meaning. Something you watch gets into your head in a bad way, like it crawls out of the screen and into your reality. Review your recent memories not only of what you watched and read but also what you witnessed. The dream imagery may represent it symbolically, a poignant sort of metaphor. Modern life experienced through a video screen, as if the soul or essence of a person is trapped behind glass, is another line of thought to pursue.

See also: Aliens, Black-eyed People, Evil, Haunted Dolls, Medusa, Possession, Witches/Warlocks

GODZILLA
See: Dragons

GOLEMS
See: Frankenstein

THE GRIM REAPER

The Grim Reaper character can appear in dreams to symbolize something related to death, such as fear of it or flirting with it. The Grim Reaper is death personified and the perfect character to play certain roles where death is a theme or idea of the story, ranging from serious illness and mortality to figures of speech like "it would be the death of me" and "the stress is killing me." Now, look at the Grim Reaper in the dream: Do you see stress personified, the mistake that embarrasses you, the fear that strikes you, the memory that shames you? Do you see *and* feel the thing eating at you? Death is a symbol, and a symbol is what the Grim Reaper really is when it appears in your dreams.

As with all dream symbols, the meaning depends on the context. Your reaction to the Grim Reaper speaks volumes because it's based on subconsciously knowing what it really means. The Grim Reaper isn't always a scary character and not always taken seriously, suggesting that you sense while dreaming that you have nothing to be afraid of—or maybe you do, but you trivialize or ignore it.

Take, for instance, a man's dream where he's working in a store and takes out the trash. On the way back, he sees the Grim Reaper and, unafraid, strikes

Obviously, the Grim Reaper is death personified, but the appearance of the deadly fellow might not mean your personal death. It could be a symbolic death of something else in your life.

up a conversation. The Grim Reaper loses the black garb and scythe and appears as a normal man. The dreamer starts making smart-ass remarks, and the Grim Reaper says, "Why do you mock me?" The question makes the dreamer uncomfortable. He tries to go back into the store, but the Grim Reaper grabs his arm and asks more forcefully, "Why do you mock me?" The dreamer doesn't have an answer. The Grim Reaper laughs sardonically and says, "Go grab me some more beer so I can cook with it!"

The clues that reveal the meaning of that dream are in plain sight. A store is associated with making choices. Taking out the trash is another way of saying "throw away." Put the clues together, and they suggest that the dreamer is making a choice that's like tossing something in the trash. Turns out that he risked throwing away his life. He went to a bar the night before the dream, drank some beers, and drove home. Knowing the risk, he did it anyway. Metaphorically, you could say that he mocked death. That context explains his action of mocking the Grim Reaper and the Grim Reaper taking offense to it. It enacts the metaphor "mock death." It also shows his disappointment with himself. The Grim Reaper's comment about getting more beer symbolizes the idea that drinking and driving will catch up with him eventually. Through the dream, he's telling himself that the next time he's in the same situation, he'll remember the lesson and get a ride.

"Cheating death" is the idea behind a dream where the dreamer plays cards with Barack Obama and realizes he can't win, so he decides to cheat but can't because his handful of cards—almost too many to hold—are facing outward, and no matter how hard he tries, he can't turn them around. Obama looks at him smugly as if knowing what he's trying to do and chuckles at the futility. He then pulls out a pack of cigarettes and offers one to the dreamer, who responds by saying, "What, are you trying to kill me or something?" He thinks he's being clever, but the look in Obama's eyes stops him cold. *Yes, fool, I am trying to kill you*, it says without a word. The man then notices that Obama's shadow is shaped like a long, hooded cloak, and he has a scythe gripped in his bony hand.

The dream punched the man in the gut, and no wonder because of the meaning behind it. Playing a card game symbolizes taking chances, and for him, the big chance he's taking is by smoking too much. That's what the dream means by too many cards in his hand. Cigarettes are white and held in the hand, and a cigarette pack is the same basic shape as a card deck. Cheating refers to fooling himself into believing that his habit won't end his life prematurely. But you can't cheat death, and that's what the dream means by his cards facing outward so Obama can see them and Obama's knowing look. In that context, the meaning behind offering a cigarette and the statement about trying to kill him is now obvious but not why Obama plays the role of Death. It's based on the dreamer knowing that Obama was a cigarette smoker. Also, Obama fits the general physical description of the Grim Reaper.

The final nail in the coffin is the card game they were playing. It's not stated outright by the dream, but when the man thinks back with that question in mind, he senses that they were playing Spades. Spades are associated with death. You reap what you sow with no way to avoid it.

Death can mean the end of a relationship or a time of life or the loss of something important. The Grim Reaper embodies the idea of losses and endings, especially ones that are dramatic and deeply felt. Take, for example, the dream where a woman's boyfriend leads her through dark woods, saying that he needs to show her something. They come to a little village in a clearing where his family is drinking wine. Spirits move about the place. She's not scared of them, but then, the Grim Reaper appears, and she falls flat to the ground, begging to be spared from dying. The Grim Reaper shakes its head "no" and moves on.

> **The Grim Reaper embodies the idea of losses and endings, especially ones that are dramatic and deeply felt.**

The dream occurred during a time when she was thinking a lot about the future of her relationship with her boyfriend. It was headed in a direction she was unsure about, and her dream symbolizes the idea as walking with him through dark woods. Her concerns about their future together center around his family's heavy drinking, which the dream refers to as drinking wine and the spirits floating about the scene. Alcohol is sometimes referred to as spirits, and the dream creates a wordplay by showing spirits in one sense but meaning it in another. The Grim Reaper symbolizes her wish to be spared from ending the relationship. The Grim Reaper says no, and it's a message to herself that you can't avoid the inevitable.

Separation is a common meaning of the symbolism of the Grim Reaper. Death is a separation from physical life, and it separates people who love each other.

Encountering the Grim Reaper can mean that something big and dreadful is hanging over you. Your head is on the chopping block. A dream could translate the idea as an encounter with the Grim Reaper, and under the circumstances, it's probably going to deeply affect you. However, a mild reaction is a clue that the subject or idea behind the dream is also relatively mild.

Take, for instance, a dream where the Grim Reaper visits a guy and says it's time to join his deceased father. He's like, okay, cool, because subconsciously, he understands that joining his father means growing up. He will soon join his father in the sense of growing into adulthood. He reported being concerned by the implications of the imagery—he wondered if he was about to die or had done something to deserve punishment—but those concerns came *after* reflecting on the dream, not *while* experiencing it, and in the field of dream interpretation, we call that sort of muddying of the water analytical overlay. Death in this context is a good thing. He's ready to face the coming changes, shown in the dream as accepting his fate.

In a dream where the Grim Reaper chases the dreamer around a baseball field, it shows that he isn't ready to grow up. The baseball field represents "the game of life," and his reaction of running from the Grim Reaper symbolizes the idea of trying to avoid the changes that are part of growing up and that enable him to progress from place to place or "base to base."

A woman falls asleep while working on paperwork at her desk, then dreams that she's simultaneously there at the desk and observing herself asleep. The room's temperature plummets to frigid, and she sees the Grim Reaper standing over her body. It gently kisses her forehead, then turns its attention to the observer part of her watching the scene and sternly forces it out of the room. She wakes up instantly. She's not scared by the dream imagery; on the contrary, the Grim Reaper is a sympathetic character.

> In a dream where the Grim Reaper chases the dreamer around a baseball field, it shows that he isn't ready to grow up.

Following that first encounter, it reappeared many times, never speaking, and always pushing her out of the scene.

Her dream presents the idea of dissociation between her mind and body, symbolized as observing her body as it sleeps. The circumstances are important to note because she fell asleep at her desk while doing paperwork for one of her jobs—she'd driven herself to exhaustion and couldn't keep her eyes open any longer. The Grim Reaper's sympathy for her body but not for her "other half" is also important to note because by pushing the dreamer's mind out of the scene, it's protecting her body. The body has a mind of its own—literally, a mind that's unconscious, but it can be overridden by the person's ego and forced to go to detrimental extremes, such as by working when she should be sleeping. It's slow suicide—the body can only hold up for so long under such strain. You could say that it's a "kiss of death."

Her dream experience also fits a pattern from reports of out-of-body experiences. The mental awareness of the mind separates from the body and can observe it sleeping in an objective reality, and the Grim Reaper is nearby. It's not scary in the same way that a vulture over a carcass is not scary—it's just doing what comes naturally. The Grim Reaper has a role to play. It doesn't judge, it doesn't warn. It's just there, perhaps as a reminder that the day will inevitably come when every person leaves their body forever. For the woman

A dreamer pushing themselves out of a dream may be in an effort to protect the body.

with recurring dreams about the Grim Reaper, a lesson can be learned from the dichotomy between the tender sympathy it shows for her body and the stern intolerance for her ego mind.

A man who'd learned how to make his mind leave his body at will decided to use his power to aid a loved one who was very ill and close to death. In the room next to her hospital room, he put his body to sleep and kept his mind awake, then separated his conscious awareness from his body. While out of his body, he observed the physical environment as being identical to physical reality, then went into his loved one's room and saw the Grim Reaper standing over her. They communicated telepathically, and he got the message that nothing could save her. A few hours later, she passed on.

If he'd had the same experience by falling asleep and dreaming naturally, the argument could be made that it was merely a message to himself about the inevitability of his loved one's death. Dreams about the Grim Reaper are known to occur as a loved one is dying, and people close to death dream about it, but the man induced his experience, and he's far from the only person to ever encounter the Grim Reaper while out of their body and near someone who is dying. Voluntarily separating one's consciousness from their body is a rare ability, for sure, but so is the ability to write a Fourier series, and no one is going to argue that that isn't real.

Becoming death is a hero's tale and, at its heart, an archetypal one. You get to be death incarnate with the power to reap souls, and the experience is not just imagined but lived in a dream. In one sense, it's a test to see what you would do with power—especially power that affects the lives of others. Pass the test, and you find greater power within yourself and to make a difference in the world. You can be entrusted with responsibility.

That idea plays out in a dream a boy had about being the son of the Grim Reaper and reaping evil souls. He plays a heroic role by battling against what he perceives as wrongdoers, and his actions in the dream are symbolic of "cleaning house" within himself. He's also role-playing a self-image in his dreams that shapes his personality. A priest or psychotherapist could dream about themself in such a role because they remove the "evil" from people. A police officer removes bad people from society, a role comparable to being the Grim Reaper.

But let's also consider that becoming the Grim Reaper in a dream can mean that the dreamer is in a role of handing out bad news. They are the doctor who gives a fatal prognosis to a patient, the marriage counselor who advises a client to divorce, the teacher who must fail a student, the manager who "terminates" an employee. They are grim roles to play.

Marrying the Grim Reaper is a fascinating variation of the theme. It may dramatize the ego bonding with or being bound to a fatalistic attitude or viewpoint. The Grim Reaper symbolizes the idea of fatalism, while marriage is a bonding ceremony. Marrying the Grim Reaper may symbolize bonding between the ego and the dark and mysterious aspects of the psyche, aka the shadow. They take on strange, distorted, and frightening forms in dreams, representing the strained relationship you have with yourself or some part of yourself. A marriage is a relationship, and the dream author uses the association to tell a story about an *inner* relationship. In that sense, the Grim Reaper embodies something dark or shadowy about you or something that feels forced on you, and marriage symbolizes your relationship with it.

Dreams are your inner world brought to life for you to interact with, and the trick to interpreting them is to figure out the idea that's wrapped in the dream imagery. Imagine how the dreaming mind would show a person their gloomy and fatalistic attitude. *Hello, Grim Reaper!* Imagine how the dreaming mind would translate the idea of being forced into assuming the role of the bad guy. It's like being married to the Grim Reaper. It's a much different scenario from a forced marriage and may indicate an acceptance of oneself and one's fate.

Dreams create symbols based on subjective perceptions of what's good and bad, and therein, you find the critical insight for understanding why a dream presents something as the Grim Reaper and how the dreamer perceives it. For example, a person may perceive something that's contrary to popular opinion as bad, then discover the good in being able to stand up for an unpopular opinion that they believe is right. The dream author needs to create a symbol that unifies the opposites and insert it into a scenario that tells the story. Marrying the Grim Reaper is one heck of a way of accomplishing it!

> **Dreams are your inner world brought to life for you to interact with, and the trick to interpreting them is to figure out the idea that's wrapped in the dream imagery.**

Let's not forget the "grim" part. In the Grim Reaper, you could be seeing a mirthless or morbid side of yourself. It may depict how you perceive a person, situation, circumstance, or condition. If you feel doom or fear death—subjects as grim as they come—the Grim Reaper is the perfect character to play the role.

Finally, people report encountering shadowy figures like the Grim Reaper during sleep paralysis, sleep apnea, night terrors, hypnagogic and hypnopompic episodes, and parasomnias. They could swear it's real, but it's really fear dressed up in hallucinatory imagery.

See also: Charon, Dark Magicians, Demons, Ghosts/Poltergeists/Spirits, Killing, Mummies, Murder, Vampires

HAUNTED DOLLS

Think of "doll" as a noun of dream language and "haunted" as the adjective that modifies it. This is the basic way that a dream creates symbolism: by beginning with a symbol, then adding details. Then, it layers more meaning by putting a haunted doll into the context of a story and pulling from the dreamer's personal experience and associations and collective and archetypal ones to embed meaning. The doll is meaningful, and so is the fact that it's haunted. The dream means something when it combines those details into one symbol.

Begin with the symbolism of a doll. It resembles an animate object, such as a person, creature, or animal. It's a plaything, and it's associated with childhood and childish ways. Dreams build atop those ideas. A doll is a blank canvas on which to project personality traits, thoughts, and feelings and to speak to anything that has a life of its own, such as a crazy idea or an out-of-control situation. As a plaything, the meaning of a doll relates to ideas like being manipulated or unappreciated. As something associated with childhood, a doll can serve as a reference to memories from long ago or unexplainable thoughts, feelings, and behaviors rooted in childhood and immaturity.

To those possibilities for meaning, we add what haunted means. One possibility is that it means that something is unexplainable about what's happening in the dreamer's life and world, inner or outer. Behind the scenes is a driving force, and it may be beyond their comprehension. The symbolic meaning builds atop the idea that hauntings are unexplainable, uncontrollable events, and a doll is under someone's control. A dream can dramatize the idea by making a doll come to life and do odd things.

Feeling coerced—that's what a haunted doll can mean in a dream. Coercion is the use of force and threat to cause someone to do something, like a doll that has no choice. We typically think of coercion as coming from an outside source—a person or authority structure—but the dream author thinks more expansively by including internal sources, such as emotions and compulsions that possess or control you. Buried memories—especially childhood memories—cause you to do things, and you don't know why. In the symbolism of a haunted doll, the dream author has a means to express the idea that the unseen influence of buried memories is affecting you.

For example, a woman dreams that her home is falling apart. She races around trying to fix problems while her family members go about their business like nothing's wrong. She feels alone and unappreciated, then she sees an animated doll dissolving in a puddle of water. It says to her, "Remember when you were 4 [years old]." She begs to know what she's supposed to remember, but the doll reverts to being inanimate. The dream ends. The woman understands the obvious message to search her memory for something traumatic that happened at age four but doesn't remember anything. She remembers a normal childhood with no traumas that would cause her issues as an adult.

Dolls in horror movies are often creepy, but in dreams they can have more complex meanings related to such topics as childhood, memories, or immaturity.

Then, she follows the feelings of the dream, and they resonate with her current situation—she feels alone and unappreciated for working her butt off to keep her home and family together. In the dream, the home is falling apart, and in that imagery, she sees a metaphor for her home life, with her trying to hold everything together while her family takes her for granted. But the feelings in the dream are much stronger and more personal than what is warranted by her current home situation, so she searches her memory again and recognizes a pattern. As a child, she felt alone. Her parents' hands-off approach to parenting didn't directly harm her but neither did it establish the strong sense of self and appreciation that children—and adults—need. The memories formed so long ago, she's not consciously aware of them. Her parents' neglect created tremendous sadness and, like the doll in a puddle of tears, she's dissolving in it. The image sums up her childhood and the feeling that, like a doll, she was given attention at times but mostly ignored. A doll is small and so is a child, creating a sense of relatability.

The important early childhood memories that dreamwork can help you uncover are usually not about the big events; they highlight the conditions and atmosphere that shaped the patterns in your life that continue to the present day and drive emotional reactions that can seem out of kilter. It's no wonder—the child within you is reacting, too. The memories and emotions are stored in the body, and in dreams, we can more readily access them. That's why some highly effective methods of dreamwork (i.e., Embodied Dreamwork) involve listening to the body and allowing it to

> **As a dream symbol, a doll is ideal for highlighting health issues and body-image issues like dysmorphia and gender confusion.**

speak through feelings, intuitions, and sensations. A humanlike doll resembles a body, and in dreams, it borrows the person's speech centers to speak to or for the ego. It can have a lot to say—especially about buried memories and emotions and the body's health and condition.

In fact, somatic dreams are the most common type of dream, and prodromal dreams are forerunners of illness and disease. Serious and chronic conditions and situations involving a person's health and well-being can be the driving force behind nightmares and other powerful dreams. As a dream symbol, a doll is ideal for highlighting health issues and body-image issues like dysmorphia and gender confusion.

A doll is a plaything, and that association opens the door for using it as a symbol for the idea of being manipulated, used, and only appreciated for one's appearance and service. The doll is dressed up to please and put on display, then put away when the show is over. That sums up childhood for some people. In their dreams, they encounter haunted dolls—it tends to be a recurring theme—and in their waking lives, they retreat behind a mask, hiding their true self and feelings. Beneath the mask is a very different reality for them.

A haunted doll is an ideal symbol to highlight what's going on beneath the surface of a person and the things that haunt them. Take, for instance, the dream that features the dreamer, a man, finding out where his ex-girlfriend lives, and he goes to her home. She isn't there, but in the living room, he sees an inanimate doll that resembles a Chucky doll sitting on a chair. He feels like it's watching him and tries to ignore it, then decides he will take a nap on the couch. When he wakes up, the doll is gone, and in its place is a note with one word: "YOU!!!" He suddenly feels immense shame and flees the home.

That one word sums up an entire situation from his life where he acted shamefully with his ex. Time has passed; he desperately wants to apologize, but she relocated, and he has no idea where she is. The dream alludes to that situation by creating a scenario centered on him finding out where she lives, but she isn't home—in other words, she's absent physically but present in his thoughts. The home represents the place in his mind where he dwells on her. "Dwell" and "dwelling" go hand in hand, one being where the mind lives and the other where the body lives. The living room represents his living situation inside of his own being, dominated by intense feelings of shame whenever he thinks about his ex. In that internal space, the doll stares at him and doesn't have to do or say anything to give off a haunting vibe; ideas and emotions are embedded in the symbol, as they are in all dream symbols.

Falling asleep in the dream alludes to the times when he can forget about the feelings that haunt him, only to "wake up" and remember his intense shame, summed up in one word: "YOU!!!" As in, "You know what you did, and I'll never let you forget." It's a mark of his shame. The Chucky doll is especially appropriate as a symbol for his situation because it's male, and in the *Chucky* movies, it says vile things that echo the dialogue in the dreamer's mind.

Movies like *Chucky* and *Annabelle* have given us a strong association between haunted dolls and fear, but the roots extend back centuries, even to prehistory when people drew doll-like images on cave walls and created burial figurines. The body of a deceased person is dressed up and made to appear lifelike, creating association between dolls and death, and death is a strong fear for most people. Nothing says "I feel dead inside" like a haunted doll.

See also: Entities, Molestation, Paralysis, Possession, Zombies

HYDRAS
See: Snakes

MEDUSA
Dream symbols can appear obscure and inscrutable, but you can decode them by thinking of them as amalgamations of ideas. Medusa is a fabulous example because she's an amalgamation of a female person, snakes, and hair, and each has possibilities for use as symbolism that gets even more interesting

when combined. Hair can symbolize thoughts because it grows from the head, and snakes can symbolize something harmful. Now, combine those ideas together, and you have a symbol for *thoughts* that are *harmful*. Thoughts that make your hair stand on end. Thoughts about vengeance, retribution, jealousy, and rage—particularly the feminine manifestations that are more subtle and devious than the blunt, masculine-oriented ones. Thoughts can be wild like snakes and lead a person astray—just ask the many warriors who tried and failed to defeat Medusa.

Medusa is the image of wildness, giving the dream author a specific association that works well as a symbol that matches with certain conditions and situations. Take, for instance, a woman's dream that starts off with her leaving her house and walking next door to her in-laws' house. It's late at night, and moonlight splashes over the scene. Instead of going to the front door, she stealthily goes to a side window and peers in. There, inside the house, are her in-laws staring mutely at her. It gives her a fright. She sees her reflection in the window, and her hair is standing straight up and writhing like snakes. She runs away.

The dream made a lasting impression on her, especially the sight of her reflection in the window. It reminded her specifically of Medusa, and the reason for her spontaneous association is because she's seeing something about Medusa in herself—it's *her* reflection. The action happens as she looks in the

A bronze statue of *Perseus Holding the Head of Medusa* by Benvenuto Cellini in Florence, Italy. Yet another image from mythology, Medusa has snakes for hair, a symbol of harmful thoughts.

window and spots her in-laws, and the simple idea is that something about being near them makes her hair stand on end. Viewing the scene that way provides her with a direction for reviewing her thoughts and feelings to find parallels with the dream content.

First, she really does live next door to her in-laws, and walking from her house to theirs is an everyday occurrence, but rarely does she do it late at night, and she never sneaks over to a side window to peer inside. Those details deviate from her patterns, and we want to know why because it may give more clues to the dream's meaning. In the dream, she sneaks a peek inside because she wants to know what she's about to walk into, and it rings a bell with her because the atmosphere at her in-laws' house is thick with unspoken thoughts and feelings, making her wonder what she's done to deserve their odd treatment. Medusa is a pariah, and that's how the dreamer feels with her in-laws.

The night setting suggests the idea of finding her way in the dark—it's how she feels about the situation—and the moonlight is a symbol for the idea of emotional undercurrents. The moon affects the tides and subtly influences emotions, and the situation with her in-laws has many below-the-surface dynamics. In the presence of her in-laws, her thoughts are intense and go in different directions. A pervasive sense of unease and the potential for danger is present. And yeah, it's making her feel a bit crazy. The comparison with Medusa's wildness is exaggerated but fits.

With Medusa, a dream can say everything in one look, and like all dream symbols, it's a picture that says 1,000 words. She's a picture of pain, anger, and anguish. She's danger personified and the poster child for the proverb, "Hell hath no fury like a woman scorned."

"Fatal beauty" is another idea for Medusa as a symbol, an alluring beauty that's also sinister. What a metaphor for beauty that drives men wild and drives women to fits of jealousy. But with dreams, you need to think more broadly because they begin with an association like fatal beauty and reach out for related ideas. Fixation is another word for the same idea. A dream can then use Medusa's fatal beauty when you are unable to break the hold that something has on you. Fatal beauty is a hypnotic beauty, and in that sense, the basic idea branches out to include anything that seductively pulls you in, that possesses, and that compels you to act against your own good.

The dark side of beauty is obsession, and it's a danger both to the people hypnotized by it and those obsessed with having it. The dream author may observe a person going to great lengths to style their hair, with strands sticking out this way and that, and compare it with Medusa's head of snakes. The visual metaphor might not fit exactly but instead match up with the person's internal thought processes and feelings and their motives for wanting to be beautiful. Dreadlocks, however, are a better visual comparison to snakes rising out of the head.

Think beyond physical beauty—dreams apply the idea across the board and use it as a comparison to, for example, desires and temptations that are alluring and dangerous, beliefs that are seductive and not what they appear to be, and certain emotions and motives that possess their own center of gravity. Beauty as an idea is the starting point, and the ending point is the outlying associations that may not be apparent or obvious.

Medusa was cursed after she broke her vow of chastity as a priestess of Athena. Her beauty was her downfall, and dreams can use her as a symbol that speaks to the curse of beauty and the repercussions of using it and sex for manipulation and power and for breaking promises, tempting fate, and committing sacrilege. It's a cautionary tale about a downfall brought on by overstepping one's bounds, and it's the very picture of a dark transformation driven by lust, deception, and betrayal.

> Medusa was cursed after she broke her vow of chastity as a priestess of Athena. Her beauty was her downfall, and dreams can use her as a symbol that speaks to the curse of beauty....

Medusa can symbolize something that grabs ahold of a person, such as an addiction or vice, and is particularly good as a symbol for injectable drugs because the fangs of a snake are like needles, and the drug has a fatal allure. But that association is only a starting point for branching out to related ideas, such as the venomous effects of a bad influence and the poisoning of the mind and heart. Medusa is the picture of a poisoned heart.

As a type of dream character, the symbolism and meaning of Medusa may be similar to a witch or the girl from *The Ring*. She's a symbol for fear of the feminine and the dark side of its traits and behaviors.

See also: The Girl from *The Ring*, Possession, Snakes, Vampires, Witches/Warlocks

MINOTAURS

The minotaur is similar to the centaur, with the difference being that the minotaur has the body of a man and the head of a bull, but the centaur has the lower body of a horse and the upper body of a human. The duality of the imagery offers many uses for symbolism, though the minotaur has darker connotations. Whereas the centaur is seen as wild and noble, the minotaur suggests the ideas of savagery and violence. The story of the minotaur in mythology is tragic, and it gives the dream storyteller dark material to work with.

The place to begin decoding the meaning of a minotaur is with the fusion of a bull's head on a human body. Nothing says "bullheaded" like that imagery. The minotaur won't listen to reason; it's obstinate, relentless, and implacable—does that remind you of anyone you know? Does it remind you of yourself? Dreams usually point inward, and as you consider ideas about dream

Compared to the noble centaur, the minotaur is more a symbol of savagery and violence. The minotaur is also associated with labyrinths, confusing places that are difficult to escape.

imagery, you always look there first. The minotaur may remind you of someone you know, and perhaps, in some way, they remind you of yourself, like a mirror's reflection.

Dr. Carl Jung says that we react most strongly to the things we see in other people that we also see and don't like about ourselves. For example, you are "bullheaded" about a particular subject but easygoing about everything else, and at first, when thinking about a minotaur in your dream, it reminds you of someone who's bullheaded. Then, you realize that the person reminds you of yourself. You may not think of yourself as bullheaded, but dreams exaggerate and dramatize, and the comparisons they make are exaggerated but true. They're metaphors.

As one learns the language of dreams, a common hurdle to overcome is the difficulty of seeing the ideas symbolized in dream imagery. You see a minotaur in your dream and immediately look for comparisons with human and animal qualities, but the same comparisons can be made to problems, situations, and circumstances. The minotaur can symbolize the problem that has no solution, the situation that leads you in circles, the circumstance that won't change. The dream author has good reasons for choosing the minotaur as a symbol, and they are often found in your subjective impressions and feelings. They may not be objectively accurate but, like metaphors, they express hidden dynamics that are sensed, felt, and subjectively true.

Wild sexual desires and other strong, instinctive drives that override one's restraint and reason are the minotaur's forte. Fuse the head of an animal known for its virility on to a human body, and the implication is obvious. It replaces the part of the body associated with thinking and reasoning with the image of an animal that's not known for its thinking and reasoning! The dream imagery may capture the sexual overtones of a situation, such as being passionate about a desire to do something. Climbing a tall mountain, for instance, is a passion driven by desire to conquer, to be "on top," to push the body to its limits with animal-like power. The image of the minotaur expresses those ideas visually. Dreaming about trying to control, trap, or tame a minotaur is one heck of a metaphor for trying to control a powerful passion or instinctive drive.

When a maze or labyrinth is a feature of a dream involving a minotaur, it suggests the idea of being caught up in something for which no escape or way out exists. Such dreams often spark feelings of desperation and hopelessness—follow them into your waking life and find the source.

The labyrinth is also great symbolism for situations such as relationships, with their twists and turns and arguments that go around and around. The imagery suggests that the dreamer is lost in something, perhaps lost in their own thoughts or personal problems. Existential questions and issues in life can be like a maze, and the way out leads inexorably to a person facing the thing about themself that frightens them the most. That's the moral of the minotaur's story.

The spiraling shape of the minotaur's labyrinth is highly suggestive of processes of the psyche. Moving inward in a spiral pattern can symbolize going inward toward the center of one's being in the unconscious mind. The center is a seat of personal power for those who master the lessons leading to it. The minotaur is a symbol for the challenges one faces on that journey, and in that way, it's similar to a psychopomp, the guide of souls to the places of the dead, which must be faced or trusted in order to progress but with the twist that the minotaur must be killed to complete the process. It could represent, for example, the attitude or stance of an ego that's self-serving or recalcitrant and must "die" before new aspects of the personality can emerge.

Going outward from the center may symbolize using one's power in the ordinary world and in the dream space. It suggests the idea of going forth to make your mark on the world, or it can simply mean "unwind," in which case the minotaur is likely to be a symbol of whatever is winding you up: stress, anxiety, fear, and so forth.

The hunger, rage, and pain of the minotaur draw parallels with the mythology of werewolves, so read the discussion in the entry on Werewolves for more insights.

When a mythological creature appears in a dream, it's a good idea to research the subject matter. The stories from mythology are archetypal, and they don't have to be consciously known for a person's dreams to use them. Oftentimes, a feeling of resonance can be found between the dream, the dreamer, and the myth. Dr. Carl Jung calls this interpretation method a tool of "amplification." The person searches for parallels in myth and literature to help illuminate and understand dream content. If Dr. Jung were around in modern times, he'd also suggest searching the stories that video games and other media tell; they are like modern myths.

See also: Centaurs, Charon, Imprisonment/Entrapment, Werewolves

MUMMIES

A mummy is under wraps. Something is hidden beneath the layers, and for the dream author, it's a great symbol to use in stories about what's hidden or unknown, especially about ourselves. Go beneath the surface to find the meaning hidden beneath the mummy's wrapping. Sigmund Freud compared the dream interpreter to an archaeologist carefully brushing away the surface layers, seeking to solve a great mystery, and with dreams, the mystery in question is of one's existence. Who are you, really, and why do you exist?

But not all dream imagery is that deep, and as we think broadly, we run across possibilities for mummy symbolism like "dead on your feet." Another idea conveyed by the imagery is that it's something dead that's been brought back to life, and that's an idea a dream can really run with, especially when telling you a story about something you pursue that should be over and done with. Still pining away for your ex or regretting that decision from long ago? Yeah, it's like a mummy: dead, but you're still giving it life. On the other hand, the mummy as a dream image can convey the idea of rejuvenation. You somehow find the strength to rise again, in which case your dream about a mummy will feel positive.

"Wrapped up" is another way of saying "constricted," and the mummy is the image of constriction and lack of freedom. The mummy's moaning is an expression of pain, and the mummy's wrapping is a way of saying that beneath the surface is great pain and yearning. Something deep inside of you may want to be heard.

Special people are mummified, making it a symbol for commemoration and remembrance. A big achievement is something about a person's past that stays with them forever after. On the other hand, a big mistake can also stay with us. Nothing says "the past is catching up with you" like a mummy catching

up with you. A dream will express the difference in meaning with details that relate to the mummy; for example, whether you encounter it in a grand temple, a symbol of commemoration, or buried in a closet, a symbol of concealment or wishing to forget about something.

What will you be remembered for, and what will people think of you after you're gone? Those are the questions that may be at the heart of a mummy dream. If you are mummified, it means that you have made an impact on the world. Then again, the same imagery can also mean "forgotten," so always search the context of a dream's story for the meaning of its symbols.

Mummy images are a bit more complex than, say, the Grim Reaper, in that they have a potential dual meaning of both death and rejuvenation and life, but life involving pain and loss of freedom.

Dr. Carl Jung once dreamed about mummies chasing him. It occurred during a midlife crisis while he was questioning his direction in life, especially as a psychiatrist. On one hand, he pursued professional recognition and respect in society; on the other, he felt a calling toward inner pursuits that ran counter to what his society and profession wanted of him. Dr. Jung struggled to rectify the two opposing desires within him and came to understand the mummies chasing him in his dream as symbols for the old ideas and notions he inherited from society. He decided to pursue his inner calling, and near the end of his life, he wrote in his autobiography that it was the right decision, but first, he had to pass through a period of intense personal questioning.

Fear of change and attachment to old ways—those are the ideas hidden beneath the mummy's wrapping in Dr. Jung's dream. Death and mortality are two other ideas you may find when you peel away the layers, and perhaps, the grandaddy of them all is secrets. Keeping a secret is like wrapping it up and hiding it away, and if you want to express the idea as a visual metaphor like dreams do, a mummy is ideal. Perhaps the secret is a truth or realization that you keep hidden from yourself. The dreaming mind is the archaeologist of the psyche, and dreams serve a purpose of showing you what you don't consciously know. Find out what's beneath the wrapping!

Finally, the difference between mummy and mommy is one letter. Dreams are notorious for creating poignant wordplays like that. Beneath the wrapping, for example, is something you are trying to tell yourself about your mom, your relationship with her, or the subject of motherhood.

See also: Frankenstein, Haunted Dolls, Possession, Zombies

PENNYWISE THE CLOWN

Oh, my, what a deep impression this character makes, judging by how often it pops up in reports of terrifying dreams. Pennywise is an evil clown that lures children to their deaths and is a character that appears in dreams about dangerous personal flaws, relentless pursuits, and alluring traps. Dreams with evil clowns dramatize parallel situations and circumstances in ordinary life, such as when pursued by unwanted romantic advances, trapped in no-win situations, or being so self-involved it's comical. It's a story we all know, even if we haven't read the book by Stephen King that imprinted Pennywise on to our collective consciousness.

Pennywise is a recent incarnation of the evil clown, a particularly dark manifestation of the trickster archetype. Its penchant for dark humor and play-

As with Frankenstein's monster, Pennywise the demonic clown has origins in fiction (the novel by Stephen King). The symbolism involves the machinations of the dark trickster.

ing tricks lends it a wide capacity as a symbol to use in stories about the dark underside of people and life. As a trickster character, Pennywise is an archetype, a universal pattern of thought, feeling, and behavior that manifests in people. As a dream symbol, it points inward at something that fools you into working against your own best interest, that deceives you into believing things that aren't true or real, and that possesses your ego. The trickster lives in the shadow of the ego, and the bigger the ego, the bigger its shadow. Pennywise as the trickster hides in the shadow of a big ego. Pennywise also hides in the sewers, a fantastic metaphor for the dark underside.

Dark underside—when the term fits, dreams can tell the story as Pennywise down in the sewers. In dream-speak, a sewer can mean "forget about it; it's useless." It's associated with memories we want to forget, talents and opportunities we waste, and relationships we cast aside—might as well flush them down the toilet. It's associated with ideas such as "taking shit" and with behaviors, feelings, and thought processes that stink. Dreams use our figures of speech and the ideas they express as the basis for creating symbolism, and with Pennywise, those ideas are powerfully poignant and personal.

In one such dream, the dreamer observes Pennywise as an ordinary man going about his business when he gets into a fight with another man, and that man curses him to forever feed on fear. The first man then goes through a horrid, full-body transformation into Pennywise and begins feeding on children. The dream dramatizes a strong split between two sides of the dreamer, one shown as the character that transforms into Pennywise and the other as the man who curses him. Duality is a dream's way of showing a person what's divided within them, and the dream's observer point of view gives the man distance to observe his deep inner conflict without getting too caught up in it.

His dream dramatizes a divide between doing and being what he wants and not doing it because he's afraid. Fear "feeds" the divide, so in a sense, he's cursed to feed on fear. As Pennywise, he feeds on children, a nod to the psychological roots of the divide in his restrictive childhood that taught him that it's not okay to ask for and get what he wants. Transforming into Pennywise dramatizes how the internal divide is warping him. The full-body transformation is a nod to the childhood memories stored in his body.

The phrase "penny wise and pound foolish" is the source of the idea behind one person's dream about chasing a red balloon and wanting so badly to catch up to it that she doesn't see the pit in the ground in front of her before falling into it. The dream pokes at her money problems caused by overspending in pursuit of social status. A red balloon is Pennywise's lure to get children into his trap, and in her dream, it symbolizes the social status she wants and her blindness to the "pitfalls."

> **Duality is a dream's way of showing a person what's divided within them....**

Pennywise is quite the slave master in some dreams. In one woman's dream, he impregnates her and bonds them together through the child, symbolizing her bondage to what the evil clown represents about her personality: a childish sarcastic streak—appropriate, considering what a wisecracker the clown is. Another person found themselves in the role of Pennywise's sex slave, a dramatization of their fixation on sex and statement about the psychology behind it. Pennywise is the perfect actor to give voice to the taunts in the person's head that belittle his sexual prowess while demeaning and debasing everything related to sex.

Pennywise is a specific character that works well in some roles and a type of character with broad uses as symbolism in stories. Use the list below to continue your exploration.

See also: Dark Magicians, Demons, Devils, Evil, Haunted Dolls, Possession, Spiders

SHADOW PEOPLE

This widely reported symbol in nightmares is not meaningful when it results from night terrors, sleep paralysis, sleep apnea, and sleep-related hallucinations (parasomnias). It's not a symbol in the traditional sense in those cases; it's a by-product of chemical and sensory misfires and a reaction to the fear and confusion they cause. Night terrors, also called sleep terrors, result from the body dumping a load of trauma-based energy and the dreaming mind translating it into the imagery of evil shadow people. In sleep paralysis, the conscious realization of being unable to move zaps the nervous system with panic signals and activates its emergency response system. During episodes of sleep apnea, the person panics from suffocation and experiences a life-and-death emergency. It occurs while they are asleep and dreaming, and the dreaming mind responds by creating imagery that expresses their terror. Whatever the cause, the hallucinations are as real as it gets.

No wonder so many people sense evil in the presence of shadow people!

The causes behind the meaningful manifestations of shadow people in dreams—fear, anxiety, and stress top the list—are explained in the discussion in the Black-eyed People entry.

Shadow people are great symbols for the dark, mysterious, and unknown aspects of life and what's feared, avoided, suppressed, and repressed. In nightmares, shadow people tend to be manifestations of what we don't accept or love about ourselves, so they hide in the shadows of the psyche, where they gain strength and power. They want to rejoin the conscious personality and be whole with it—runaways who just want to be welcomed home.

Shadow people are both shadowy and people, and it's a combination for using them in the stories that dreams tell about people and their shadows—namely, their psychological shadow. The most common misunderstanding about the psychological shadow is that it's bad or evil, but it's just split off from the ego. Dr. Carl Jung said that it's everything that could be conscious about a person but isn't, including what's good about them. The parts of oneself that are left unlived—especially the rejected parts—eat you from the inside. They must be faced, a recipe for our most powerful and meaningful dreams. If healing and reconciliation happen in the dream space, they carry over into waking life and enable deep changes in the person and an outburst of creative energy.

The psychological and physiological reasons for why shadow people appear in dreams are deep, but in some cases, it's simple. A shadow person is simply something that can't be seen in detail. Take, for instance, the dream a man had that puts him in his childhood home in front of the door to the basement. He dreads opening it—on the other side is something purely evil. An invisible force swings open the door and sucks him in. Now, he's in the basement, in the dark and scared out of his mind. He looks around to get his bearings and discerns darker, human-shaped shadows coming out of the walls and closing in from all sides. He falls to the ground and covers himself,

The shadow person is a fairly clear metaphor for the psychological shadows that dwell within most troubled people.

screaming, "No, no, no!" The shadow people are symbols for his phobia of the dark—it's more than a fear, and the dream reflects that fact by creating a scenario that causes extreme terror. It also chose the perfect setting to play out the story. As a child, the basement of his home terrified him, and he often froze outside the door and would only enter if he absolutely had to. His phobia is driven by not knowing what lurks in the shadows of a dark room. His imagination fills in the details with his worst fears.

See also: Aliens, Black-eyed People, Dark Magicians, Evil, Slenderman

SIRENS

See: Witches/Warlocks

SLENDERMAN

This urban legend and its variation, the Hat Man, infiltrates into more dreams than one might think. It's a legend about a tall, slender man who can be ritually summoned, then it wreaks havoc in waking life and in nightmares. That idea caught hold in the popular imagination of teenagers, but as a type of dark, ill-defined dream figure, it also appears frequently during adult episodes of sleep paralysis, night terrors, and parasomnias, and in those cases, it's a variation of the shadow people phenomenon.

Slenderman falls into a category of the creature that's summoned and has the power to possess, and that's a subject covered extensively in our discussion in the Girl from *The Ring* entry. Summoning is a long-tailed story with numerous variations. It appears in literature and myth going far back in history, particularly in stories about genies and other types of magically summoned spirits. At their heart, they are cautionary tales about the desire for power and what a person is willing to do to have it, and they provide great fodder for dreams. Here's an example:

A teenage girl dreams that she summons Slenderman, and it tells her that it'll grant her greatest wish if she agrees to kill her best friend. She objects, saying she can't do it by herself, and Slenderman assures her that it has possessed a group of popular girls she knows at school, and they will help. The dream ends with her unsure of what to do.

She wakes up and wonders what sort of horrible person she must be to even consider such a thing, but the dream is figurative, not literal—a common mistake people make when they fail to understand why they create a dream experience for themselves. It asks what she's willing to sacrifice to be popular and gives her a choice. Popularity is a sort of power, and she doesn't have it, but she does have a close friend. Her friend would never fit into the popular crowd, she thinks, and she will never be welcomed by the popular girls unless she ditches her dorky friend. The dream asks, is she willing to sacrifice that friendship?

With origins in urban legend, Slenderman is a wicked entity that can be summoned by people. Slenderman, therefore, is a cautionary figure for being careful what you wish for.

The importance of understanding dreams as self-created experiences really stands out in her case because her dream dramatizes her thoughts and tests her character. It's not like the popular girls said to her, "You can be one of us if you lose your friend." The choice is based on a hypothetical, and the point is to make her search herself to define who she really is and what she *values*. It's okay if she makes a bad choice—in the simulated reality of dreams, bad choices are opportunities to learn before we blunder into making them in ordinary life. A situation may come up in the young woman's life that tests her friendship, and she'll be better prepared because she's already been tested in her dream.

> **Slenderman is fear incarnate—especially fears based on the extremes that people will go to get what they want.**

The dream author observes the tales and legends about Slenderman and sees the perfect type of character to pull out when the dynamics are right. One obvious dynamic is when something from within a person overpowers or deceives their ego. It seems to come out of nowhere like an evil spirit because it's the ego's blind spot. Slenderman is a walking, talking symbol that interacts with the ego in the dream space, and it's a type of character used in dark dreams to help you discover what you're really made of—and (hopefully) to find out that it's more than you thought.

Slenderman is fear incarnate—especially fears based on the extremes that people will go to get what they want. Like the Dark Magician, it's the inner voice that convinces you to set power in motion that can't be controlled. It's the repercussions for bumbling into something without thinking about the consequences. It's the hubris of the ego that thinks it knows everything and invites a hard lesson in reality. It's the trouble a person invites into their life.

In other words, Slenderman is a trickster character. Read about Dark Magicians and Pennywise the Clown in their own entries, two of the better known tricksters.

The list of entries below points you to extensive discussions of various aspects of the symbolism and psychology behind Slenderman as a type of dream character.

See also: Black-eyed People, Dark Magicians, Demons, Evil, Girl from *The Ring*, Pennywise the Clown, Shadow People, Vampires

SNAKES

It may be the most common symbol in scary dreams, and it even features in the scary dreams of people who normally don't fear snakes. The following discussion offers many reasons for why snakes make such great symbols for fear and related ideas, but as with all dream symbols, the meaning depends on the dream's context and the person who experiences it.

A snake can hurt you—that's reason number one. Sure, lots of things can hurt you, but snakes are deliberate about it—they don't bite to say, "Good morning!" We fear what hurts us because it's a survival instinct. Snakes are survivors, and people are, too. That association gives the dream author a great symbol to use when in survival mode, when feeling hurt or hunted, or when someone "as mean as a snake" has it out for you. It's a role given to snakes in fables, myths, and modern storytelling, too.

Pain and suffering are reasons number two and three. The snake's bite inflicts pain—sharp, sudden pain—and suffering ensues, which spreads and lingers long after the initial strike. Those associations give the dream author a symbol that matches well with situations and conditions that cause lingering pain.

The suddenness of a snake's attack and the major pain it inflicts are big reasons why people hate dreaming about them, and the dream author loves them as symbols that mix fear, pain, and suddenness. Take, for instance, the woman's dream where she's walking in a forest, enjoying nature. A snake falls out of a tree and lands on her head. A life-and-death struggle ensues. The snake bites her on the neck, and the implication dawns on her that it could be fatal. It terrifies her so much, she's shocked awake, grasping at the air as if still fighting the snake.

Notice the suddenness of the attack, how it came out of nowhere, and the drama of the ensuing struggle. It's a perfect symbolic way of describing the notice to vacate her apartment that her property-management company dropped on her "out of the blue" (the snake drops from above while she's outside) the day before the dream. Her life went from peaceful, shown in the dream as walking through a forest, to a panicked emergency. She then found out that she had no legal protection because she paid her rent month to month and wasn't under a lease. In the dream, she's exposed and vulnerable, and that sums up her situation.

Also, she suspects treachery—the company knew what was coming and milked her for all the rent money it could get before kicking her out. The snake symbolizes the property company, and the bite to the throat symbolizes their "go for the jugular" mentality. The nightmare is the type that processes the memories and emotions associated with sudden, shocking events. Treachery is a common association with snakes, and her dream turns the idea into a scenario.

In another example, a woman dreams that a snake slithers into bed with her and her husband, a symbol for treachery in her marriage—she suspects him of having an affair. The bed where they sleep together is the perfect setting to tell the story, and the snake is the perfect symbol for betrayal. In her dream,

Pain and suffering that strike suddenly, sometimes out of nowhere, are concepts embodied by snake imagery.

she tries to wake up her husband to do something about the snake, but he's dead asleep, another perfect symbol that matches with the situation because he acts oblivious to the trouble in their marriage.

Trouble is the simple idea that provides a good starting point for understanding the dream. The snake is a character playing a role in the story, and knowing that, you try to understand the thinking of the storyteller, the dream author. The snake enters the scene, spelling trouble. Then, the trouble gets into bed with the woman and her husband, and it raises questions like what's the trouble in their marriage and where's the danger really coming from? We know those answers. Danger is reason number four on the list of most common meanings of "snake dreams," and treachery is reason number five. Answering the above questions gives her the information to readily deduce the dream's meaning.

That process is the essence of dream interpretation, and you can use it to decode the meaning of most dreams. Begin with the main symbol and think of it as an idea, then analyze the symbol in the context of the overall scene or story. If you run from a snake in a dream, ask what it symbolizes that you are running from. If you battle a snake, ask where the battle is in yourself and your life. If a snake hurts you, seek out the places where you are hurt and the sources of your pain.

Even long and complex dreams follow that outline. Take, for instance, the dream where a man is a warrior in a huge battle and gets injured. Natives take him to their village and nurse him back to health. They live in a giant tree, a picture of harmony with nature. Time passes and his health improves, so he ventures out to exercise and take stock of the situation. He joins the villagers who do martial arts training with wooden staves, catches on quickly, and masters the weapon. The villagers are in awe and begin referring to him as the savior promised by an ancient prophecy. He denies it.

Then, he notices more about the grand tree they live in. It is sentient and protects them from the mostly unseen dangers that lurk beyond its reach. It asks in return that they dress and act as it dictates, never leave its protective radius, and return indoors before sunset—for their safety, of course. The arrangement makes the dreamer uneasy.

Then, one day, outsiders attack the tree. Slaughter ensues—the villagers take the worst of it. The man observes the tree closely and finally notices what he had sensed but couldn't see. The tree is a mother snake, and its branches are its babies! At the base of the trunk, the bark opens and reveals the snake's heart. It's a rare moment of vulnerability brought about by the heat of the battle, so the man rams the end of his staff into the tree's heart and kills it. The battle ends, and the surviving villagers pick up the pieces of their lives and leave.

The dream fully reveals its simple idea in the final scene: a "bad bargain." The tree offers protection to the villagers in return for their obedience. It seems reasonable considering the many dangers that lurk, but the tree is unable to keep its end of the bargain. Summarizing the dream as a simple statement helps the dreamer identify the parallels with his life.

The tree symbolizes a religious cult he used to be part of, having joined it after devastation struck his life. That's the meaning behind the opening scene when he's wounded in battle and taken to the tree village to heal. Everything is great at first—the cult is the image of harmony, and as he recovers, he quickly grows in knowledge and strength, symbolized as training with the staff. The dream creates another parallel by including the storyline about the villagers gaining the tree's protection in return for their obedience. Cult members give their obedience, and the cult's structure protects them from the dangers of the outside world. Another bad bargain.

The final scene encapsulates the man's departure. The cult collapsed under pressure from outside forces, and he delivered the fatal blow by using his knowledge and strength—the staff—to reveal it as the serpent it really was. The dream's comparison of the cult to a tree that's really a mother snake with many babies—symbolizing the cult's power structure—is a beautiful metaphor.

Something is hidden—that's reason number six for snake dreams, and the above dream is a prime example. Snakes hide in unexpected places and lurk unseen. They ambush, striking suddenly and powerfully. So not only is something hidden, but it's also a danger. It may cause pain and suffering. It's treacherous. Oftentimes, multiple reasons on our list show up in one snake dream.

Anger is reason number seven. Some snakes look angry, and it creates a strong association with anger, spite, vindictiveness, and cold-blooded hate. Snakes are cold-blooded and superb symbols for predatory behaviors and for lashing out and striking and protecting territory. Sex, mating, and desire are also instinctive, which is why we find those ideas in many fables and myths about snakes.

Reason number eight for nightmares and dark dreams about snakes is their role as serpents like the one in the Garden of Eden. It's evil in physical form.

All told, the many associations with snakes provide a grand buffet for storytelling, but for every dream that features common associations with snakes and reasons why we dream about them, one defies the norm and draws its meaning from deeply unconscious processes and content. Snakes live underground, and in dream-speak, underground means unconscious. The unconscious is the opposite pole of the conscious mind, and it's the part of the mind that nature alone creates. Its ways are mysterious. Dr. Carl Jung said that snake dreams happen when life gets serious, and the unconscious has a most important message to deliver.

So, number nine on our list of reasons encompasses the first eight, which all say "shit's gettin' real," plus the most important one: you need to understand what's happening deep inside of you, get the message, and respond. Nightmares are the shock therapy of dream life, and nightmares featuring snakes may be the biggest jolt of all.

> **Nightmares are the shock therapy of dream life, and nightmares featuring snakes may be the biggest jolt of all.**

Extra difficulty in understanding snake dreams enters the picture when they pull from archaic associations in the collective unconscious. Such dreams are critically important to understand, but most people do not possess the base of knowledge for decoding the obscure symbolism. Human interactions with snakes—both for good and ill—began during our prehistory, and the further we as a species distance ourselves from our instincts and roots, the more our consciousness creeps away from its foundation in the unconscious and our instinctive ability to interact with it.

You've heard of the reptilian brain, but most people don't understand what it means psychologically to have an advanced cortex of brain tissue layered over a "primitive" substructure, the reptilian brain stem. For thousands of generations before modern humans, our species lived much closer to nature, and we developed cultural structures during that long span to help us understand and interact psychologically with the unconscious. Those structures have all but vanished, leaving today's humans exposed to merciless internal forces that we don't even know exist—merciless in the same way that nature can be merciless by design, not intent.

The following example demonstrates the problem and the solution. The dreamer stands atop a mountain, looking up. High above her, she sees an eagle flying. Suddenly, the ground beneath her quakes, and a ginormous, five-headed, white snake emerges. It rises into the air and blocks the sky from view. Her heart beats frantically, and she thinks she's going to die. The dream ends. She's so frightened, she turns on the lights in her bedroom to check under the bed and make sure the snake isn't there.

It's no wonder the snake scared her so much. It's like something out of mythology: massive beyond measure, pure white, and oh, yeah, it has five heads! A puny human is helpless against it.

The woman who experienced the dream is Hindu, and two years later, she made a pilgrimage to Vasuki Nag Temple at the top of Mandar Mountain. There, she was stunned to see paintings and other depictions of the five-headed, white serpent god Vasuki. In Hindu mythology, the giant eagle Garuda hunts Vasuki, his half brother, with the intent of killing him and is stopped by their father, a sage. Her experience at Vasuki Nag opened her mind to the connections between the myth, the dream, and herself, and especially stunning is the fact that she did not know much about the mythology before having the dream.

That means that it arose from the collective unconscious, and those dreams rank at the top of importance and potency. As time passed, she found out why. The mountain in her dream symbolizes her quest for spiritual enlightenment, and it may have foreshadowed her trip to Vasuki Nag. And like the symbolism of the eagle that soars above her in the dream's opening scene, she is overly cerebral in her quest. Her distant and dry orientation lacks the awesomeness that firsthand experiences of bliss and revelation impart. She shifted her spiritual practice to body-based practices such as yoga and gained what she needed to make rapid progress.

That personal dynamic adds a dimension to her dream about the giant, white serpent erupting from the ground beneath her. Underground can be a dream's way of saying "the unconscious." The unconscious, wanting to support her spiritual quest, shows her the earthiness and feeling that are missing from her spiritual practice, and it does so grandly. When the serpent rises over her in the dream, it shelters her from the sky and cuts off her cerebral orientation. At the beginning of the dream, she is looking upward, a depiction of her mental focus. The serpent's action says symbolically, "Your answers are not here."

What began as the most frightening nightmare of her life became her biggest blessing once she understood its message.

The white color of the snake is common to dreams where the unconscious sends messengers to aid the conscious mind, and its five heads are significant numerologically as a number portending big changes. Vasuki the serpent is commonly depicted with five heads but can have anywhere from one to seven. The dream appears to deliberately give it five heads as a sign of the big changes coming up in the dreamer's life.

The ouroboros, visualized as a snake bending in a circle to eat its own tail, is a common dream sign that the person is entering a time of transformation. Two snakes intertwined and rising upward is a symbol of transformation—a visualization of kundalini energy, which, when awakened, produces powerful transformative experiences—and so is the shedding of a snake's skin, which it does to allow room for growth. Times come in life when our old ways restrict us, and we shed our skin and grow.

The ouroboros originated in Egyptian and Greek iconography and represents cycles of life and death.

Embrace those opportunities, and your dreams reflect it positively. Run from those opportunities, and you invite nightmares. The unconscious mind won't allow you to ignore or avoid what the snakes in your dreams symbolize, and it may even put snakes in your path in your waking life to double down on the message.

Dreams may use snakes as symbols to highlight the dangers, fears, and threats that come from one's environment and the people in it, but the wise person looks inward first when penetrating the meaning of their dreams by asking, "What do I see about myself in the snake, its behavior, and the conditions involving it?"

The following is a rundown of examples:

- ✖ Recurring dreams about being trapped in a room with hundreds of dangerous snakes. It symbolically sums up the dreamer's internal conditions—stuffed full of terrible fears and anxieties and seeing no way out.

- ✖ A teacher's dream about finding a dangerous snake in the schoolyard and intervening before it can bite a student. It bites her instead and leaves deep puncture wounds. The dream dramatizes the stresses of her job that "leave a mark" on her.

- ✖ A mom's dream about pulling a snake out of her young daughter's throat, symbolizing her situation of being unable to vocalize her unhappiness. She loves her daughter dearly, and her dedication as a mother is unquestionable, but she's paying a major price for it by neglecting her own needs.

- ✖ Fighting a huge, black snake that sneaks into the dreamer's home symbolizes the dreamer's struggle against gloomy feelings. The dream sets the scene by making it noticeably gloomy and giving the snake a black color.

- ✖ A woman's dream where a snake tells her point-blank that it's going to kill her and she's powerless to stop it. The snake symbolizes late-stage brain cancer.

- ✖ Locking the door to keep snakes out of the dreamer's home, but one gets inside, slithers underneath the carpet, and heads straight for the couch where she was sitting. She grabs a knife and savagely hacks through the carpet to kill it. Locking the door to keep snakes out of her home is a symbolic way of saying that she tries to keep men out of her life, but her ex-boyfriend is the one "snake" who can get past her defenses by using "underhanded" tactics to slither back into her life—and into her pants! In the dream, the snake would come up from below her if it managed to reach the couch. In that sense, the carpet could represent pubic hair, but in the context of the dream, it's more likely to be a symbol for "sneaking up."

The snake is a classic phallic symbol that appears as a predatory creature in the dreams of people who fear and/or hate male sexual energy and the act of intercourse. (Conversely, people who love male sexual energy and intercourse experience snakes in phallic dreams very differently, sometimes as hypnotic and irresistible creatures.) The dreams rise to nightmare level for people who have been sexually abused, raped, or traumatized.

Phallic symbolism also appears in the dreams of men and women alike who feel victimized by patriarchy. Attacks by snakes in their dreams dramatically express their feelings and perceptions about situations and conditions that

The snake can also be a type of phallic symbol and, thus, hints at sexuality and eroticism.

involve dominance and submission, violence and the threat of it (including psychological and emotional), authoritarian hierarchy, and "the law of the jungle."

Constriction is a theme that appears frequently in snake dreams, and now that you understand how dreams use snakes to create symbolism, the main possibility for the meaning may be obvious: you feel constricted! Something has its hold on you and won't let go. The dream begins with a situation or condition like the coronavirus lockdown and dramatizes the feeling of being restricted to your home. You feel constricted, and next thing you know, you are dreaming about a boa constrictor being wrapped around your body or preventing you from going outside. Or a dream begins with the anxiety and stress that causes tightness in the chest and visualizes the feeling as a python squeezing your torso.

Jobs and relationships are two main culprits behind dreams about constrictor snakes, but the symbol is appropriate for just about anything that locks you into a way of being that you want to leave or outgrow. Another culprit is the lack of options and opportunities. It's a simple formula; dreams use something physically constricting as a symbol for something figuratively constricting. It's common to experience powerful dreams about constrictor snakes when a person's attitudes, beliefs, or lifestyle inhibit their freedom and self-expression. Add sexual repression or restriction to the mix, and it gives the dream author even more raw material. Snakes are sensual and phallic creatures that have long been associated with sexuality and temptations of the flesh. The more a person's ego is antagonistic toward their instincts for self-expression, sexuality, and freedom, the more the unconscious mind compensates by taking an equally antagonistic stance toward the ego. And when the imbalance is severe, it results in nightmares.

The source of the dream imagery may be a physical condition. Sleep apnea can feel like something is choking you—your airway is being constricted. Blood flow to a limb is constricted as you sleep. Your intestines are tied in a knot, or a tapeworm has made them its home. Those dreams are often startling. Some are downright scary. And if the physical condition threatens your health, you are likely to have dreams that demand your attention.

Associations between snakes and healing originated millennia ago. Healthy, green snakes are common symbols for good health and fertility and black snakes for illnesses of the body and mind. The symbolic connection builds atop the fact that snakes are highly sensitive to their environment and attuned to the rhythms of nature. Snakes are also symbols of the body's subtle energy channels, long and sinewy, called meridians. The personal side of the unconscious mind is centered in the body and acutely aware of everything happening inside of and around it, and it possesses faculties for correctly interpreting signals from the brain stem and nervous system that the conscious mind may lack or ignore.

> **Healthy, green snakes are common symbols for good health and fertility and black snakes for illnesses of the body and mind.**

Venom is a common theme of snake dreams. A dream doesn't just use a snake as a character, it uses a venomous snake. It may be a way of heightening the sense of danger, but if you dream about a venomous snake biting you, the door opens to an array of possibilities for meaning. The simple idea is that something toxic has gotten inside of you; it's "under your skin." The discussion in the entry on Spiders offers more ideas for the meaning of biting that relates to pain and irritation.

Venom is a toxin, and a dream can begin with that association to use venom as a symbol for anything that's toxic to you. A bad influence is toxic. Negative thoughts and feelings are toxic. Substances are toxic. Dreams about a venomous snake hidden inside one's home correlate frequently with hidden environmental toxins, such as pesticides and radon. Why radon? Because it emerges from the ground.

The dream chooses a snake to deliver venom because of associations with biting and injecting. Intravenous drug use is an obvious parallel—the needle injecting the drug is like a snake's fang injecting venom. In one addict's dream, he allows a venomous snake to bite him on the arm, a parallel with shooting up—he does it voluntarily. But a dream can go the opposite direction to mean that something gets into you involuntarily, such as when an environment of pervasive gloom or a bad influence rubs off on you. For one person who dreamed about a venomous snake biting them on the chest near their heart and latching on, the symbolic connection is to their emotions. The dream creates a scenario where the snake belongs to their ex, and the dreamer's experience with that person has poisoned their heart!

A bite can lead to infection and necrosis, giving the dream author a symbol for expressing ideas related to situations and conditions that "rot." Rotting flesh is a visual metaphor for the idea that a person's inability to make needed changes is killing them from the inside. The discussion in the entry on Zombies offers more insights.

A hydra is a snakelike monster with multiple heads attached to long necks. Now, imagine a bad problem that has multiple facets and a long reach. You fix your attention on one part of the problem, and while distracted, another part sneaks up behind you. It's like a hydra. A health issue can be like a hydra if it spawns multiple symptoms.

A hydra is a monster with multiple snakelike heads. Hydras in dreams can, therefore, represent a problem with multiple facets such as a health problem that causes numerous adverse symptoms.

The "one thing leads to another" use of a hydra as symbolism has many parallels with situations in life. Your computer crashes or you lose your phone, and it spawns other problems. You say or do something that causes an uproar, and now you've got angry people in your face. You make a bad decision, and the consequences snowball. When a hydra's head is cut off, two more grow in its place—talk about problems that multiply! You think something is finished or completed but it's not, and it just grows worse. If a hydra's heads attack each other, it suggests the idea of internal division.

Another approach to interpreting the symbolism is to think of a simple idea behind the imagery of a hydra. One is, "It's too much to handle." Too much is happening at once. You don't know what to focus on. The message in such a dream may be to tackle one thing at a time, to use your head and think things through, or to see the multiple dimensions of a situation or person. They say that two heads are better than one. Well, the original Hydra of Greek legend had nine heads!

A hydra is a huge problem. Its body is huge, and it presents a problem for anyone who wants to defeat it or at least get beyond it. It might be an unwinnable situation. That's the simple idea.

See also: Dragons, Medusa, Rape, Spiders, Teeth, Zombies

SPIDERS

"Spider dreams" may be as creepy as a horror flick, but behind the scenes, something may lurk that's not so bad once you understand it.

No "one size fits all" interpretations exist for the creatures in your dreams, but common associations form the basis of the same symbolism found in the dreams of people everywhere. Take webs, for example. They are great symbols for sticky and entangling situations and for lies, deceit, and intrigue. Get caught in a web, and next thing you know, along comes the spider!

Being in the clutches of a spider is one heck of a metaphor for situations where a person is helpless against something that overpowers them, such as a tangled web of thoughts and emotions. Intrigue is like the sticky strands of a spiderweb. It's no wonder that being caught in a web and in the clutches of a spider is the metaphor of choice for destructive relationships, cults, and pyramid schemes. Spiders are physically weak as far as predators go, but, for good reason, they are among the most dangerous and feared.

> Spiders are physically weak as far as predators go, but, for good reason, they are among the most dangerous and feared.

A young man who was home from college for winter break dreams that a guy he knew in high school lifts sewer lids and shows him a network of tunnels running beneath the town. Spiderwebs stick to the dreamer. He peels them off. The black widow that made them is stuck to him, too. He brushes it away without getting hurt, but it keeps coming back. It's a scene straight out of a horror story, but once you understand the symbolism, you'll see that it's more satire than horror.

Since returning to his hometown, danger has been stalking him—his ex-girlfriend! She weaves webs of intrigue for him to blunder into, but he dodges her traps. The underground tunnels are a visual metaphor for dodging his ex, and they also symbolize the idea of being "underhanded." He perceives his ex as being not only underhanded but, like a black widow, something dangerous that devours its mates. The dream chooses the guy he knew in high school as a character to show him the tunnels because he's wise about avoiding webs of intrigue, and the dreamer is picking up lessons from his example.

His dream shows that he's wary of his ex but doesn't fear her. In another guy's dream, a fear is front and center. The dream puts him in the lab where he works, and his lab partner traps a spider in a glass jar and holds it up for him to see. The glass magnifies it—the hairy legs, the many eyes, and—gulp—the fangs!—and he says nope, keep it away from me. By magnifying the spider's size, the dream says that his fear of spiders is blown out of proportion. The dream chooses his lab partner as a character to show him the spider because he perceives her as being fearless. The dream is saying that when it comes to his overblown fear of spiders, he can learn a lesson from her example.

Confront the fear while dreaming, and it lessens or eliminates the fear response while awake. If you can't muster the courage to confront a fear while dreaming, do it while awake by bringing up the memory of the fearful imagery and meeting it with feelings of courage and calm. Recall a person you know, a fictional character, or a character from your dreams that embodies the idea of courage. They are your allies.

Fear is an association dreams use to create the symbolism of spiders, and generally, the bigger the spider, the bigger the fear. A spider is a particularly good symbol for fear that makes your skin crawl or spine tingle and for fear of entrapment and ambush. The fear you feel in response to the spider in your dream may warn you of real danger that you sense but don't fully comprehend. After all, spiders are incomprehensible to most people, and they can be dangerous. Take, for instance, the dream a young woman experienced where she lies in bed with a female friend, who uses a spray bottle to herd a bunch of spiders over top of her on the ceiling. She asks her friend to stop, but the friend acts oblivious and keeps spraying. The spiders start dropping from the ceiling and landing on the dreamer. They are white and translucent. She wakes up, hyperventilating from fear.

The first thing to know about the dreamer is that she's deathly afraid of spiders, making them superb symbols for fear in her case. The second thing to know is that she's starting to feel like the "meal in reserve" for her friend's appetites. When the friend doesn't have anything better to do, she hangs out with the dreamer and pretends like they are close friends, symbolized as being in bed together. But gradually, the dreamer is realizing her friend's true feelings, and the dream shows it symbolically in the action of moving the spiders into a position where they can de-

> **A spider is a particularly good symbol for fear that makes your skin crawl or spine tingle and for fear of entrapment and ambush.**

scend. Spiders wrap up their meals and leave them hanging until convenient to eat, and that's how the dreamer feels in this friendship. The spiders' translucent color symbolizes that she is "seeing through" the facade. And it's a real danger because she is super sensitive and could easily get hurt.

A person who isn't afraid of spiders is less likely to dream about them as a symbol for fear. Dreams create symbolism atop personal associations, and without fear as an association, the dream author has nothing to work with, seemingly.

But a symbol is information wrapped in an image, and responses while dreaming are driven by subconsciously knowing what lies beneath them. It's why people who aren't afraid of spiders can still fear them in their dreams—for example, you may not fear spiders but do fear death, and it's the idea of death in the form of a spider that you see and respond to while dreaming. It may be a dream's way of saying that you fear something that you shouldn't or that you sense something hidden: an agenda, a secret, a plot, a personality trait. Dreams are well known for alerting us to things that we detect subconsciously—things that, like spiders, can hide in plain sight and leave telltale signs of their presence.

Spiders can represent the dark side of you that lies hidden within, revealing itself in an attempt to get you to acknowledge *all* aspects of your personality.

However, maybe what's hidden is something about the dreamer. The spider lies in wait in the recesses of their mind and pops up unexpectedly. For example, you are coolheaded but can lash out when under pressure, like how a spider is generally harmless unless disturbed. Or something in your personality or emotions seems to drop out of nowhere, and it startles or frightens you. Spiders are known for that kind of behavior.

Or—here's some nightmare fuel for you—the darkness in a person is antithetical to their self-image, and they deny it exists. Imagine how a dream could tell the story as the dark spider hiding in the shadows, a symbol for what they ignore, deny, suppress, don't know, or don't understand. Or, better yet, the spider crawls across their skin—now, it's undeniably close!

The source that creates dreams, the Self archetype in the unconscious mind, wants you to know and love yourself—everything about yourself, not just the parts you agree with. A spider nightmare may seem like a strange way of matchmaking, but it simply reflects the antagonistic relationship a person has with aspects of themselves. Those aspects may be foreign and incomprehensible to the ego—especially when they're deeply unconscious—and that's why the dream author chooses a spider as a symbol for them. Make a friend of the spider while dreaming, and you make a friend of the dark and unknown aspects of yourself.

Anxiety is an emotion that spider dreams spotlight. It's a natural fit. One spider means one anxiety, and many spiders mean many anxieties. Dread also fits naturally with spiders—like dread, they are "creeping," "unnerving," and "hair-raising." A spider may symbolize the cause or source of dread and anxiety or the feelings and emotions themselves. It may symbolize a situation, person, or problem you must confront. The spider isn't going anywhere, and neither is the person nor the problem until you deal with it.

A minor spider bite in a dream may be a sign of irritation. Irritation, whether emotional or physical, is commonly felt on or near the skin. "Prickly" is a good word for it. If you feel prickly about small things, your dream may symbolize it as small spiders. In dream-speak, one irritation translates as one spider, and many irritations translate as many spiders. Also, check for skin irritations and bite marks. Usually, a bite is symbolic in a dream, but it may be a response to something physical—even to spider bites!

A major spider bite is another story. Dream imagery corresponds with the personal and situational dynamics it dramatizes. In that sense, you could say that a major spider bite is a major irritation. But dreams usually reserve the big guns for big situations, and irritation falls short in comparison to the implications of a major bite. Irritation is a thought process, and it can lead to behaviors related figuratively to biting, such as "bite your head off," but a major bite is tailor-made for situations that involve getting in touch with painful feelings. The skin, particularly the hands, is sensitive to touch, and in dream-speak, it can mean "in touch with my feelings," and sensitivity means "sensitive feelings." By that logic, a major bite means majorly hurt feelings.

Instinctive behaviors, such as the bite reflex of an animal or insect, may symbolically connect with the dreamer's instinctive behaviors. For example, the reflexive response to a painful bite is to withdraw and protect oneself, which is also the response to emotional hurts and wounds. Or, conversely, the response is to lash out at whatever causes you pain. Yeah, the spider that bites in a dream may symbolize *your* behavior.

After dreaming about being bitten, it's wise to search your memories for painful experiences that occurred in the past day or two or something painful that's anticipated to soon materialize. A bite may be a dream's way of foreshadowing what's developing in your attitudes and feelings and helping you see trouble brewing. Monitor yourself the following day for reflexive responses and behaviors and in general for warning signs.

A venomous spider is a powerful dream sign. Combine the symbol with the other symbols outlined above, such as spiderwebs and bites, and it's a red flag. You are wise to be on alert not only for external conditions, like devious plots and psychological manipulations, but also for internal conditions, like illness and dark emotions. Venom is a dream's way of saying "danger." It's also a great symbol for something that causes damage from the inside. Don't ignore the warning sign because, like a spider, once it's taken up residence, it's not going away on its own.

"Spider dreams" may highlight issues and conditions of the body, such as one woman's recurring dreams about a spider crawling down her throat as she's sleeping, a symbol for the airway blockage her sleep apnea causes. It's a recurring situation and, thus, a recurring dream. A guy experienced a dream where he drinks from a can of cola and feels something crawling inside of his mouth. He reaches in and pulls out a black, venomous spider! The dream compares venom with the effects of soft drinks on his body.

> **Venom is a dream's way of saying "danger." It's also a great symbol for something that causes damage from the inside.**

Dreams can create imagery in response to what's felt physically while sleeping, and if you dream about spiders crawling on you, it may be all too real or a sign of frayed nerves. Dreams also use the imagery to warn of danger while sleeping. A fascinating example is the nightmare a co-ed had about a big-ass spider (her wording) descending from the ceiling over top of where she was sleeping. Just before it landed on her, she woke up screaming, sure that the spider was real, but she was safe. Her screams woke up her roommate, who then looked up just in time to see a big spider hovering over her and about to descend the rest of the way!

Spiders aren't all bad. They're marvelous creatures and appear in good dreams as well as bad ones. A memorable example comes from the dream a young man had about a mother spider in his home that spun soft webs to cocoon him in comfort and protection, a beautiful metaphor for feeling cared for and safe.

See also: Aliens, Paralysis, Imprisonment/Entrapment, Snakes

VAMPIRES

Dreams can be funny even when they're scary by making satirical comparisons that are spot-on and express how you really feel. You step back from the dream, realize what it's really saying, and see the humor in it. Granted, it's gallows humor, but it makes the point effectively. With vampires, the comedic gold is found in the use of their common associations as part of a story, such as the "emotional vampire." The vampire in your dream is dark and scary and relentlessly pursues you. It traps you with no escape. You see its sharp fangs emerge as it closes in on your neck, and something about its eyes reminds you of your ex, the one who brought endless drama into your life, and you think,

Wait a minute, you moocher, I'm not going to let you feed on me again! The vampire is a symbol for your ex, the emotional vampire you cut out of your life, and the characterization is satire.

It's not to say that vampire dreams are always the *Love at First Bite* variety, but dreams are rarely as they appear. Pretty much everything in them is symbolic, and vampires as symbols are not necessarily meant to be scary. The emotional punch and poignancy of dreams can certainly be heavy—it's what gives them their energetic charge and memorability—but look deeper because it might not be what it seems, and the lovesick vampire in your dreams isn't actually out to kill you.

But it might be out to drain you—vampires are terrific symbols for things that drain. Vampires suck blood, and blood is a symbol for vitality and energy. The dream author can expand the basic meaning to include the idea of feeding on the goodness and productivity of others. It's an image of selfishness and callous disregard. Because vampires are, or were, people, they make great symbols for the people who drain and take advantage of you and for your personal qualities and aspects that suck the life out of you. Situations, conditions, and circumstances can also suck you dry, too, and the storyteller behind your dreams matches symbols to suit.

Take, for example, the dream that creates a scenario where vampires infest the dreamer's house, symbolizing the drain on time, energy, and money for him to maintain it. In a darkly humorous way, the house—an old Victorian he bought to renovate—seems to be cursed, and the dream chooses vampires to symbolize the idea because they, too, are cursed—"the damned." The focus of the dream's story is less on the vampires and more on the house because it is the subject, and the vampires symbolize the issues with it. When you want to tell a story about something or someone being cursed, vampires are your symbol.

For another dreamer, the vampires that live in her basement symbolize difficult, subconscious memories and emotions draining her vitality—and nothing says "subconscious" like a basement. Her dream's use of vampires as symbols to tell the story is especially suitable because they are night creatures, and the dead of night is when she feels closest to her *buried* memories and emotions. Vampires are ancient creatures that work great as symbols for things associated with the distant past.

The vampire in your dreams can have meanings other than being a physical threat. They can have erotic implications or represent how something in your life is draining you of energy.

Sleeplessness leaves you feeling dull and listless like a vampire's victim. Illnesses and health conditions can be like vampires, too, when they drain vitality and energy—especially blood-based diseases such as anemia and diabetes and blood-borne pathogens such as HIV and hepatitis. Addictive and toxic substances are associated with vampires because they travel in the bloodstream. A sleep schedule of being awake at night and sleeping during the day is a vampire's schedule.

Dreams enact their symbolism by showing it rather than telling it. If a dream wants to say that something is draining, one way to show it is with a vampire's bite, but a bite is also a way of expressing pain, and the discussion in the entry on Spiders offers more insights about its meaning. If a dream wants to say that something is addictive, it enacts a scene where a vampire uses hypnotic power or you turn into a vampire—then, it's not just beneath your skin, it *is* your skin.

> **Vampires seduce. That association is a fun one for the dream author to play with. Seduction gets the juices flowing and is a raw ingredient in stories that grab your attention.**

Vampires seduce. That association is a fun one for the dream author to play with. Seduction gets the juices flowing and is a raw ingredient in stories that grab your attention. The easiest correlation for people to understand is the one between seduction and people—mysterious, dark, seductive people—but ideas, emotions, compulsions, and morbid curiosity are seductive, too. The appeal of the idea to quit the job that drains you; the dark emotions that lure you into their sphere of influence; the compulsion that leads to destructive behaviors; the morbid thoughts that are oddly comforting. They seduce you.

For example, a woman dreams recurrently about a vampire that wants to marry her. She responds strongly to its erotic magnetism, but before she can accept the offer, she wakes up feeling sexually charged and frustrated. The dreams dramatize her temptation to have an affair to gratify the desires that are unmet by her loveless, sexless marriage. The idea is *seductive*, like the vampire. Marrying it means accepting what it symbolizes in place of her current partner.

The temptation isn't just about sex; it's about wanting love and passion. Seduction in this example illustrates the powerful internal dynamics of it. We tend to think of seduction in terms of an outside influence, person, or force, but it's more of an internal affair, a psychological interaction between the person and the thing that's seductive. Her interaction with the vampire in her dreams is her ego dancing with the decision it's facing.

Seduction is a type of ego possession, and the discussion in the Possession entry explains it.

Cold, predatory, remorseless—if a dream uses those associations to create the symbolic meaning of a vampire, the story will highlight it and the dreamer will feel it. Dreams embed meaning in their symbols and reinforce it with how they tell a meaningful story. If a dream means "predatory" when it shows you a vampire, it backs that idea with other clues—not only is the vampire predatory, but the story is dark and features other details that say "predator" or "predatory." The story paints a big picture with details that interconnect symbolically and as part of the narrative. In dream interpretation, we call it "story context," a shorthand way of saying "analyze how a dream ties together details to tell a story."

Portrayals of vampires in modern media expand the vocabulary for dreams to work with, such as the *Twilight* series, which portrays some vampires as emotional and moody. You can imagine the legions of lovesick teenagers who respond to such portrayals and how their dreams pick up on them.

But for all the dreams where vampires are portrayed—do I say it—sympathetically, you have ones that are downright scary. The vampire is the image of the ruthless thing that hunts its prey, the supernatural evil that feeds on the life of others, the monster that cheats death. Those associations are the basic ingredients for the darkest dreams and most potent nightmares. They tie in with the worst sorts of people and situations and the worst personal qualities and disturbances in the mind, body, and spirit.

We already discussed the symbolism of the act of feeding on others as meaning something that drains the life out of you. The examples we reviewed are mild in comparison to the other end of the spectrum, the vampires that represent a psychological complex, neurosis, or dark side of the ego that's particularly nasty. Think like a storyteller and ask why the dream author chooses the vampire over other symbols, and the answer points toward the seriousness of the situation. The vampire represents something entrenched in the psyche. It's the thing eating a person from within and driving them to self-destruction or even suicide.

The vampire is the right symbol because with one image, it sums up the dynamics of what's happening inside of the dreamer, and perhaps the one word that's most appropriate is *black*. Black as Nazi leather, as the heart of a psychopath, as the black widow that devours her mate.

Vampires cheat death, a dark subject, and one behind the most potent nightmares. Avoidance of the subject of death invites the dream author to focus on it. We commonly think of cheating death as extending one's life beyond its expiration date. One popular conspiracy theory even says that elite Satanists

Because vampires are immortal and come back from death—as represented by the coffin—they might be implying in a dream that you are avoiding something you need to face.

drink the blood of children to rejuvenate their bodies and keep them alive—a myth about modern vampires. But cheating death is also a way of saying disrespect it. You cheat death by not grappling with the facts about mortality and by putting off until tomorrow what needs to be done today, pretending that you have all the time in the world to live the life you want and to make things right. If you aren't making the most out of life, you are cheating it, with death waiting to swoop in and claim you kicking and screaming. When that moment comes, you want to be able to say you did your best. People who passively let life pass them by are asking for nightmares to shock them out of their stupor.

Dr. Carl Jung said that he reckoned with death by reminding himself every day that it's inevitable, and by doing so, he energized his daily existence and kept his priorities straight. It was a driving force behind his prodigious output of work and intense focus on the mysteries of consciousness. But it also reminded him to spend quality time with family and friends, mentor promising students, nurture connections with nature, and revere all that is beautiful. By contrast, his preoccupations with gaining professional prestige and status in society were trivial. This is what the vampires in your nightmares may be asking of you.

> **Males can dream about female vampires in a dark and seductive content as symbols for psychological dependence.**

Males can dream about female vampires in a dark and seductive content as symbols for psychological dependence. He feels like a slave to something more powerful than him. All males have a feminine subpersonality, the anima, that is the face of their internal relationship with the deepest aspects of their psyche, which are often unconscious and therefore far outside of their awareness. It can be the driving force behind addictions, sexual fixations, complexes, neuroses, and other entrenched patterns. They feed on the person and can be perceived as something supernatural, evil, and vampiric, characterizations that sum up the person's dysfunctional internal relationship with their contrasexual subpersonality, the anima.

The same thinking applies to females in relation to the nastiest male vampires in their dreams. It may represent the dark side of the animus, their male subpersonality, which is similar, but not identical to, the anima. The opposite polarities of these structures of the psyche make them a source that brings out the best, or worst, in a person. It depends on their relationship with it. *Relationship* is the key word because the relationship a person has with the structures of their psyche colors their interactions with them as characters in their dreams. The structures take form, and the dream space is where the ego interacts with them.

A simple idea about vampires is that they are dead things brought back to life. In dreams, they can represent resurrecting or reliving the past. Something won't go away on its own; it must be faced.

Finally, on a humorous note, vampires in dreams can symbolically tie in with situations that involve giving blood. "Oh, no, it's the annual blood drive at work—the vampires are coming!"

See also: Black-eyed People, Dark Magicians, Evil, Rape, Suicide, Teeth, Witches/Warlocks

WEREWOLVES

A werewolf is one heck of a metaphor for the hidden, dark side of someone, the Mr. Hyde lurking beneath the surface. The idea extends to situations, too, when something dark and ugly hides behind a facade, such as when someone's friendliness is driven by ulterior motives. The simple idea is that something is not what it seems to be, and simple ideas are where you begin interpreting a dream.

Why does a dream choose the werewolf as a symbol over other monsters to represent a person's dark side or an ugly situation? One reason is that werewolves transform from human to monster. Imagine the parallels in life, such as when stress, deprivation, and greed bring out the worst in people. A werewolf is the image of the worst coming out in a person. It visually conveys the idea.

Werewolves transform during the full moon, suggesting the idea of an environmental factor influencing behavior. Internal factors also influence behaviors and cause changes in personality: emotions and feelings; illnesses and diseases (think rabies); drugs and alcohol; mood disorders and phobias; PTSD and mental illness. Bipolar disorder may cause drastic swings in behavior and personality. The change from human to werewolf is a metaphor that captures the dynamics.

Now we enter the territory of "the monster within," an idea that the werewolf as a dream character captures with its imagery and mythology. Observations about people are the basis of many myths, and the myth of the

The transformative nature of the werewolf is a clear message about how we are hiding a monstrous side of ourselves that we fear might be released uncontrollably.

werewolf and lycanthrope leaves a trail leading back to ancient Greece. In those stories, a person is possessed by something that turns them into a savage animal. Legend has it that notorious serial killers and heinous murderers were werewolves. It's an attempt to explain the unexplainable; the person must have a monster within them because why else would they commit terrible crimes?

Since dreams exaggerate and dramatize, their comparisons don't need to be factual or objectively accurate, and whatever the werewolf in a dream symbolizes is all but certainly not as bad as a deranged killer. But a dream's use of the comparison between a person and a savage monster to create symbolism does suggest powerful underlying dynamics about the dreamer and their life.

Many folktales and urban myths about the influence of the moon on behavior persist to this day and make for good storytelling. Dreams can pick up on that association with the moon to tell stories about things that influence you—the influence of someone close to you, for instance, and of belief systems, education, culture, society, pack mentality, and more.

In stories about werewolves, the full moon influences their change from human to beast. Associations between the moon and feminine dynamics show up commonly in dreams that speak to a strong female's influence and the strong influence of the feminine on the psyche. Take, for instance, the boy in early puberty who dreams about being out in the woods at night, entering a clearing, and seeing the full moon. It transfixes him, and he fails to notice the werewolves emerging from the woods until it's too late. A powerful she-wolf then jumps in by his side and intimidates the werewolves, preventing their attack. They leave the scene, and he looks down and sees long hair growing from his body.

The she-wolf represents the boy's mom, who is very protective of him. He's wrapped up in her world, a world of beauty and harmony symbolized in the dream as being transfixed by the beauty of the moon. The werewolves that emerge from the woods represent potential dangers for this sensitive boy as he ventures out into the world—dangers he is only vaguely aware of but senses to be coming. The final scene where he sees long hair growing from his body represents the changes of puberty.

Humans transform into werewolves by growing fur. Hair or fur growth can symbolize a growth process, a rite of passage, and maturation. It can symbolize the development of instincts. In the above example, growing body hair represents puberty, and with the imagery of the threatening werewolves covered in fur, the dream hints at other dangers that are approaching as this boy transforms and ventures outside his mom's protective sphere. The werewolves are symbols for dangers in the world he can't get away from—the hair is part of him; it goes wherever he goes.

But for children closely attached to their mother, another sort of danger is the changes to their relationship with her. Psychologically, growing apart from her is akin to experiencing death because the child's relationship with her dies in a sense; it's gone and will never come back, and new hair growth is a sign of what's coming. The werewolf's transformation is a point of no return, making it a good symbol anytime such a point is reached in life.

Werewolves are ordinary people who transform under certain circumstances, then wake up and don't remember what happened. Dreams can use that association to create symbolism meaning "out of it." You aren't your normal self. Time is missing from your memory. Your behavior changes inexplicably. The symbolism is demonstrated in a dream where a man wakes up covered in blood. He thinks he must have turned into a werewolf, and he

One symptom of the werewolf is that when they turn back into humans they do not recall being a wolf. This can serve as a kind of excuse that one was not behaving as they normally would for some reason out of their control.

panics because he can't remember. The dream reflects his fear of doing something to permanently screw up his life. He knows he's capable of it because he has spells where he loses touch with reality and doesn't remember much.

As with other monsters in dreams, the symbolism of a werewolf varies from amusing to terrifying, and the difference is seen in the story and the dreamer's felt sense of the experience. Take the following example when, after a night out drinking and having fun with a group of male coworkers, a woman returns home, goes to bed, and dreams about a pack of werewolves that come to her bedroom window and invite her out to run wild and howl at the moon. She politely declines and makes sure to lock her doors and shut her windows. The dream humorously captures the horniness she sensed in the men as the night wore on with the heavy drinking bringing out their animal side, and they started looking at her as a potential bed partner. Before things could get out of hand, she extricated herself, thanked them for a wonderful evening, and went home—alone.

The werewolves' mild behavior, coupled with her mild reaction to them, is far from terrifying. Instead, the dream treats the subject with a humorous touch, reflecting her feelings about the situation. But if she didn't handle male sexual attention well, the dream would reflect it darkly. She'd sense a danger or threat from the werewolves that visit her home.

Animal passion, sexuality, lust, the wild side—those associations make werewolves good characters in stories that dreams tell about a person's sex life. Dreaming about transforming into a werewolf strongly suggests the idea of passion and sexuality taking over. Sex is a powerful, instinctive drive, and werewolves are powerful, instinctive creatures. Transformation is a creation process, opening the possibility of using a werewolf as a symbol to mean that a *creative passion* takes over a person; they are *completely consumed* with or by something. It can mean that something is trying hard to find expression in the person. It may be hidden even from themselves.

> **The mindless, involuntary, reflexive, and instinct-driven qualities differentiate the werewolf from other monsters as a dream symbol.**

You could dream about a werewolf in connection with the potential for trouble. With werewolves, a situation can quickly spiral out of control. In their terrible form, they are a picture of pain, anguish, rage, and despair and of explosive emotions and palpable threats. In their milder form, they can symbolize resistance to restraint, disdain for society, and the idea of lashing out. The mindless, involuntary, reflexive, and instinct-driven qualities differentiate the werewolf from other monsters as a dream symbol.

Of course, what a werewolf means to you is the most important factor for interpreting it. Think about the werewolf in your dream and allow thoughts to come to mind spontaneously. Those associations may be the basis of the symbolism. Look at the werewolf in the context of the dream's story. A werewolf in a cage is an entirely different picture from one running loose in a bar district or terrorizing a family. Your feelings and the context of the dream are your guides to decoding the symbolism and deciphering the meaning.

See also: Evil, Killing, Minotaurs, Vampires

WITCHES/WARLOCKS

The mythology of witches and warlocks grows in the soil of superstition and ignorance. It's an attempt to explain the unexplainable and know the unknowable, especially about people, and it's rooted in how we process our observations and experiences. The dreaming mind takes note and gets ideas for how to tell us stories that reflect us back to ourselves in the same way that myths do. Jungian psychology relies on mythology, folklore, and other tales as blueprints for understanding what we see in our dreams—that's why we look to stories for guidance when decoding the meaning of a symbol such as the witch and warlock.

Imagine the lessons one can learn through the observation of how people react to what they don't know and are prejudiced against. Witches and warlocks are characters that play roles in stories crafted to mirror us back to ourselves. This is why you should always ask what you see about yourself in your dream characters, knowing that it's likely to be something you don't know or recognize about yourself—the prejudice and ignorance—but it exists, all right, and you need to see it. Otherwise, you project it onto others and hate it, and what people hate, they fear and destroy.

The dreaming mind observes how we justify such darkness to ourselves and each other, and since its focus is on our inner life and development, our dreams are full of such stories and can use a witch-burning as an allegory for a wrong that we justify as right. We help ourselves by approaching the interpretation of a witch as a symbol through how a dream tells a story involving it.

Sure, dreams are not always that complex, and the witch could fit the popular mold as a symbol for scheming and wickedness. In an exaggerated way, it can symbolize people who seem cranky, nosy, reclusive, manipulative, and divisive and situations that seem cursed, dark, and unexplainable. Those associations with witches are common, and dreams commonly use them as the basis for symbolism.

Witches can symbolize the darker aspects of the feminine, while their male counterparts, the warlocks, can do the same for all things masculine.

However, you are likely to find deeper ideas that your dreams express through symbols, and nothing is deeper than the inner workings of a person's psychology. In this way, the witch and warlock work superbly as symbols that embody an idea or set of ideas about dark, gender-based qualities. The witch is a symbol specifically for the dark side of the feminine and the warlock for the dark side of the masculine. The witch is the image of dark power to seduce and manipulate. If she can't win openly, she schemes behind the scenes. Men caught up in their psychological shadow, which also schemes behind the scenes, tend to dream about the witch in terms of their internal relationship with feminine energy, sexuality, influence, and aspects of themselves. When it's more powerful than a man's ego, his dreams may use the witch to represent a shadow side of himself that he is unable to control or understand or that he feels powerless against.

The seduction of addiction is a particularly apt role for a witch, which is demonstrated in the recurring dreams a man has about a witch who summons spirits to possess him. She symbolizes an addiction to spirits—alcohol—and how it possesses him. Another man's recurring dreams about fighting a witch who can pop in and out of reality show his struggle with a dark voice in his head that attacks his masculinity. The voice seems to come out of nowhere, like the witch. She's the shadow side of his Anima archetype, the unconscious feminine side of his psyche. Animus is the term for this archetype in females, and it represents how the same idea manifests differently in the female psyche.

The warlock is the image of the dark side of the masculine: overbearing, aggressive, inflexible, emotionless, and emotionally manipulative. Women caught up in their shadow can dream about the warlock as the embodiment of what they hate or fear about men in general or a specific man in their life, but more likely, it's something about herself that she sees personified in the form of a warlock. It could mirror her when *she* is the one who is overbearing, aggressive, or manipulative.

The warlock may be a symbol of something she feels powerless against, an idea one woman's dream uses in a story about a warlock that rapes her in a men's restroom. The restroom represents a secret sphere of influence in her mind related to male sexuality, and the warlock represents her powerlessness against it. The dream creates a scenario of rape because the influence overpowers her. In her waking life, she wants to say no but can't resist jumping into bed with another lover as if against her will.

> **Both the witch and the warlock make good symbols for something destructive, whether about the dreamer or in general—particularly due to it working behind the scenes against them.**

Dreams of this type use a warlock or witch character up close and personally, whereas if the witch symbolizes a milder idea, such as crankiness, it's likely to be a secondary character in the story, or another symbol may reference the idea, like when a witch's hat references the idea of covering one's true intentions, symbolism based on a hat covering the head and a witch as a schemer. A witch's black cat can reference the idea of being watched from the shadows or the feeling of being unlucky or cursed.

Both the witch and the warlock make good symbols for something destructive, whether about the dreamer or in general—particularly due to it working behind the scenes against them. They can symbolize something that wants to cause harm and that's perceived as wrong or evil. In dream language, "she's acting like a witch" translates as the image of a witch doing something witchy. Women having trouble with other women or with aspects of their gender dream about such situations in ways that involve witches. Men, too, can dream about their relationship with other men in warlock terms. A witch or warlock in such dreams is given simple symbolism based on the idea of it meaning trouble, and it causing trouble enacts the meaning.

But lest we forget, witches and warlocks can be benign symbols, too. They are masters of the arcane and great symbols for one's mastery of a rare or valuable skill or for the acquisition of arcane knowledge. They are fantastic characters for stories about finding one's spirituality or coming into one's power and for working outside of traditional structures to reach one's goals. Witches and warlocks do things their own way and dare to do what others only dream of, and those two ideas are present in many of the myths and legends about them.

In dreams about such a character pursuing the dreamer, the underlying personal dynamic may be the avoidance of assuming power or accepting a role in life that's outside the mainstream. It may symbolize some sort of mastery, creativity, or quirk. The character symbolizes the idea, and the action of pursuing tells the story about it wanting acknowledgment and acceptance by the ego. On the other hand, dreaming about *being* a witch or warlock may dramatize the idea of assuming power, accepting a nonmainstream role, mastering a skill or knowledge, embracing one's creativity or quirkiness, or doing things your own way.

See also: Dark Magicians, Evil, Fire, The Girl from *The Ring*, Ghosts/ Poltergeists/Spirits, Medusa, Possession, Rape, Shadow People, Vampires

ZOMBIES

The zombie is the picture of mindlessness, and it makes you wonder if zombie lore has grown up around the exaggerated portrayal of mindless people. What a metaphor! One look at a mindless, shuffling zombie says it all, and that's the magic of dream symbols. It's a picture that says a thousand words by symbolically connecting ideas.

The dream author possesses a symbol in its arsenal that it can insert as an idea into a story and provide the context to understand its meaning, like in the dream a college student had about zombie students all over her campus. They don't threaten her, but they don't make for stimulating conversation, either. The dream is about her inability to engage mentally with her classmates—they are like zombies to her. It shows mindlessness in the sense of being unable to meet mind to mind. She feels like she lives among "the walking dead," a common metaphor for a low opinion of people and society. It's an easy symbolic connection to make, bearing in mind that the comparison with zombies is exaggerated.

In an exaggerated way, a zombie is an image of a person driven by primitive instincts and desires. They'll do anything to get what they want with no thought of the consequences or impact on other people. It's a picture of single-mindedness, and it's great satire for a person's blank expression. They can't think of what to say. They freeze in panic. Or something holds their attention so strongly, they are unaware of what's happening around them, like when watching TV or scrolling on a phone. Extend the idea further, and it can mean bored to death, dead on your feet, or wandering aimlessly. It means "lifeless"— no energy or inspiration, particularly in dreams where the dreamer turns into a zombie, a transformation that symbolizes what's happening within them. Te-

What is particularly frightening about the zombie is its mindless evil, something with which you cannot reason like a primitive, animal instinct.

dious conversations and deafening silence, grifting and mooching—these are ideas that zombies can symbolize.

A zombie can symbolize something that won't die, such as a relationship or difficult situation that just goes on and on. It's given new life when it should be "dead" and over. Take, for instance, the dream a woman had that features her ex-boyfriend as a zombie and her wanting him to bite her so that she can be a zombie, too. It's a wicked satire of her desire to get back together with him despite knowing how stupid it would be.

Another humorous use of zombies as dream symbolism derives from the fact that they are neither alive nor dead—they're stuck in between. The zombie is a picture of an incomplete transformation or change. When a person can't decide or act, they are like a zombie, particularly when the situation is chronic. It's the adult who still lives like a teenager, holding tightly to their old ways, or the relationship that ends but one person continuing to give it life when it should be dead and buried. Take a whiff of the moldering and decay—it's long past the time to move on.

The zombie is a symbol for addiction and compulsion—*Must eat more brains!* Sadly, it's also the image of the damage done. Longtime meth addicts end up looking (and acting) like zombies. When you can't help yourself from doing something damaging, the zombie is the picture that tells the story.

But addiction applies to more than substances. It's a seduction of the ego and a type of possession, and the discussion in the Possession entry offers many useful insights. The dream author can pick from a lineup of usual suspects as characters in stories about the seduction of addiction and possession by something stronger than the ego—aliens, demons, vampires—and it has reasons for choosing the zombie as the right symbol. A common reason centers on the idea of being unable to think for oneself. The zombie eats brains, after all, and can't think for itself. Blindly following someone else's lead is a situation comparable to being a zombie. Compulsive consumerism is another one.

But the psychological dynamics are deeper when consumerism (root word: consume, as in "consumed" by something) and zealotry fill a hole in a person's self-identity. Fearing emptiness, they latch on to consumer items, ideologies, dogmas, philosophies, and so forth to project the image of themself that they want the world to see: poor substitutes for authentic being. Zombies are the picture of emptiness and animation by forces beyond a person's control and of ego projections that end up taking over.

With zombies, the dream author has a great symbol for expressing ideas about subjects like instant gratification and mindless obsession—obsessions possess people, and zombies are mindless creatures possessed by the need to gratify their cravings.

The art of dream storytelling uses symbols like language uses words. A symbol is like a noun, and a dream inserts it into a context: who else is in the scene, what it does, where the action takes place. The context is the rest of the sentence where the noun appears, and it tells the story. The zombie means something symbolically, and the story context defines the meaning.

For instance, a woman dreams that she's standing in line with her daughter in a futuristic building. In another line, her ex-mother-in-law transforms into a zombie and lunges at her. She doesn't fear her, though, and nearby police officers arrest her and take her away. The story dramatizes a situation where her mother-in-law turned against her during the divorce with her husband, becoming raving mad. The dream tells the story in the context of her ex-mother-in-law transforming into a zombie and attacking her as she stands in line in a futuristic building. The building symbolizes the future, and the lines of people are the flow of time. The ex-mother-in-law is in a different line, meaning she's going a different direction in life than the dreamer and her daughter. They are going their separate ways. The daughter is in the scene because Mom wants to protect her from her ex-mother-in-law.

> **Zombies are the picture of emptiness and animation by forces beyond a person's control and of ego projections that end up taking over.**

Through the action of police arresting and taking away the ex-mother-in-law, the dream says that her threat is neutralized and she's no longer within "striking distance." The legal proceeding may have something to do with it—the police symbolize legal protection. The dreamer's reaction of not fearing her ex-mother-in-law speaks volumes because it's a clue to the underlying personal dynamics the dream dramatizes. She doesn't fear her ex-mother-in-law; therefore, she doesn't fear the zombie!

The Apocalypse is a common scenario for zombie dreams due in part to it being a common storyline in zombie stories. As the popularity of those stories rises, so do reports of zombie dreams, such as when the hit show *The Walking Dead* became a cultural phenomenon. But the correlation only explains why the imagery of zombies and the Apocalypse appears more often in dreams, not what it symbolizes or means personally.

The fact that such dreams are frequently remembered is a testament to their deep psychological impact. The dreaming mind uses a show like *TWD* as a starting point, then weaves a personal story around it about the apocalypses of ordinary life, such as when a huge change hits, life being a struggle, and shit getting real. Be sure to read the discussion in the Apocalypses entry.

Zombie dreams are often coupled with apocalyptic visions. Perhaps people are having more of these dreams thanks to the popularity of TV shows like *The Walking Dead*.

The slow movement of zombies and their tendency to appear between a person and where they need to go combines to make them great symbols for obstacles, like in the dream a student had during exam week that puts her in the campus library, trying to get to a private study area, but she keeps encountering zombies in her path, symbolizing her struggle with overcoming obstacles to studying—namely, interruptions by friends who'd rather socialize than cram. The zombies symbolize not only obstacles but also lack of focus. It's how she perceives her classmates, who are unfocused. The dream provides the context for defining the zombies' meaning by putting them in the dreamer's path between points A and B. Plus, the campus library is a place where she likes to study, and throughout the dream, she carries her backpack with her, which is packed with study materials.

Fear and dread are common uses of zombies as symbols. The fear correlation with zombies is obvious, and dread is a kind of fear that lingers and grows. Words such as *creeping* and *insidious* come to mind, and zombies embody them. Another word that comes to mind is *uncontrollable*. Good luck with trying to control a zombie. The key to figuring out the thinking behind the dream author's choice of a zombie to symbolize something uncontrollable may be found in the reasons why it's uncontrollable, such as lack of reason and empathy, overpowering rage and pain, and insatiable hunger. When a person's pain overwhelms their reason or their hunger overpowers their empathy, it's a ripe situation for zombie dreams.

The words "craving" and "zombie" go hand in hand. A craving is a desire or hunger that's all-consuming. The dream author looks for a way to express the idea, and a zombie that craves flesh is the perfect metaphor.

And speaking of perfect matches, a zombie horde is a mindless horde and an ideal metaphor when a person is caught up in situations involving groupthink, consumerism, mass movements, and pack mentality. "Come on, people, stop and think about how stupid you're being!" That's the feeling or sentiment, but expressing it to a pack of people whose minds have been made up for them is about as effective as reasoning with a zombie horde. Unfortunately, we live in times of such uncertainty, duplicity, and confusion that the comparison between modern society and a zombie horde is not a stretch. Usually, when dreams make such strong statements, they're not meta-statements about society's conditions; they're personal expressions of thoughts, feelings, and perceptions.

As with other monsters, zombies work best for certain roles, and if you can think like a storyteller and figure out why the zombie is the best choice to play a role in a particular dream, you give yourself a direction for interpreting its meaning.

See also: Apocalypses, Black-eyed People, Evil, Frankenstein, Mummies, Possession

Violence and Crime

The shooter who walks into the scene and opens fire; the violent confrontation that ends in death; the war scene with guts blown everywhere—now we're talking nightmares! The three scenarios outlined above are typical of nightmares, and they are symbolic enactments. Look only at the surface, and you see terror, horror, violence, and death. Look below the surface, and you see ideas related to fear, conflict, struggle, and so forth. It's not what it seems to be at first glance, but the tendency is to view the dream imagery as literal and respond in kind.

The mass-shooter dream scenario, for example, makes people want to avoid going out in public for fear of it coming true, but perhaps, the better response is to turn off the video screen that's feeding the imagery into their brains. Figure out how the dream uses the imagery to tell a personal story. The idea could be as simple as fear of something related to being in public because of social pressure, germs, scrutiny, incomprehension, danger, violence, or displays of anger.

Imagine how a dream visualizes the idea of doing violence to oneself. We use wording like that to describe situations where a person causes themself harm. Even if the harm is only psychological, it's still felt and experienced by the body; it's still an act of violence. A dream could visualize it as doing violence to oneself through self-harm such as cutting and mutilating. But what if the person is not aware of how bad it is or the reasons for it? Then, a dream projects the action onto a character that acts violently and inflicts the wounds or is the target, visually depicting the gap in the person's awareness. They think the world is out to get them, but ultimately, they are the source of their troubles. The dream character that acts violently or is the target of violence is a projection of the dreamer.

The discussions offered here demonstrate how dreams visualize ideas. They don't cover all contingencies; instead, they show you how to decode the symbolism. Begin with the simple idea and utilize your knowledge of common dream scenarios and techniques of interpretation. Say that a stranger pursues you in a dream. The simple idea in that scenario becomes the question of what's strange that's pursuing you. A dream about a raging war becomes the question of where the raging battle or conflict is in your life. It may be difficult to equate the dream imagery with a situation, condition, or circumstance from ordinary life, but view it as a comparison that's exaggerated and dramatized, and maybe, the connection will be clear. And always remember to work from the inside out. The war scene in your dream may dramatize a war going on inside of you, not the conflicts and battles of ordinary life, and it may be exaggerated to help you recognize just how powerful and important it is.

APOCALYPSES

A personal apocalypse is a dramatic way of saying that a person's life is headed in the wrong direction. It's next-level trouble, beyond ordinary tribulations. The dream author observes how we use figures of speech and says, "Hello, metaphor!" when the situation is right, like when something is beyond control or your comprehension or your world is falling apart. It delivers a dream about an apocalypse because the metaphor sums up the situational and personal dynamics.

The most common overreaction to an apocalyptic dream is to assume that it's going to come true. Countless false prophecies and predictions have been uttered by well-meaning people who completely misunderstand their dreams, which are full of apocalyptic imagery because their minds are full of it. They dwell on fear, negativity, and worst-case scenarios. Even for people who are not so inclined, an apocalypse nightmare can send their thoughts in the wrong direction toward assuming it's a warning about the future: the world is going to end or something like that. But the simple fact that millions of people have apocalyptic dreams but the world is still here points toward interpreting them as figurative, not literal.

Apocalypse is another word for huge change, and apocalypse dreams are known to accompany situations in life such as entering puberty, leaving home, joining the workforce, retirement, relationship declines and breakups, and even marriage. The dream author finds just the right way of mirroring a person's perceptions and feelings, and if, for example, getting married or retiring is "the end of life as you know it," an apocalypse may capture the idea better than other symbols or themes. In that way, it's the perfect metaphor.

By understanding how dreams create symbolism, it's easier to make the correlation between an apocalypse dream and what it dramatizes. Reflect on what's happening in your life and ask if the metaphorical idea of apocalypse fits. You may find the source in the events, situations, and conditions of your outer life, but the dream author observes your inner life, too, and tells stories about it, and it may be trickier to discover the parallels between the dream content and what's happening inside of you. Many dreams forecast the future and predict where things are heading, and you aren't as likely to see the connection until afterward.

It may be obvious why you dream about an apocalypse when you are ill, in distress, or psychologically imbalanced but not when you are entering puberty or feeling depressed. The dreaming mind, though, knows that we equate apocalypses with situations that have unknown causes—we don't know why they happen, which is what a teenager can think when their body changes or what anyone can

Just because you dream about the apocalypse doesn't mean it is a premonition that it will happen. Such dreams are symbolic, not literal.

think when they are inexplicably depressed. An apocalypse characterizes how they feel, and dreams respond more so to feelings than to rationality.

"I have no reason to feel depressed," the man said. "Life is fine—no setbacks. I'm in great health. In fact, I just got promoted at work to a coveted position." But then, he dreams about an apocalypse and sees his name written on a tombstone, and he wakes up feeling like his world is not just ending but over. It puzzles him because no rational reason explains what the dream imagery implies. He's in his prime, doesn't fear death, and has nothing but appreciation for his success and everything that led to it. He doesn't feel depressed; why dream about feeling not just depressed but as low as a person can go?

It's because tacitly, he realizes that this really is the end. He can rise higher in his career, but it won't have the same thrill. He can live a charmed life, but it's only a continuation of what he knows all too well and can't find any more challenge in it. He will meet expectations, which is great, but he's 27 years old, and his life is over.

The social point of view says that he should feel on top of the world, and he's been trying hard to convince himself that it's true. It's not, though, and his dream captures the idea with the imagery of the grave. His rise in life has locked him on to a path that can only offer contentment until his inevitable death. He won't consider a change of career—why would he when he's doing the high-technology job he set out to gain and beat the intense competition to get there? The grave symbolizes the idea that the life he's made for himself is also a trap that he can't escape even if he wanted to.

An apocalypse is the biggest sort of shake-up, and that's why the above dream uses it as a theme. The dream doesn't speak to what is happening or has happened, it speaks to what's needed. He needed it to see how he feels beneath his rationalizations.

The experience of the dream is where the answer is found. It's a self-created experience, and we work backward by asking why he created it (subconsciously) for himself. The lack of apparent connection between himself and the symbolism of apocalypse requires him to dig deeper and ask existential questions. And when the answers start flowing, it makes sense why the dream chose an apocalypse as the story's theme and the grave as its main symbol. Now, with the lesson in mind, he has a new way of framing the most important issue in his life, which accounts for the other half of the equation that he isn't honoring: his true feelings.

Dreams amplify our little voices, and the man's dream is a prime example. The Apocalypse, like most nightmares, is the volume cranked to 11. It's a desperate attempt to get the attention of the ego. It's the message that's screamed instead of spoken. Only one level exists above the Apocalypse and that's Armageddon, the worst it gets, like war is to nuclear war. A dream has reasons for presenting an apocalypse that's felt as if the world is ending, and tracing those reasons is how you think like the dream author and work backward to find the meaning. You're looking for something happening in you and your life that's especially urgent.

But when an apocalypse is not felt so deeply, the dream might have something else in mind that's comparatively mild. Take, for instance, the dream a woman experienced where she's riding out an apocalypse at home with her children, and her husband knocks at the door to let him in. She refuses to open the door because she thinks doing so will allow bad things into her home. She had the dream the night after a bad fight with her husband, and it reflects the explosive situation and her desire to protect her children from the poisonous atmosphere. Allowing her husband into the home would mean allowing trouble back into their lives. The dream characterizes the situation as an apocalypse because it's bad, but as far as apocalyptic dreams go, it ranks low on the "holy shit scale."

The "meltdown" nature of the trouble is why the dream chose an apocalypse as the theme that fits the situation. It's the same metaphor we use in everyday life to describe bad situations, except that it's shown instead of told by the dream. The writers out there—especially fiction writers—may recognize the number-one rule of story craft: show, don't tell. Show what you mean instead of putting it into the mouth of a narrator or character. Dreams follow the same logic. And no one in a dream has to say "apocalypse" for it to be understood; like in the above example, it's just known, a precondition of the story.

> **Only one level exists above the Apocalypse and that's Armageddon, the worst it gets, like war is to nuclear war.**

Dreams offer you a look into their inner workings when they communicate their meaning in ways other than saying it. It's especially true of a dream's preconditions and the things that happen "offstage," meaning outside of the dreamer's view. Preconditions and offstage happenings are taken right from the dream author's story outline, enabling you to read the author's mind. When a dream says "apocalypse," you know what it could mean as a metaphor: a sudden downturn; a barrage of challenges and tribulations; a fight for your life; a big breakup; a terrible loss; a major illness; an explosion; a meltdown. Look for the parallels with yourself and your life.

And look, too, at the emotions a dream brings out. In most cases, they are easy to correlate with what you've been feeling and experiencing lately if you take the time to reflect. An apocalypse dream can bring up the worst sorts of fear, dread, anger, and anxiety. Those emotions arise in response to what happens in a dream and what you know about it subconsciously. From the dream's point of view, a good reason exists to feel that way—the emotions grow out of the soil that is you and your life; they don't come out of nowhere.

Even when emotions don't match the tone or actions of a dream's story, they are still informative. For example, feeling happy during an apocalypse is understandable when you know that it symbolizes a badly needed do-over. It's exactly what you need, and that's why you are happy.

Another sort of discrepancy can be apparent when a dream uses an apocalypse to set the stage for telling a story about what you'd do if it was the end of the world. It's an opportunity to say and do what you really want to say and do. These "what if?" dreams explore possibilities and test scenarios by giving the ego an excuse—*hey, what does it matter, it's the end of the world*—to, for example, confess your love to your honey, tell the boss to screw off, or jump on an international flight with only a suitcase and a one-way ticket—let the adventure begin! They're also opportunities to speak your truth, and that's a big reason why you should never cringe when you say or do something awful in a dream; it's probably how you really think and feel, expressed as symbolism, and it's exactly what's needed.

Apocalypse can mean simply "the end," and it could be the end of your vacation, for example, or a much bigger end, such as the end of life as you know it. The difference is gleaned from the dream content and your felt sense of it. When "the end" means a big sort of ending, an apocalyptic dream delivers a bigger wallop.

In one apocalyptic vision, a woman dreamed that the sun was getting larger and larger until it filled the sky. In this case, the sun may have been symbolic of her parents.

A woman dreams about the sun getting bigger and bigger until it fills the sky. News reports say it's the end of the world. She goes inside her home and tells her parents that she loves them, and together, they wait for the end to come. Her dream shows that she recognizes the inevitable change in her relationship with her parents as she grows into adulthood. The dream shows it as the sun—the source of life on Earth, a symbolic parallel with her parents as the source of her life on Earth—growing bigger and causing the end of the world. Her action of telling her parents that she loves them is an expression of her gratitude to them for providing her with a good life. She doesn't run in terror or freak out when she thinks the world is going to end because she knows subconsciously what it really means and accepts the inevitability. People who are not ready to accept the end of something react negatively when they dream about it.

A man dreams that he's traveling in a car with his parents and sister. Behind them, the moon grows massive in the sky, and he knows it's the end of the world. They stop in a desert town. A handful of random families are there, and after he grabs supplies and readies to depart, his parents say they are choosing to stay and accept their fate. He pleads with them, but they are adamant.

His dream uses apocalypse as a theme to tell a story about the inevitable changes coming in his relationship with his parents. One, they're getting older and won't be healthy forever, and two, he's coming into his prime of life and assuming the adult role they have played until now. It's a transition symbolized as the moon, which changes shape as it goes through phases, making it a great symbol for changes during different phases of life. Leaving his parents behind in the desert town is the dream's way of saying that his life must go forward without them playing their familiar role in his life, and their adamance about staying reaches behind the scenes to touch on the dream's meaning. The transition must happen. His sister is in the scene because they're close in age and experiencing the same transition. Traveling together in the car is a great metaphor for a family life together. The time has come for the dreamer to get behind the wheel and assume full control and responsibility.

In rare cases, a dream may offer a view into what's happening in the world and the very real possibility for apocalypse. War conditions and mass slaughters are known to spark dreams that put a dreamer in the scene to view what is happening, about to happen, or could happen. But even with prophetic dreams, the future they show is usually not a foregone conclusion. And the dream author doesn't discriminate between the big, collective apocalypses and the more personal ones.

Someone somewhere is experiencing an apocalypse *right now*—the world is full of miseries big and small, and powerful, emotional responses to events and circumstances send out signals that the radio receiver in the mind picks up. People receive the distress signals and dream about it because they are attuned to it; for example, when a crisis strikes a loved one and the dreamer sees it as if present as an observer or experiences it through the loved one's eyes. Other times, the personal connection is to a place, such as one's hometown that's hit by a disaster; you dream about the event and its aftermath, even though you could be halfway across the globe at the time.

> **In rare cases, a dream may offer a view into what's happening in the world and the very real possibility for apocalypse.**

The rarest type of apocalyptic dream is the one that comes true and the dreamer has no personal connection to the event. The dreamer may play a passive role as a witness or an active role when they feel compelled to respond. Praying for help or going to a disaster site in spiritual or astral form to lend a hand are two common responses. One fascinating type of dream replays a real apocalypse as it happens or soon afterward, and the dreamer sees or participates in a spiritual response to it. One woman dreamed about her recently deceased husband as an angel at the site of the World Trade Center attacks in 2001 helping the confused spirits of people who died there. She said it was just like him to respond to a crisis that way, and her dream's vivid intensity and accuracy of event reproduction set it apart. To her, what she saw in her dream was more real than what she saw on the television news reports.

See also: Armageddon, Crashes, Fire, Ghosts/Poltergeists/Spirits, Nuclear War, Storms/Blizzards/Hurricanes/Tornadoes, War

ARMAGEDDON

The discussion in the Apocalypses entry delves into how dreams choose story themes and symbolism to match with situational and personal dynamics, and Armageddon can be thought of as the top of the apocalyptic scale, the worst of the worst, as bad as it gets. The dreaming mind reviews the information it has about a situation, condition, or circumstance, and from its point of view decides to tell a story as Armageddon instead of apocalypse because of a spiritual or religious slant, for example. Let's say that the dreamer is a member of a church, and something happens that blows up their world: a prominent member is caught in a scandal, or something sinister enters the picture. Or, say, that a person is in a spiritual crisis or fears judgment. Those situations could be characterized as an apocalypse, but the better metaphor is Armageddon.

A meltdown that's worse than an apocalypse is Armageddon. Mom and Dad not only had a terrible fight, but they're also divorcing. Failing a test not only means a bad grade, but it also blocks you from getting a coveted honor. Breaking up means not only the end of a relationship but also the loss of important friends or the loss of home and income. The world just blew up. It's more than an apocalypse; it's Armageddon.

Dreams choose symbolism with precision and accuracy based on how the dreaming mind sees things from its big-picture perspective and on your subjective feelings and viewpoints. A situation doesn't have to be Armageddon in order to feel or be perceived that way.

The subjectivity of dreams opens a wider possible use for Armageddon as symbolism and as part of a story. Take, for instance, the dream a woman experienced where Armageddon strikes while she's at work and her task is to figure out how the work can continue (it's somehow critical for humanity's survival), but her computer equipment will be useless. The dream dramatizes a situation at her workplace involving the crash of its computer system that will take weeks to fix, but work must continue, and everything she did via computer will have to be done manually—which is pretty much everything. It's Armageddon because it's a monumental disaster, as bad as it gets. Plus, it means a return to relatively primitive conditions. Other employees who aren't impacted as deeply might dream about the situation as a vacation because their subjective experience of the disaster is different from hers.

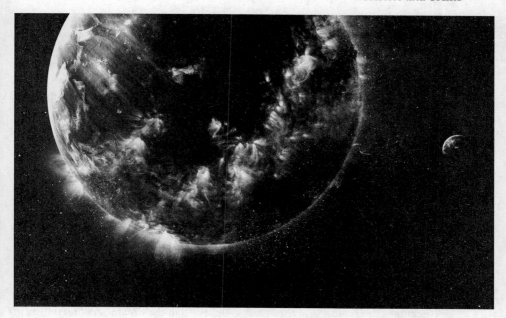

Armageddon is the worst version of apocalyptic scenarious—basically, the end of everything, the entire universe, existence itself.

In the dream a teenage male had, Armageddon is like a video game. His task is to save the world, and he's given the powers of flight and clairvoyance so he can zoom to wherever he's needed and fight the bad guys. The dream uses Armageddon to create an atmosphere of heroism, and it reflects an internal process of learning what he's really made of. This type of existential dream puts you in extreme situations—do or die, sink or swim—that force you to do your best to save the day. By doing what the dream asks you to do, you gain more power and ability to meet the challenges of ordinary life. It's known as "leveling up" in video game terminology, and in dreams, you are given opportunities to unlock latent or dormant powers, talents, and abilities if you pass the test or just respond as best you can.

A variation of the story theme uses the idea of foreboding. Armageddon is a terrible, cataclysmic event that will happen in the future. Exactly what will happen and when is usually vague, but a sense exists that it'll be really bad. Now, imagine how the dreaming mind can run with that idea. A dream one woman experienced starts with an angel telling her that Armageddon is coming and she will be given the ability to get through it. She wakes up knowing it will be the day she ends a relationship with a dangerous boyfriend. During the breakup, he attacks her, and she suddenly feels supernaturally fast and powerful, enabling her to fend him off and get away. Her dream came true, and Armageddon is the best story theme for expressing the ideas of violence and special powers that also came true.

A dream could use Armageddon to refer to something specific the dreamer knows is coming or to capture feelings of fear, dread, and anxiety. Apocalypse carries the same idea, and Armageddon is stronger symbolism that dreams generally use in relation to stronger feelings and situations. For example, a change in life that's imminent isn't just big, it's epic and dangerous.

> A dream one woman experienced starts with an angel telling her that Armageddon is coming and she will be given the ability to get through it.

Prodromal dreams—ones that warn of impending illness and disease, sometimes years in advance—are another good example. If an illness is coming and it's not life-threatening, a dream can use the theme of disaster or apocalypse, but if a life-threatening disease is developing, Armageddon is a better theme. It's a guideline for dream interpretation, not a hard rule.

Armageddon is a popular theme in the dreams that people who view life as spiritual warfare experience: angels versus demons, God versus Satan, good versus evil. As an idea, Armageddon captures the tone and substance of what occupies their mind, and they tend to believe that the dreams are literal instead of figurative or reflective. But the number of these dreams could add up to billions, and Armageddon hasn't happened. The dreams are not prophetic or predictive in the traditional or religious sense, but they may dramatize the inner life of a person or even predict that something important or major is soon to come, especially if it involves the idea or reality of death and mortality.

Finally, Armageddon is one heck of a story theme that captures ideas that relate to it: guilt, judgment, terror, finality. It's a terrible end for the bad people and unbelievers and the ultimate reward for the good people and true believers. Dreams may use the theme to speak about fear of punishment or judgment or about rewards expected for faith and good behavior.

See also: Fire, God, Hell, Jesus, Lucifer, Nuclear War, Storms/Blizzards/Hurricanes/Tornadoes

INCEST

If you want instant freak-out, bring up the subject of incest dreams. Or have one. You wake up from a dream—maybe nightmare is the better word—

about having sex with a relative and feel disgusted. How can you ever look them in the eye again? Do you need to see a psychologist?

But like everything in dreams, incest is a way to tell a story; for example, a story about feeling too close to a relative. Your lives are so enmeshed, you don't know where their life ends and yours begins. That's the idea behind an incest dream where an adult man has sex with his mom. During the dream, he wants to stop, but she talks him into continuing. He knows it's wrong but does it anyway because it's his mom and he loves her. It's what she wants, so he does it, but it's not incest, it's symbolism in motion.

In his waking life, he has been trying to move out of her house, but she talks him out of it, or he talks himself out of it. She's dependent on him emotionally, and that's a big reason why the dream chose incest to tell the story. It's a way of expressing their emotional closeness—too close for comfort. He loves his mom dearly, but their relationship crosses the line to dependency.

Crossing a line—that's an association with incest that the dream author can run with. You cross a line when you go too far with something or violate a taboo. The dream author wants to visualize the idea by making a colorful comparison, a metaphor, and it uses incest to tell the story when the dynamics of the situation match up. The comparison works especially well in situations that involve family, but it's applicable to any relationship that feels too close, smothering, or dependent or that crosses a line.

A dream discussed in the entry for Rape features a young man having sex with his mom, and the line that's crossed is both psychological and physical. She's coercive and too touchy with him, and he can't say no to her.

A young woman dreams that she is in a bedroom dry-humping her cousin as all her other cousins watch. She feels like she's on display, and that's the idea behind the dream. She's from a big family with many cousins in her age group, and they're all up in each other's business. She can't say or do anything without everyone finding out and turning it into a soap opera. Her life is on display, and she has no privacy—especially from her cousins—and her dream very effectively expresses those ideas! Dry-humping is symbolism in motion for the idea of putting on a show for her cousins that lacks substance.

As with many other images in dreams, having a vision involving the taboo of incest should not necessarily be taken literally. It might have a more general "crossing the line" meaning involving a relationship.

The examples given do not conform to the best-known interpretation of incest dreams as expressions of a secret desire to usurp a family authority. Sigmund Freud's theory of the Oedipus complex views the incest dream as an expression of a secret desire to take a parent's place as an authority figure. It's an infantile, jealous desire, and it's a real psychological dynamic, but it's far down the list of the most common reasons behind incest dreams. Family and gender dynamics have changed tremendously since Freud's day, but in today's incest dreams, we still see variations of the basic idea.

Take, for instance, a young man's recurring dreams about having sex with his mother. During the dreams, she moans with pleasure and makes him feel like a conqueror. He feels power transfer from her body to his and enter him through the sacral area. The dreams are about his relationship to the Mother archetype within himself and how his ego feeds on the dark side of it. The power is illusory and comes at the terrible price of possessing him. In the dream, he feels like his mother is "his" in the truest sense—no one else can make her feel like he does. But it's a twisted head game that he's on the losing end of because the power he feels is a substitute for the authentic experience of his personal power. He'll always need a sexualized mother figure to conquer in order to feel powerful.

A young woman had similar dreams about having sex with her father. His penis feels like a magic wand inside of her, and she revels in her power to taste the forbidden fruit. But like the above example, her dreams illustrate an internal dynamic of substituting a sexualized form of power for the authentic personal experience of it.

Incest is another word for regression in the sense of wanting to return to a child's position in the relationship dynamic with a parent. The child's position is passive and receiving, every need taken care of, every pleasure indulged.

Some incest dreams are tender and loving. One woman's recurring dreams feature her having sex with her brother. Actually, "making love" is a better term; it feels natural and enjoyable. Her initial reaction to the dreams is to wonder what's wrong with her, but they are expressions of her closeness with her brother and their deep love.

> Incest is another word for regression in the sense of wanting to return to a child's position in the relationship dynamic with a parent.

The symbolism of sex adds another layer of meaning to incest dreams that's summed up in the word "integration." Sex is the union of two bodies, and it can be more when it's a union of hearts, minds, and spirits. Now, put yourself in the shoes of the dream author, who wants to speak to the things that you take into or give of yourself. Things that become part of your personality. Things that "rub off" on you. We use sexual terminology to describe it, and the dream author follows our lead by visualizing the idea. The woman who dreamed about having sex with her brother described him as being a huge influence on her. In that sense, you could say that he had gotten inside of her. The dream author merely found the best way to express the idea visually. While having intercourse, he's inside of her, she takes him in, and they integrate!

Now is a good time to remind you that the dream author doesn't follow social conventions. It only wants to tell the story as best it can by using symbolism.

Incest dreams can amplify feelings of attraction for a relative, like in the dream a man had about having sex with his female cousin. He woke up feeling dirty, and during the dreams, the main thought in his mind was, "I shouldn't be doing this, but damn, is she beautiful!" Behind the dream is his observation that his cousin has blossomed from a twiggy little girl into a sensuous and beautiful young woman. And yeah, it really bothers him. "Don't look at her that way, you perv!" But just like in his dream, he can't help himself. His dream is making him come to terms with the situation by exaggerating it as a scene involving incest. And by going too far in the other direction toward the extreme end of attraction, the dream responds to his suppression of his feelings—a classic case of psychological compensation. He needs to be all right with noticing his cousin's beauty and feeling attracted to her.

A college-age man's nightmare put his stepsister in the bedroom next to his as she has sex—loudly—while a demonic little boy in the room with him makes vile suggestions about barging in and taking his turn with her. The dream is a vivid learning simulation. He's been studying abnormal child psychology, and sexual abuse is a commonality among truly disturbed children. The torment of hearing her have sex while the demonic boy tempts him gives him a taste of what it's like to be inside of the mind of a disturbed child.

Now the door opens for us to talk about incest dreams that express fantasies and immaturity. A child is immature, and sex with a child can be a dream's way of saying "immature sexuality." It's a simple idea that's often missed because the dream content is so disturbing, but the simple message may be "grow up." People who are sexualized at a young age become fixated, and incest in their dreams may express the dynamics of their situation. It's true also of recurring dreams involving immature expressions of sexuality—the key word being "immature."

Also, addictive pornographic material involving children is way too easy to acquire. It traps the viewer in a world of fantasy and may crosswire their brain to be attracted sexually to children. It's the reason behind one man's graphic dreams about children being sexually abused. He said his child porn habit began innocently as curiosity and even nobly as an attempt to understand the lure of it. It sucked him in, and he watched it even after he got sick with himself. His dreams replayed the porn as a sort of noire, with him as the audience. It's hard to say exactly what the dreaming mind was trying to accomplish, but as with any addiction, the beginning of the end is when you can say "no!" in your dreams. Dream imagery wires directly to the parts of the mind and body associated with it, and interactions with the imagery, whether while dreaming or awake, is the most powerful sort of therapy.

See also: Molestation, Possession, Imprisonment/Entrapment, Rape

KILLING

Dreams create symbolism by making comparisons between things that on the surface don't appear related, but a connection does exist. Killing is a potent example. It appears to be nothing but bad, and dreaming about it is often misunderstood as revealing violent tendencies and wishes or worse, but beneath the surface is likely to be a metaphorical expression of meaning that's not so bad in comparison.

Take, for example, when a person says, "I'm so mad I could kill somebody!" It's a strong expression of feeling and may be a harbinger of an explosion coming, but it's not intended as a literal statement of intent (usually). It's just blowing off steam, and the same can be said of statements like, "I wanna kill my boss" and "I wish my ex would die." If we took such statements literally, we'd overwhelm the police with people to arrest. The dreaming mind visualizes ideas and draws from a storehouse of personal and collective memories to create symbolism, and when it creates scenarios that involve killing, it's meant figuratively, not literally.

Killing in a dream is an expression of powerful emotions, frustrations, fears, and, of course, anger.

"Kill" is a strong word for use in strong situations, and dreams follow the same pattern of using it for strong situations, behaviors, feelings, attitudes, and so forth. It captures strong emotions, such as anger, revenge, hatred, and loathing. Dreams pull no punches when it comes to expressing emotions, and a common misunderstanding arises when people compare how they feel with how a dream expresses it. They say they don't feel as strongly as the action of killing implies, but when they dig deeper, they find and feel the truth in the metaphor.

Dreams create scenarios that trigger emotions. It's part of normal memory processing while dreaming. A dream triggers an emotion to release it and process it, transforming emotional memory to dream memory and creating psychological distance from the emotion. As a result, the energetic charge carries less voltage. In that way, it's good to dream about killing. It may prevent a bad mistake or overreaction down the road.

The exaggeration and drama of killing in a dream are why it is commonly misinterpreted. For example, a man has disturbing dreams about killing people. He is in an ordinary dream, and suddenly, he just goes off—hacking and slashing and enjoying it. His reaction of enjoyment is a big clue that killing represents something symbolically that he understands subconsciously while dreaming. It's also out of kilter with the action of killing, another clue. The characters he kills represent his anxieties and fears—that's why he enjoys it. The meditation and relaxation techniques he's been practicing are helping. The same sort of imagery appears in the dreams of people who are changing their ways by ending bad habits and taking care of problems. Killing is a dramatized way of visualizing progress.

> **Metaphorically, the dream uses the idea of being forced at gunpoint as a reference to her do-or-die attitude about making big changes.**

"Making progress" is the idea a dream expresses when one woman finds herself forced at gunpoint to fly an invisible plane to an alien planet. She gets out and witnesses carnage as aliens slaughter humans and the bodies are stacked 10 feet high around her, but she's nonplussed. Her reaction is a telling clue because it shows that the killing symbolizes her progress in "killing off" her old ways by forcing herself off the couch to exercise, focus on college classes, and take a second job. The dead bodies in the dream represent her old couch-potato ways.

Metaphorically, the dream uses the idea of being forced at gunpoint as a reference to her do-or-die attitude about making big changes. The changes are new; thus, they are "alien," another word for foreign. The invisible plane expresses two ideas symbolically: one, she is "going places" now that she has changed her ways, and two, the changes are noticeable, visible to everyone who knows her or just witnesses how she's remaking her body and improving her health and life.

On the other hand, dreaming about killing people and enjoying it can express masochism and sadism. The people are symbols for inner aspects of the dreamer, and killing is a dramatized enactment of violence the person self-inflicts through self-hatred, self-criticism, and self-abnegation. The psychological source may be negative voices the dreamer absorbs and makes their own. They repeat narratives to themselves about how bad they are, and they think they deserve their misery. Masochism and sadism are opposite poles of the shadow of the Warrior archetype, and a person locked into that duality can easily flip from one to the other, saying that they hate people and that's why they enjoy killing them in their dreams, but they actually hate the self-reflections they see in their dream characters and the people in their life. They hate people because they hate themself.

A dramatic type of killing dream involves opening fire in a crowd of people. It often happens spontaneously with no reason given in the story except that the dreamer wants to do it. Now, think of how a dream can symbolize hating social pressure and anxiety. It puts the dreamer into a crowd of people and sparks the same feelings experienced in similar ordinary-life situations. The dreamer reacts by acting out their feelings.

The same dream imagery of opening fire on random people can express the feelings in a statement like, "I hate people so much!" The frustration, anger, and loathing are dramatically acted out through killing, and you could call it a public service because killing dreams are like a safety valve for releasing emotions that otherwise might boil over.

On the other hand, in some dreams, killing is merely a way of acting out symbolism, like in the invisible plane example, and the difference is noticeable in the dream content and the dreamer's felt sense of it. Take the example of a dream where a student kills her teacher. During the dream, she doesn't think much of it, but afterward, the implication freaks her out. The true meaning of killing, however, is that she's killing her chances by bombing the class (in the figurative sense), and the dream uses the teacher to symbolize the class.

Experiencing a dream in which you are a mass shooter could be about a generalized frustration with society as a whole or, perhaps, with one's entire life.

Her "oh, well" attitude about killing the teacher reflects the stance of her ego about killing her chances. But during the dream, she realizes that she'll be caught for the crime, and she ruined her life. It's a dramatization of her sense that bombing the class is part of a downward trend. She's screwing up, and the consequences will catch up with her. The real crime is the one she's committing against herself. The dream amplifies the situation, hoping she'll respond positively and address it.

Some dreams that feature killing are shock therapy to break a pattern and "wake up" a person. Their ego is creating imbalance in the psyche, and their unconscious mind compensates by creating powerful dreams. The greater the imbalance, the more psychological force it uses to compensate.

Killing in a dream may branch off the idea of what people do when they don't fear consequences, such as the dream a man had where he becomes aware that's he's dreaming. Thinking to himself that no consequences exist in a dream, he decides that he wants to experience what it's like to kill something. He then sees a horse in front of him, and suddenly, he's armor-clad and holding a big sword. He hacks triumphantly at the horse until it's a bloody pile of meat and immediately regrets it so intensely that he falls to his knees in despair and wishes more than anything to bring the horse back to life.

He knows it's "only a dream." He's even lucid during the dream and makes a conscious decision to experience something he wouldn't dare do in ordinary life, figuring that since it's a dream, no consequences or ramifications exist. Without success, he tried to use those rationalizations to assuage his guilt, and he learned an immensely valuable lesson from the experience that dream characters are living aspects of oneself. Dr. Carl Jung says the psyche is their home, and they continue to exist there regardless of whether a person is dreaming. For people who treat everything in their mind as a plaything, that revelation is like the sky opening and the most powerful beam of light striking them full in the face, and for the man who had the dream about killing the horse—a rational, scientifically minded person—his perception changed radically.

> **Dr. Carl Jung says the psyche is their home, and they continue to exist there regardless of whether a person is dreaming.**

One common dream theme features killers breaking into the dreamer's home. To decode the symbolism, you take the main symbol, the home, and figure out what the dream means by killers breaking into it. Inside the home might symbolize your inner life, and someone getting killed inside the home means "dying inside." The same idea can be expressed in a multitude of ways, such as dead bodies being buried inside the home, and they all mean the same thing.

Think of the home as a symbol for the body—the body is where you live—killers breaking in can symbolize something harmful or dangerous getting into it or trying to.

Think of the home as your mental space; killers could symbolize intrusive thoughts and feelings and anything that harms through the mind, such as excessive self-criticism and negative personal narratives.

Think of the home as your sphere of influence; killers could symbolize a threat to it. The killers could symbolize a financial, personal, or psychological threat or a threat to a relationship. After all, a relationship is like a shared space, and a home is a space that people share.

Think of the home as a storehouse of memories; killers could symbolize memory loss, neuroplasticity (rewiring of the brain's neural pathways), or just the effects of time. The suppression of memory is comparable to killing because it's an intentional act to make the memory go away.

Think of the home as a boundary; killers could symbolize anything that crosses your boundaries. Dreams can express the same basic idea by using burglars and intruders, but by using killers, they up the ante and express different emotions. Killing an intruder can mean, "I've had enough—no more!"

Think of the home as an ego boundary; killers could symbolize a threat to the ego.

Killers inside your bedroom is a common dream theme during sleep paralysis episodes. Sleep paralysis is a normal condition while dreaming; usually, you're not aware of it, but when you do become aware, such as by waking up while still paralyzed, it's natural to react with fear, which the dreaming mind then translates into the fearsome imagery of killers. Your bedroom in the dream represents the space you occupy at that moment; killers represent the sense of danger and threat.

Danger, threat, fear—these are common symbolic meanings of killers in dreams.

Much can be learned by analyzing how killing is done in a dream. Do you do it, or does someone else? The invisible airplane dream discussed above gives the role of killers to aliens in order to express the idea that the source within the dreamer driving her to drastically change her ways is outside her conscious awareness. She just woke up one day and knew that the time had come, and she went about it like her life was at stake. The source of her motivation to kill off her old ways is "alien" or unknown to her. When someone else does the killing, it may indicate that an external source is affecting you, like when the stress that's killing you originates externally, but when you do the killing, it can mean that you are the source of the stress and whatever is causing harm and distress.

Playing the role of a killer can dramatize a stance and attitude of the ego. Killers play God by taking lives. They feel powerful. They are cold and

The dream experience can very much be like looking into a mirror and confronting yourself. Dreams point out aspects of your personality by exaggerating them to give them clarity.

remorseless. The dreamer feels and acts that way during their dream but objects to the implication, saying they aren't a killer, and they miss the point. The dream is going to an extreme to show them something they don't know about themselves, exaggerated to make it obvious. *Hey, killer, who are you really hurting in the end?*

And deeper meaning occurs when dream characters represent aspects of yourself. The ego is a small part of the psyche's system, but it can do tremendous damage, especially when it's hostile toward other parts. It doesn't like what it sees and suppresses it. As far as the dream author is concerned, suppressing something about yourself is like killing it.

How is the killing done: gun, knife, bomb, drowning, flamethrower, bare hands? Analyzing how killing is done in a dream can yield clues to the meaning. For example, a gun is a less personal weapon than a knife for killing. In the discussion in the entry on Creatures is an analysis of a dream where a creature comes at the dreamer with a knife with the intent of killing her. It dramatizes a legal battle with a former employer and a recent development where she found out that her former manager was spreading rumors and "killing her chances" of getting another job. The dream puts a knife in the creature's hand to symbolize the personal nature of the conflict.

Killing with a gun can symbolize an idea as mild as "I hit the target" or "I absolutely killed it," meaning a big success, or as major as "I have it out for you" and "revenge is best served cold," in which case the use of a gun is simply the most efficient means of inflicting pain and damage. Shooting from a distance can symbolize personal and emotional distance. Conversely, shooting from a close range implies a closer personal connection and impact. Dreams commonly represent loud arguments as nearby gunfire—it symbolizes "shooting" words at each other, the emotional impact of threats and insults, and the loudness, heat, and explosiveness of such situations.

Killing with bare hands is even more personal than killing with a knife, but alternatively, it can mean an idea like "I did it with my own two hands." In a darkly humorous dream, a man strangles himself to death. He jolts awake, gasping. He'd been having an episode of sleep apnea, and his dream expresses the idea as strangling himself.

Killing by using a flamethrower or fire suggests the idea of hot emotions. Arson carries a similar implication symbolically—the underlying situation is very personal and may involve burning anger. It may express the desire to completely wipe away the source of the dreamer's troubles or the associated memories and feelings. For example, burning down a childhood home in a dream can speak volumes about how a person feels about their childhood!

> **A bomb is a symbol for a threat or a situation waiting to explode, and you can imagine how a dream can use the idea to parallel situations such as a major shake-up, big mistake, or self-sabotage.**

Killing with a bomb can symbolically express ideas like "bomb the test" and "blow your chances." A bomb is a symbol for a threat or a situation waiting to explode, and you can imagine how a dream can use the idea to parallel situations such as a major shake-up, big mistake, or self-sabotage. In dreams about planting a bomb, the imagery may symbolize the idea of sabotage or trepidation at what the dreamer knows is coming once the truth is found out or word circulates. Imagine how a dream could symbolize the idea in the phrase, "It will kill me if anyone finds out." The dream author chooses the best way of enacting the idea, and a bomb about to explode is the perfect metaphor.

A woman dreams that she plants a bomb in her boyfriend's car and sets it to go off after the car has traveled a few miles. The scenario mirrors her pattern of sabotaging her relationships, and she's seeing it play out presently with her boyfriend. She thinks it's just a matter of time until the inevitable conclusion. That's what the dream means by the bomb going off later. She's the character who plants the bomb because she's the source of the pattern.

Killing by drowning brings in the idea of submersion and opens a discussion of a common source of killing dreams: when a person hates something about themselves. In this case, submersion means symbolically "make it unconscious." Bodies of water are symbols for the unconscious mind, from which everything about the personality arises. When a person hates something about themselves and just wants it to go away, killing by drowning aptly expresses the idea.

Take the example where a man dreams that he deliberately drowns a kitten. The implication horrifies him, but drowning the kitten is merely a way of acting out a suppression of his naivety and boyishness. He is sick of being perceived that way by his peers, and recently, he'd toughened up by suppressing the "soft and friendly" character traits that made him such a "kitten." Killers are hard. They are tough. Kitten killers … eh, not so tough. Killing something that's much weaker than you may reflect a pattern of the ego to act meek around stronger people and like a bully around weaker people. Donald Trump is a classic example of the big dog who turns into a puppy around people more powerful and macho than him.

As symbolism, drowning is a great way to express dismissiveness and the idea in the phrase "you're dead to me." The imagery also carries the idea of a person slowly and passively dying inside; dreams can express it symbolically as a dead body underwater or as watching a body float away, a symbolic way of saying their life is floating away. But on the milder side, the imagery can express ideas like "drowning in debt," "overcome with emotion," and "overwhelmed."

A woman who dreamed about violently hacking to death a snake that slithered beneath her living room carpet symbolically enacts how she feels about her ex trying to "slither" back into her life. Her expression of deep frustration and anger by hacking up the snake is a reaction to a pattern in her life of being used by men. Seeing the snake ignites a hatred in her toward all men and particularly toward her ex.

A different woman dreamed about her ex as a random man who steals her phone as she's trying to use it to navigate to her family home. She chases him down, knocks him to the ground, rolls him over, looks him dead in the eyes, and rams a big knife into his heart! The man in her dream only fits the general description of her ex—the giveaway is in her reaction of hunting him down and killing him. Subconsciously, she knows that the character is really him. Navigating to her family home symbolizes her attempt to get her life back on track after he lured her into using hard drugs. Now, her reaction to sensing his presence in the dream is easy to understand. Stabbing him in the heart points right to where he hurt her the worst.

> **A woman who dreamed about violently hacking to death a snake that slithered beneath her living room carpet symbolically enacts how she feels about her ex trying to "slither" back into her life.**

The dream a man had about killing himself by hanging dramatically illustrates that nothing is getting through to his head. In the dream, he states his intention to hang himself, then ignores the pleas of his loved ones as he carries through with it. By ignoring their pleas, he enacts the idea that he ignores all opinions except his own. Nothing gets through to him, comparable to how no blood or air can get to the head during strangulation.

A woman dreamed vividly about being handed a knife and told she had to kill someone strapped to a table. She begs not to have to do it, but it's either her or the sacrifice who gets the knife. Thinking she has no other choice, she apologizes profusely to the sacrificial woman on the table, who is oddly cheerful and seems okay with what's about to happen. The dreamer then goes about slicing up the sacrifice, who is not dead at the end.

The dream dramatizes a sacrifice the woman is making by giving up a career she wants to pursue another one. She can't do both, so she must sacrifice one, and she's having difficulty with it, which the dream expresses by showing the killing unfinished at the end. The odd behavior of the sacrificial lamb is how the dream reflects the dreamer's true feelings that she's okay with pursuing another career and how it's not a huge sacrifice. And killing with a knife in this case—or at least attempting to—reinforces the idea of sacrifice. How are human sacrifices usually carried out? With a knife.

See the entry for Murder for a discussion of what it means to kill by poisoning.

Killing in a dream can simply mean starting over, and when the underlying subject is not very stirring, dreams tend to express it by using secondary characters and vague references. Take, for instance, the dream that refers to the idea of starting over after moving away by delivering news that an acquaintance from the dreamer's old town was killed. That time of life is over—it's dead, metaphorically, and the acquaintance represents the time of life. The dream tells the story as killing to dramatically express the idea of a messy break from the past. But the person who had the dream wondered if it was prophetic and he should warn his acquaintance, a common misunderstanding about dreams that feature death.

When killing dreams recur, patterns in life may be the underlying cause. Dreams recur in some cases because situations and conditions in life recur, feelings and thoughts recur, and things don't change despite the need to. For instance, the stress that's killing someone is a recurring condition, the shame that's eating at them is a recurring feeling, and their anxiety is a recurring thought process. Killing may boil down to the need for change. The ego is locked into patterns that began earlier in life and perhaps once suited a person well but are now hindering development.

Stress and depression can build up relentlessly requiring some form of cathartic release that a killing dream can provide.

In one such case, a young woman has recurring dreams about killing people, then trying to get away with it. Two police officers show up and she makes up a story about how the people died, but the officers don't seem to care. One says, "Look, they needed to die so that they could live fully." Statements by dream characters can be very revealing, and the officer's statement speaks to the heart of the dream when understood figuratively as meaning, "These parts of *you* need to die so that *you* can live fully."

Some of the most dramatic killing nightmares feature cold-blooded murder committed by the dreamer or other main characters, and at their heart, they are desperate pleas for change. The person is so messed up, they wish they could just start over. The plea for help or change is sometimes carried out by a killer hunting down the dreamer and executing them, a way of saying that the person is so locked into a pattern of destruction, nothing short of drastic action will break it. Killing by execution can also mean that you feel like you deserve harsh punishment or that a failure is likely to bring down harsh consequences.

As symbolism, killing can mean causing harm and destruction through one's actions and attitudes. When it's unintentional and done against the people closest to the dreamer, represented as dream characters, it may express the idea that the person sees what their personal problems are doing to the people closest to the fallout. In their dreams, they kill family members, friends, and loved ones but don't mean to. It expresses the idea that they don't mean to cause harm to the people they love, it just happens. The same idea can apply to unintentionally causing oneself harm, and it shows up frequently in people with major learning disabilities and behavior disorders. They are cognizant of how messed up their life is and the issues it causes the people closest to them, but they can't help it.

When killing is intentional and committed by the dreamer, the dream author may give them the role to highlight something about their behaviors and attitudes. It may dramatize the harm and destruction they cause to themselves and others. Through decoding the symbolism and reflecting on what it says about the dreamer, the connection may become clear. An example is given in the discussion in the Nuclear War entry where a woman has a choice whether to press the button that launches nukes. She does it spitefully, the dream's way of showing that she's fully aware of her spite and feels justified.

People who are passive in life can suddenly turn aggressive in their dreams, and the connection is murky because their actions are antithetical to their self-image. "I'm no killer," they say, but their dreams show a strong desire to change coupled with a bouncing between the polarities of the archetype that governs aggression, the Warrior. Secretly, they want to do a 180 from masochist to sadist and start giving out the pain they've been taking, but they don't know how to manage their aggression when it's directed outward. Inwardly, the sources of their trouble are their bruised ego and negative personal narratives. By navigating through the initial wild swings in attitude and emotion, the person can find the middle ground where they belong and learn the healthy use of their aggression as needed in emergencies and other situations that require it.

The meaning of dreaming about killing animals or being killed by them is a chapter unto itself. We discussed examples where killing an animal symbolizes suppression—the kitten drowning dream—and where it expresses hatred—the snake dream. The animal symbolizes something, and killing it enacts a meaning, the same basic formula for all dream symbolism. An animal doing the killing is also basically the same as any other killer doing it, except you know that reasons exist why the dream author uses an animal as an antagonist character. One reason may be that the underlying psychology involves instincts—animals are instinctual creatures, and when they kill, it's for reasons related to their programming. Human instincts are programmed, too, and programming also comes from sources such as personal narratives, life patterns, and environmental factors. Other reasons for animals that kill in dreams are the same as those discussed already: a need to change, self-abnegation, and conditions and situations that cause harm and damage.

> **The animal symbolizes something, and killing it enacts a meaning, the same basic formula for all dream symbolism.**

Look for the metaphor. With animals, the metaphors are numerous. For example, the giant bear that smothers a teenage male symbolizes his overprotective mother—his "momma bear." She's giant in his dream because her power and influence in his life are overwhelming. The tiger that one dreamer sees mauling multiple people to death symbolizes the person's aggression that comes out in competitive situations—it's the "eye of the tiger." The "murder of crows" that descends on the dreamer and eats her symbolizes a drastic attempt to save her from the accumulation of worries, regrets, and guilt that's killing her. The crows pick away her soft tissue so that all that's left is muscle and bone. It's one heck of a way of saying "eat the waste" and "start over."

Finally, killing in dreams is commonly an expression of fear. A dream creates a symbol for something you fear—a dream character, usually—then puts you in a scenario to interact with it. Killing it is an instinctive response and an expression of strong emotion. A common feature of those dreams is that the victim comes back to life or isn't harmed by the attempt to kill it. In other words, the fear isn't going away, the situation isn't changing on its own, and the truth is the truth whether you accept it or not.

See also: Apocalypses, Fire, Ghosts/Poltergeists/Spirits, The Grim Reaper, Murder, Serial Killers, Suicide

MOLESTATION

If somebody dreams about being a child who's molested or about a child being molested, what do you think it means? The most common guess is that the person may have really been molested and their dream is exposing hidden memories. And if they have no memory of being molested, they are told that it is suppressed and that the sooner they admit it, the sooner that healing begins and that justice can be served. Such ignorance is well-meaning but sows confusion and is potentially destructive if the person believes something that's not accurate or true. Plus, imposing a suppressed-memory hypothesis violates the dreamworker's top ethic that only the dreamer truly knows what their dream means.

Dreams do expose hidden memories, let's be clear. And people who have been molested do certainly dream about it and, sometimes, suppress the memory until it erupts from their subconscious mind as a dream. But that answer to the meaning of a molestation dream ranks dead last among reasons for dreaming about it. The most common reason is that it's a way of telling a story about ideas such as vulnerability, mistreatment, and loss of innocence. The dream shows molestation in the physical, criminal sense but means it in the figurative sense.

Take, for instance, the dream experienced by the mother of a prepubescent daughter. They are walking in a zoo when a sketchy man jumps out of the shadows, grabs her daughter, and runs off. The woman knows without being told that the man is a child molester wanted by the police. She desperately chases after them and cries out for help, but soon, they are gone, and she bitterly chastises herself for not being ready for danger.

After waking from the dream, the mother thinks it may be a premonition, but it's really about her daughter growing up. Her little girl is maturing and losing her innocence naturally, but to Mom, it feels like she's being forcibly taken away. The child molester in her dream is a representation of that idea. It won't be long until her daughter will be going out at

A dream about molestation might emerge from a painful memory, but it could also be about less sinister subjects such as a loss of innocence.

night with her friends and—God forbid—maybe even "doing it" with her boyfriend, and that sweet little girl is gone forever.

Mom sees it coming even though that phase of life is still a few years away. She knows how fast things change when puberty hits. But why choose a child molester as an antagonist character? A kidnapper could play the role, and the basic idea is the same. Analyzing this detail uncovers another layer of meaning. The basis for the choice of character lies in Mom's greatest fears for her daughter. She remembers what it was like to start looking like a woman while still feeling and thinking like a child. She remembers the unwanted and creepy attention from males and the jealousy from her female peers as her body matured before theirs. Her innocence made her a target, and she can only do so much to protect and prepare her daughter without prematurely ending her childhood. She's walking a fine line. Plus, by including the detail that the child molester is wanted by the police, the dream reflects the drumbeat of fear messages she hears about child molesters running loose in society.

The zoo in the dream is a symbol for the idea in the phrase "it's a zoo out there." The world is full of hazards, temptations, and bad people. Her cry for help that isn't answered is basically a way of saying that she wishes the world was a better place for her daughter to grow up in, but it's impossible to change the way things are.

> Compulsive masturbation and other sexual behaviors such as voyeurism and inappropriate touching are comparable through association with child molestation and have roots in early childhood development.

Child molestation is incomprehensible to most people. How could anyone get sexual gratification with a child and do such a terrible thing? Those associations open the possibility of using a child molester as a character in a story about incomprehension over a person's motives and their inexplicable and inappropriate behavior—especially when the flavor is sexual, but it still doesn't have anything to do with actual molestation. It's simply a symbol like any other, with meaning based on association. For example, immature sexuality brings together associations with children—they are immature—and sexuality. Molestation is an immature expression of sexuality.

The idea stretches further to include compulsions, perversions, and self-gratification. Everyone has heard the excuse, "I just couldn't help myself"—how does a dream express the idea? Compulsive masturbation and other sexual behaviors such as voyeurism and inappropriate touching are comparable through association with child molestation and have roots in early childhood development.

"As bad as it gets" is an idea that dreams associate with molestation. It's the worst sort of crime, and a dream can compare it with other things that are perceived as the worst, especially behaviors. Molestation can symbolize disgust and the perception that something or someone deserves the harshest punishment.

Mistreatment is a simple idea behind molestation, and a dream may express the idea as molestation because of other factors, such as taking advantage of vulnerability and innocence, or that a situation or circumstance has sexual undertones. Take, for instance, the dream a woman had that her autistic younger brother was molested at school. It expresses her fear that people will take advantage of his naivety and she won't be around to notice and stop it.

Social convention dictates that mistreatment and molestation are two very different categories, especially when it comes to children, but the dream author doesn't follow convention; it simply looks for the best way to tell the story.

Molestation is a prevalent theme in the dreams of people who were mistreated and abused as children. The comparison is easy to make, and a dream may bring in associations with neglect and other commonalities with mistreated and molested children. Molestation can be a dream's way of expressing the condition of a person's inner child. In a word, it's bad. The ideas of mistreatment, neglect, and abuse that a dream symbolizes as molestation arise from the psychological dynamics between the dreamer and their inner child. The interpretation of such dreams and the resolution of them points inward to that internal relationship, but unfortunately, it's all too common to look outward for the sources, reasons, and causes.

Unfortunately, child molestation is all too real for the people who experience it. They may wander in the dark for many years, then suddenly experience an eruption of dreams that take them back to what they don't want to remember. But rather than regurgitate specific memories of molestation, their dreams usually (but not always) incorporate them into stories that link the past with the present. The discussion in the Paralysis entry details the case of a woman who was molested as a child. Her dream mixes imaginary details with glimpses of the cold reality she experienced.

The discussions in the Haunted Dolls and Imprisonment/Entrapment entries offer great insights for the psychology behind feeling like you're under someone else's control and trapped in a place in life, two strong correlations with molestation.

See also: Haunted Dolls, Incest, Murder, Paralysis, Possession, Imprisonment/Entrapment, Rape

MURDER

Like other dark and difficult dream themes, murder is easily misunderstood. Dreams use it as symbolism and as part of a story, as figurative instead of literal, but the tendency is to get wrapped up in the "Oh my God, I dreamed about murder!" trap. Then, you lose sight of the fact that murder is like anything else in a dream and understood by stepping back and asking what it really means.

Decoding the symbolism of murder works similar to the way it does for killing in a dream: search for the metaphor. Metaphor is a favorite way for dreams to create symbolism, and metaphor uses murder to express a higher level or degree of something. A person may say "I could kill someone" as a metaphor that expresses frustration and anger and "I could murder someone" to express a greater degree of frustration and anger. The author of our dreams uses the same precision when expressing meaning and may create a story about murder to say metaphorically that something is "top of the scale."

That way of understanding the symbolism helps you see the meaning behind the action. Take the example of a dream where a man waits in his car outside the home of a woman he'd been dating who suddenly cut off contact. In the car with him is his best friend. Tired of waiting, he pulls out a gun, shoves it into the mouth of his friend, and pulls the trigger.

On the surface, it looks like cold-blooded murder, but more is happening than meets the eye. He's frustrated about the situation with the woman and has been waiting for her to get in touch with him, symbolized as waiting outside her home. Now, he's realizing that it's probably not going to happen, and his worst fear about the situation is coming true. But why take it out on his friend? Because his friend has better luck with the ladies and always knows just what to say, whereas the man who had the dream habitually blows his chances, and he enacts that idea in the dream by blowing away his friend. The action looks like murder, but "blow his chances" is its meaning. He shoots the friend in the mouth because it symbolizes the source of his dating troubles—he "shoots off at the mouth"—and some frustration and envy show in his action, too, but not malice.

Decoding the true, underlying meaning of a dream about murdering someone can take a bit of work and analysis as to a person's current life situation.

A variation of this dream theme played out in a guy's dream where he plots with his best friend's girlfriend to "get him out of the picture" so they can be together. The dream seriously disturbed him, and he swore he'd never put a girl before his best friend. What does that fact rule out? That the dream is in any way literal or even expresses a secret desire. Instead, it expresses the dreamer's desire to have a girlfriend like his best friend's. He says that she's everything he wants and that he tries hard to avoid feeling attracted to her, sometimes going to the opposite extreme by ignoring her. The suppressed feelings reemerge amplified as murder, a common reaction of the dreaming mind to focus hard on anything that's suppressed or denied.

Another variation of the theme showed up in a woman's dream where her boyfriend and his former best friend fight to the death in brutal, hand-to-hand combat. She feels horribly guilty knowing that she's somehow responsible, but the dream doesn't say how. To interpret it, she focuses on her guilty feelings and traces them to the circumstances that brought her together with her boyfriend. She broke up with his best friend—yeah, *that* best friend—to be with him. Now, the two men are "former best friends," and the tension between them makes the atmosphere wildly electric.

As the above examples demonstrate, interpreting dreams requires stepping back to view them objectively. It's necessary in order to provide distance to observe and notice what you may miss because of the strong subjective perceptions and feelings that dreaming about murder can involve. The examples highlight three ways that dreams use murder to say "top the scale" of frustration, importance, and emotions. The situations are not comparable to murder, some may say, but subjectively, the comparison is easy to make, and the story themes involving murder are poetic with how they capture the situational and personal dynamics. Shakespeare would approve.

A comparison is usually at the heart of a dream symbol; it's how the dream gives meaning to it. The comparison may be between two things that appear unrelated and unlike each other, but a connection does exist, and understanding it leads to the "a-ha!" moment that powerfully drives home a realization or lesson.

A woman dreams that a murderer breaks into her home and slaughters her family. She reflects on the dream content, and the fact that she doesn't live with her family is the first difficulty she has with wrapping her mind around it. She lives alone and has done so for years, so why dream about them living with her when the murderer breaks in? It's because murder is the comparison that drives home the realization of what her self-imposed isolation is doing to her spirit. Her family life was messy but freezing them out of her life isn't really hurting them, it's hurting her by feeding her spite. The murder occurs in her home because the damage she does is to herself. Murder is the appropriate symbol because her actions with her family are cold and calculated. That association is what can differentiate murder in a dream from ordinary killing.

A variation of the idea plays out in a dream another woman experienced where she protects her two younger siblings from the murderous intentions of their stepfather. She wonders why she'd dream about a time of her life that ended years ago, thinking that the dream could be warning her that her siblings are in danger. They still live at home with their stepfather. She reflects on the time when she lived in the same home as him and remembers his foul moods

A woman who lived alone dreams that a murderer enters her house and kills her family. The fact that she lives alone is a clue that the dream is not literally about killing people.

after coming home after a bad day at work and how everyone in the home would walk on eggshells. She follows the instruction to always look for what you see about yourself in your dream characters, and the "a-ha!" moment strikes her: *she* is now the one who returns home after a bad day at work and takes it out on the people closest to her: her two children. Her two siblings in the dream symbolize them, and her efforts to protect them from the murderer symbolize protecting her children from herself when she's feeling foul. Murder in her dream characterizes a behavior pattern. It's exaggerated and dramatized but accurate when understood as a metaphor.

The threat a dream chooses to symbolize as a murderer is usually internal, and here's another way that people tend to misunderstand dreams: by looking externally for the source instead of internally. The mistake is easy to make, but you can avoid it by always asking what you see about yourself in your dream characters. In the above example, it didn't take long for the woman to realize how her behavior is like her stepfather's. She just needed to be pointed inward.

Sometimes, though, whatever a murderer symbolizes is external of the dreamer and more literal than figurative. In one such dream, a woman is like a fly on the wall observing her husband having an affair. She senses that the other woman is setting him up to murder him, and she catches glimpses of a dark, male presence in the background. A dream of this type is likely to dramatize an internal situation, such as feeling like she could murder her husband—figuratively, of course—or that the other woman is a symbol for something about herself that's killing the relationship. However, she confronted her husband and found out that he really was having an affair and knew little about the other woman. It turned out that the woman had a history of setting up married men by having affairs with them, then blackmailing them, and she had a partner in her schemes, a male lover. The wife's dream was spot-on, and by "murder," it means the cold and calculated nature of the scheme, with a second layer of meaning that expresses how the affair was killing her marriage and may have led to bad trouble for her husband.

While dreaming, you play a role in the story that follows a script written subconsciously, and that insight is crucial for understanding why you would play the role of a murderer. The action is symbolic and part of a story, and the following dream demonstrates that idea. A woman dreams that her mother persuades her to poison her pet dog. She objects, but her mother counters by giving a reason she can't refuse, so she pours poison on her dog's kibble, then watches as it goes limp and dies. She realizes what she's done and flies off in a rage, pulverizing her mother's face with her fists. Then, she seeks out members of her extended family, who are in a nearby room, and tells them that her mom forced her to murder her beloved dog, and they tell her that she's overreacting as usual.

Murdering her dog appears to be a heinous act, but it's symbolic and part of a story. Think of her dog as a symbol that means "best friend." After all, dogs are man's best friend. Now, consider that symbolic meaning together with the action of poisoning; what does it really say? "Poison a relationship." Recently, her mom had manipulated her into asking her human best friend to marry her. She did it, despite her misgivings, and it almost ended the friendship. As a character in the dream, she enacts the idea by poisoning her dog, her other best friend, under the influence of her mother. Her family's reaction when she tells them about it enacts her feeling that they don't support her. She has a long history of conflict with her mom, and they always take Mom's side.

In a dream where a man finds out that his ex-boyfriend was murdered and experiences a feeling of relief, murder symbolically expresses the idea that he is over the breakup. His ex is "dead to him," and the dream chooses murder as the symbolic reference because of the bad blood between them. During the darkest times, the dreamer found himself wishing his ex would die. If you ever think or say, "I wish you were dead," watch how your dreams respond! When understood symbolically, murder is not a stretch for how to interpret such a thought or statement.

> **Murder is a crime of passion and works superbly as a symbol for the idea of the extremes of passion and the damage they can cause.**

Murder is a crime of passion and works superbly as a symbol for the idea of the extremes of passion and the damage they can cause. Now, take out passion, and we're left with just the idea of extremes. Murder is extreme, and in dreams, it can parallel extremes such as the strongest feelings and emotions, harshest and craziest thoughts, and direst situations and conditions.

Murder is wrong, and dreams can use it as a symbol for *anything* that's wrong but probably very wrong. The interpretation begins with that simple idea. Murder is also unimaginable. It's insane. It's done by volatile people and occurs during volatile situations. Look for those ideas expressed in the dream content. Also, look for parallels in your life with what's wrong, unimaginable, insane, and volatile.

Another association with murder that dreams can use to create symbolism is that it's forbidden—by committing murder, you enact the idea of doing something that's forbidden. In a dream that features a milder variation of this idea, the dreamer's sister calls him and says that something is wrong with their dad. The dreamer then finds his dad lying on a table under a sheet, seemingly dead, but then, he sits up and starts telling stories about his youth. The underlying situation that sparked the dream is the dreamer's knowledge of a secret that his sister is keeping. She started having sex before marriage, which is forbidden by their dad, but the dreamer also knows that his dad's forbiddance of sex before marriage is a "do as I say and not as I do" situation. Dad, when he was their age, broke his own rule, and that's what the dream means when he rises from the dead and starts telling stories from his youth.

When murder is a big part of the story and the action occurs close to the dreamer, it shows a close connection personally to the underlying subject. Take, for instance, the dream that puts the dreamer in the role of murdering by reading from a forbidden book. The more she reads, the more that people close to her die. She can't help herself; she continues reading. The dream reflects a situation where she's been gaining knowledge that's changing her mind about the strong beliefs of her community, and subsequently, her relationship with them is changing. Murder and death are permanent changes, and the idea of the forbidden comes into play because her community forbids the knowledge she's gaining.

A darkly humorous twist on the above idea plays out in a dream a man had about killing people as he reads bad poetry at an amusement park and relishes it. It shows that he likes to say and do things for the shock value—it amuses him.

When murder is a secondary action or reference, it shows personal distance between the dreamer and the dream's subject. The best way to understand the difference is to contrast a dream where you hear on the news that somebody you don't know died in a place that means nothing to you with a scenario where a cold-blooded murderer hacks to death your family right before your eyes. For example, in a dream where the dreamer finds out that a famous politician was murdered "offstage"—not shown as an action in the dream—the parallel in her life is with the news she received that the president of the company she works for was forced out. When a person forcibly loses their job, they are said to be "terminated," an idea her dream translates as murder. The murder is a reference and not an action in the dream because she's not personally affected by the drama happening in the executive suite.

One woman dreamt that she could kill people by reading from a forbidden book, a symbol of knowledge that is freeing her from an oppressive community.

Personal distance from a dream's actions can also mean dissociation, lack of awareness, and avoidance of responsibility or blame. Think of when a person points the finger at everyone else and they point back. *No, you are the one, you are the source.* A dream can show the dynamic as the action of murder carried out by a dream character instead of by the dreamer or by the dreamer denying involvement. The person refuses to acknowledge their culpability in whatever issue, difficulty, behavior, attitude, and so forth the dream highlights, so it gives the role of murderer to a character rather than to the dreamer, or the dreamer commits the murder and denies involvement. Dreams that involve a murder that the dreamer tries to cover up or hide can highlight this sort of "who, me?" dynamic.

In a variation of the above idea, a young man dreamed recurrently about helping family members cover up their murders. He worries about the bodies being found but feels like he must help. It's family, after all. The recurring nature of the dreams is the first big clue to their meaning—it directs him to look for an ongoing situation or pattern in his life, and he finds it when he thinks of helping to hide the bodies as symbolism for participating in his family's dysfunction. In the figurative sense, the dysfunction is killing him—all of them, really— and he has enough awareness to realize it for what it truly is, but he justifies it by saying his family life is not that bad, and by doing so, he enmeshes himself deeper in the dysfunction. He becomes an accomplice and plays a hand in the family game and the cover-up that allows it to continue. Hiding a murdered body is another way of saying "a cover-up." Justify-

> **Hiding a murdered body can symbolize covering up something shameful. Murder is shameful, and when combined with the action of hiding the body, the meaning is obvious.**

ing, enabling, and denial are dishonest, and honesty dies—you could say it's murdered—in places and situations where people can't speak their truth.

Analyzing the dream begins by simply asking himself what he's helping to hide or cover up that's wrong. What's wrong is the murder and what it symbolizes, and from there, he can follow the trail of clues to understand what being an accomplice means. When you get away with doing something wrong, feed into negativity, repeat a lie, or make yourself believe something that's untrue, you are an accomplice. It doesn't have to be on par with crime or killing to be fair game in dreams.

The dream depicts you as an accomplice as a clever way of illustrating a situational or personal dynamic. For example, helping someone cheat does them an injustice, and you play a hand in it, or by taking the easy way out, you may suppress inner voices that have other ideas. You are an accomplice to your own downfall.

Hiding a murdered body can symbolize covering up something shameful. Murder is shameful, and when combined with the action of hiding the body, the meaning is obvious. The simple question is, what are you trying to hide? The body symbolizes it. A likely answer is that it's something shameful, but it's not the only one. Hiding a body can also symbolize wanting to hide something about oneself, such as a defect of character or a suppressed aspect of the personality. Maybe it means you want to hide something about *your* body.

"Crossing a line" is an association with murder that a dream can build a story around. It may be a line that forever separates the person from the people close to them and society in general.

Your emotions guide you into the dream. In fact, one approach to dream interpretation is to simply identify the emotions you experience while dreaming and find how they parallel with your waking life. You may find a direct parallel between the emotions you experience by day and in your dreams by night or a more subtle connection that highlights emotional content that the ego avoids. Murder in that situation is a good analogy because the person is doing something to themselves that's destroying their spirit. Here's an example. A teenage boy dreamed that a porn website sent a contract killer to his home to murder him over an unpaid debt. While dreaming, he realizes that if he's murdered, the police investigation will uncover his secret porn habit and his parents will find out. The thought of it triggers his shame. Shame is the emotion he's been avoiding, but his dream makes it unmistakable, and a simple question leads him straight to the meaning: what would fill him with shame if his parents found out? The dream makes it even more obvious by creating a scenario where murder will be committed because of a debt to a porn website!

Murder by contract killing—that's an interesting variation on the idea. It's a fusion of "contract" and "murder," and both are symbolic. One way of interpreting it is that a contract is an obligation, so you ask, is an obligation killing me? A marriage is a contract, a job is a contract. They are obligations. If they're killing you, in dream-speak, it's a contract killing.

Dreams cleverly fuse ideas together, and once you learn how to speak their language, interpreting them becomes easier. Running from a murderer, for example—you know what murder can mean as a symbolic action, so what does it mean to run from a murderer? Well, murder is serious, and it may mean that something serious is pursuing you. A checkered past is catching up. Danger is right behind you. The trauma of a bad situation lingers. Something you can avoid by day pursues you by night. That's what running from a murderer can mean.

A dream about putting a hit out on someone combines the symbolism of murder with that of some kind of contractual obligation.

Running away *because* you're a murderer implies greater personal culpability or involvement. Murder means that you are doing or have done something wrong or even just plan on doing it and running away means symbolically that you're avoiding responsibility and don't want to stop. It's a frequent theme in the dreams of people who are screwing up their lives and know it but do it anyway. It's also a theme that pops up frequently in the dream lives of people who indulge the darkness within themselves. After all, murder is dark, and in dream-speak, dark means the dark side of the ego.

Dr. Carl Jung said that all dreams in some way account for the ego. The ego is "you" in the dream world, and the interactions between you and your dream characters illustrate your internal relationship with your larger (beyond the ego) self, including with autonomous aspects of the psyche that show up in dreams as distinctly intelligent characters. The ego "murders" whatever it doesn't like about itself or the system it operates within by squashing it psychologically. Murder is a dramatization of an internal dynamic between the ego and the rest of the psyche. Nature created the ego as a mediator between a person's inner and outer worlds, and ideally, it weighs all competing interests equally and makes decisions based on what's best for all involved, but most people are unaware that they are anything more than an ego, and when theirs is out of balance with the psyche, they tend to squash any voices or priorities that compete with it. The resulting dreams dramatically illustrate it as murder and other violent themes.

Power is commonly at the heart of ego-driven dreams about being a murderer. It's the power to impose one's will; to take what's wanted; and to frighten, intimidate, and rule ruthlessly.

For one woman, her dreams tell the story as the murder of her children by a character who's her age and gender and roughly resembles her. The murder happens in her house, and during the dream, she screams "bloody murder" and promises terrible retribution, but the character only smirks at her and hands her a phone to call the police. The woman grabs it but then realizes that the police may find incriminating evidence in her home. The other woman says, "Told you so."

The dream dramatizes the woman's ego-driven approach to parenting her children. She's harsh and critical and uses fear and intimidation to control their behavior. She feels justified, saying to herself that raising four children with their docile father requires her to be a disciplinarian. Her self-justifications prevent her from changing her ways, shown in the dream as her unwillingness to call the police. To illustrate her lack of self-awareness, the dream gives the role of murderer to the other woman, but deep inside of herself, she knows that she's the source of the problem. That's why she fears that the police will find incriminating evidence inside her home.

Murdering can mean that something inside of the person is dead, and it's a comparison that dreams can use to say that the person feels dead inside or has lost something essential, such as the connection between their head and heart or between their mind and body. For one man with PTSD, his dream tells the story as him being a spirit looking for his murdered body. He finds it and sees his open, lifeless eyes, a picture of what he feels like—he feels dead inside, his mind dissociated from his body. Then, he sees his body stir, a way of saying that he senses the life stirring within him and an opportunity to reconnect. For another man, playing the role of a detective trying to solve a murder is his dream's way of dramatizing his internal search for what went wrong in his life. He lost an essential part of himself after his girlfriend left him, and he dissociated from his body to escape the pain.

A murderer in a dream may represent a lost or split-off inner aspect of the dreamer, and their dreams characterize it as a murderer to symbolize the antagonistic or tragic relationship between them and what's lost or split off. It needs to be reincorporated. The same idea applies to dream characters that are murdered—in them, you see something about yourself that's dying or lost.

Dreams can symbolize fighting a bad depression and other conditions as fighting a murderer. Disease is another killer that's fought against and described in terms of fighting for one's life. Anything that you fight or struggle against could be characterized in dreams as a murderer: negativity, pessimism, a bad influence, bad luck, a bad attitude, or a bad environment or atmosphere.

Dreams about an ex coming to murder the dreamer are often dramatizations of their sense that they will never find love again because of the damage done by past relationships. The dream author chooses murder as a theme when feelings about the situation are hot and the damage is lasting. A common variation of the theme involves an ex coming to murder the dreamer's new boyfriend or girlfriend, a way of expressing fear that the past will catch up with the person and spoil the new relationship.

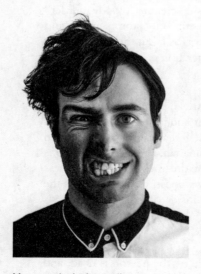

Most people don't actually go out and kill people, so the idea of doing this in a dream shows how people often have a kind of split personality between what they think and what they will actually do.

In an extreme instance, a woman's recurring dreams about her ex-boyfriend coming to murder her reflected her reality while in hiding from him. Fear is behind the dreams, and it's a constant presence in her life because even though she's in hiding, she must be vigilant to avoid doing anything that might lead him to her. He'll murder her if he can find her. Providing help in cases like hers requires advanced tools of dreamwork that few people possess outside of shamanic and therapeutic circles. If a solution exists, it's to reclaim the power taken by the murderer and what or who it represents or even to develop power that's beyond ordinary human abilities. Abilities such as precognition are said to have developed to enhance survival by warning us when danger is coming, and precognition is experienced most often while dreaming.

Even the most violent dreams present opportunities for healing and creating a sense of safety, and it begins with confronting the murderer rather than running from it. Shamanic ritual and dreamwork techniques such as Active Imagination use dream imagery as a starting point for empowering the person and conjuring protective energy. One way to respond during a dream or

> **Abilities such as precognition are said to have developed to enhance survival by warning us when danger is coming, and precognition is experienced most often while dreaming.**

vision is by allowing the murderer to do what they will, even if it means murdering you and fully experiencing it ritually. It allows the worst-case scenario to happen ritually so that you can say, "Okay, now what?" It also must happen in order to heal and let go. Stop running and face it—this is the only way.

See also: Evil, Ghosts/Poltergeists/Spirits, Killing, Serial Killers, War

NUCLEAR WAR

If war is Hell, nuclear war is somehow worse, and that's what differentiates a nuclear war from a conventional one. Dreams may choose nuclear war to express an idea when the underlying dynamics rise to a higher degree of emotion, severity, and importance.

Nuclear war imagery is common in dreams that speak to the biggest sorts of changes in a person's life. Life afterward will be completely different. Teenagers on the cusp of adulthood dream about nuclear war as an idea that captures the dynamics of their situation. Deep down, they know that life will never be the same. The dream content reflects their subjective thoughts and feelings about the impending changes, and the more they dread it, the worse the conditions in the dream. Conversely, the better prepared they are, the better the dream.

Divorce and other sorts of separation are also situations that dreams can symbolize as nuclear war, especially if the impact is huge, the fallout is major, the emotions are especially hot, or the effects are lasting. A bad breakup can be like a war, and a complete meltdown is like a nuclear war.

"Wiped out" and "devastated" are ideas the imagery expresses, and nuclear war is the highest degree. A devastating illness or financial disaster, for example, are situations in life that dreams express as nuclear war.

Nuclear war is a symbol for something in one's life that they find absolutely devastating.

But also think in terms of a fresh start—the past is wiped away and everything starts over after a nuclear war. In dreams that express the idea, the dreamer's reactions can be out of sync with the imagery. *Yay, the nukes are dropping!* It shows desire for what a nuclear war symbolizes, and the reaction is a big clue to the meaning because it's driven by the dreamer subconsciously knowing what the symbolic imagery means.

To understand how reactions in dreams are affected subconsciously, take the dream a woman experienced where she's in her home with her family and sees a nuclear explosion in the distance. The blast wave will incinerate them, and her last thought is that at least they are together one last time. The dream dramatizes her family situation—they are getting older and drifting apart, and the inevitable day is coming when what's made her family life so special for her will be history. The nuclear blast is seen in the distance from her family home, the dream's way of saying that the changes sweeping closer are yet to arrive. "The end is coming" is the simple idea. Her reaction of thinking that at least her final moments on Earth will be spent with her family is the clue that reveals the dream's true subject. Her family life is what's most important to her, and it coming to an end is a dreadful inevitability. She will cherish it while it lasts.

The association method of dream interpretation is your best tool for figuring out what the imagery means personally to you. You may be surprised when you reflect on a nuclear war dream and make associations off the top of your head like "sudden, bright, and big," and it symbolizes being struck suddenly by a big, bright idea or that the path to a goal suddenly becomes "illuminated" or obvious. In that sense, a nuclear blast is like the world's most noticeable signpost.

From a distance, a man watches a nuclear bomb detonate and can't take his eyes off the mushroom cloud. He says it's "beautiful" and "alluring." The dream is about his fascination with erotica. It grabs his attention and won't let go, same as the mushroom cloud. Plus, the shape is vaguely feminine and erotic, and feminine sensuality is something he experiences through erotica. Erotica gives him a taste of the power of feminine allure from a safe distance, same as the dream that places him at a safe distance from the nuclear detonation. Dreams can use the mushroom cloud imagery to parallel with anything that's said to hold power over a person or has a hypnotic effect, such as obsessions and ego drives, and that sets off powerful emotions and instinctive drives.

Nothing says white-hot passion like a mushroom cloud. Nukes and passion both require only a flip of the switch to set off a big bang!

Power is another association with nuclear bombs. So much power packed into a relatively small weapon. It suggests the idea that something is ready to explode in a big way. It can symbolize a "powerhouse," for example, or a small person who packs a big punch, or anyone who commands respect and attention. Another simple idea is that you shouldn't overlook anything.

The implication of a dream using a nuke instead of a conventional bomb is that the nuke has more power. Plus, it burns longer, whereas a conventional bomb explodes in a flash. In life, we say that a bomb goes off when something sudden and messy happens. On the other hand, a nuke usually means huge, lasting, and perhaps life life-changing. If an outburst of anger is like a bomb going off, a nuke is all-powerful rage. The same thinking applies to "explosive" emotions and situations—if they top the scale in power and severity, they are like a nuke.

If war is a consequence, nuclear war is the worst sort. "Nuke your career" is an example of using a phrase that expresses the idea metaphorically. It's bigger than a mere screw-up. Now, you're dreaming about being at work when a nuke goes off or coming to work and seeing the place being devastated by a nuclear blast, and what you're really seeing is the meaning of the phrase being depicted visually.

Fear of a nuclear war dream coming true is common—it's taken literally when it shouldn't be, a failure to see what it dramatizes and exaggerates. "It's not that bad," a person says about a situation or other dynamic that their dream symbolizes as nuclear war. And maybe that's objectively true, but subjectively, the situation really is that bad, and a dream amplifies it to the max to make it unmistakable. This is usually the case when a person minimizes something and their dreams come down hard on the other end of the scale, maximizing the drama and exaggeration.

Dreams of living in a bunker clearly represents a desire for deliberate isolation from the rest of the world, a "bunker mentality."

Take, for instance, the dream a woman had about being in an underground bunker and pressing the button that launches a nuclear war. She does it spitefully, thinking that the enemy deserves it. Behind the dream is a situation where she's aware of her dark behavior and emotions but justifies it. She has a "bunker mentality," symbolized as the underground bunker, and her dream poignantly shows her alone in it. Her behavior and mentality isolate her from the world. The dream amplifies the scenario in the hope of breaking through her ego barriers. It's a function of the psyche that Dr. Carl Jung calls compensation; the unconscious part of the psyche creates imagery and scenarios that compensate for the imbalance and extremes of the ego.

Pressing the button that starts a war can mean "the nuclear option." It's an act of desperation, the strongest of responses, all or nothing. It may be the trigger for a chain of events that ends in a big bang.

The scenarios and stories that use nuclear war may be more important to the meaning than the symbolism of it. A nuclear war is thought of as the right imagery for extreme situations, conditions, and circumstances, but it's also a pretext for telling a deeper story. Take, for instance, the dream a man had about emerging from hiding after a nuclear war. He walks through a deserted city where the structures still stand but all the people are gone. He comes to realize that he's the last person alive on Earth. Nuclear war is a pretext for telling a story about his extreme loneliness. He feels like he's the last person alive because he has no one else in the world he can relate to or love. Nuclear war in his dream sets the scene to tell the deeper story about the nature of his existence.

In a similar way, nuclear war can set the scene for a story about a huge threat, a big consequence, a major fallout, or inescapability. You can't escape from a nuclear blast, after all, and the fallout is widespread and severe. Then, consider death and the fear of it, the biggest, most inescapable change of all, that a mushroom cloud says with one look.

And lest we forget, a nuclear blast may be the metaphor that matches with a condition of the body, such as high fever, bad heartburn, or last night's five-alarm chili burning through your digestive system. It's also one heck of a way of symbolizing a heart attack. The clock stops ticking when the big bomb goes off.

See also: Apocalypses, Armageddon, Killing, Storms/Blizzards/Hurricanes/Tornadoes, Terrorism, War

RAPE

One of the first lessons of dream interpretation is to see beyond what a dream presents overtly and surmise a hidden meaning behind it, and nowhere is this lesson more important than with dreams involving rape and sexual assault. Read the action as literal, and misunderstanding is all but sure to follow. Read it as figurative and symbolic, and it may be correctly understood. It's true of all conventional dreams, but rape dreams are among the most likely to be misinterpreted because the dreamer can't be objective with a subject that's so loaded.

The dream author follows our example when it uses rape to mean something other than actual rape. We say rape to mean exploitation and violation, such as "rape the planet." We say it to mean humiliation and domination, like when one side in a game or sport "rapes" the other. A dream presents rape in the literal sense but usually means it in the metaphorical sense, the same as we do when we say rape but don't mean it literally.

As with molestation dreams, a rape dream could stem from a literal memory, or it could be symbolic of some other type of trauma.

Before digging further into the metaphor and symbolism, let's look at the literal usages. People who have been raped are likely to dream about it, and if those dreams follow the pattern often seen with PTSD, the dreams are experienced literally and viscerally. Traumas are reexperienced similarly or exactly as they happened, and for survivors of rape, it's a horrifying cycle of reliving their waking nightmare in their sleep nightmares. It may seem cruel to make a person relive their traumas, but behind their nightmares is an attempt to help.

First of all, PTSD results from reliving trauma as an ever-present reality instead of being in the past, so dreaming about it aids the process of creating a psychological cushion by "putting it behind you"—in the past, not still happening, because once a nightmare is over, it's in the past. Second of all, the nightmares serve the same basic function that all dreams do by processing emotions and memories. When the job is left unfinished, the nightmares recur. And third of all, dreaming about a rape scenario may give the person the ability to react in case it ever happens (again); the nightmare is a threat rehearsal.

A young woman passed out at a party, then woke up to find a random guy spooning her. Soon afterward, she started dreaming about a random man forcing himself on her. The dreams are giving her opportunities to rehearse how to handle a threatening situation like that and to know how to respond if it ever happens again—and to avoid putting herself in a vulnerable position in the first place.

Vulnerability is the idea behind some rape dreams that beg the person to recognize the dangers they put themself in. Their dreams respond by creating vulnerable situations and playing out worst-case scenarios and are likely to continue until the lesson is learned. A young woman's rape nightmares started after she accepted, while wasted and alone, a ride from two men she didn't know. Their creepy remarks about what they could do to her while she lay helpless and locked in the back seat made her realize the danger. They didn't hurt her, but she is raped in her nightmares, showing her what could have happened, and, more importantly, asking her to never be so stupid again. But she resists the message because responding to it means tempering her partying, so the nightmares recur with increasing intensity.

The revenge scenario is a theme in dark dreams that's known to follow a rape or assault. It's a reaction on the "fight" end of the fight–flight–freeze response spectrum, but it's not a threat rehearsal—it's psychological bondage to the event. For one woman, her revenge dream begins with her finding her rapist working on a car. She pulls out a gun and coldly fires rounds into him until she's sure he's dead. The character is a depiction of the man who really did rape her, the brother of her former best friend, and the setting is the auto shop where he works. She sees him around town and seethes with anger that he's not rotting in prison, but she didn't report the rape, and it adds to the psychological dynamics behind her revenge dream. She told her former best friend that her brother raped her, and the best friend denied it really happened! Now the desire for revenge consumes her life—whether waking or sleeping—and the wound keeps bleeding. Getting revenge in her dream may seem like empowerment, but it really shows her bondage to the hot and humiliating feelings that linger two years after the crime.

When rape dreams are figurative and symbolic, they express an idea that relates to rape through the use of language and other associations. Take helplessness, for example. A dream creates a scenario of being helpless—overpowered physically and/or psychologically and unable to escape—and has options for adding beating, bondage, torture, drugging, terrorizing, kidnapping, and paralysis to it. Now, add rape, and the dream author can conjure up a hard-hitting story and speak to specific personal and situational dynamics of one's life. The author chooses rape over other options because it's the best way to tell the story.

Take, for instance, the young man who dreamed that his mother raped him. The setting is his bedroom, and she enters the room in the middle of the night and says that if he's a good son, he'll go along with what's about to happen. She then climbs on top of him, rides him, and finishes by pinching him hard on the nipples and leaving the room.

It's understandable why the dream disturbed him—his mother just raped him! But she's a character in the story, and the rape is symbolic of something else.

> **When rape dreams are figurative and symbolic, they express an idea that relates to rape through the use of language and other associations.**

The trail to the meaning is found in her statement about him being a good son. It speaks to the many years that he has tolerated her physical violations like pinching and grabbing. What can he say or do in response? Nothing. His mom makes remarks that he's flabby and soft, then pinches or grabs him, and he endures it without objection because he's male and is expected to be tough and uncomplaining. Her behavior started during his early childhood, and it taught him that his body is not his own and his boundaries are not respected. It makes him feel helpless, and that's the main idea behind the dream. He lies there helplessly as his mom rapes him. Pull no punches, it's the truth of the matter.

Coercion is another idea that's unsaid but understood in his dream, and it's a common driving force behind rape dreams. Coercion is a psychological force that bends a person's will, and giving in to it sparks feelings of helplessness, powerlessness, and shame. And now, we see why the dream author uses rape to express the idea by reaching behind the scenes to touch on his feelings and perceptions. He is powerless to stop his mom's inappropriate touching, and he's ashamed of his body. His dream translates the feelings as coercive rape.

The damage goes deeper into his psychology, too, because the flip side of shame is rage, and his rage is set loose whenever he feels shame. If he can't answer a teacher's question, he rages. If his father makes a sideways comment about how he chooses to dress, he rages. Then, his parents wonder why he's being so "touchy"!

The dream author is aware of the hidden dynamics, and once exposed through dream interpretation and introspection, they're easy to trace to the source of his feelings, and it's easy to see why the dream author chooses rape to tell the story about his mother's coercive tactics. Same goes for the dream lives of people everywhere who feel ashamed—especially after experiencing assault or violation of any kind. Shame and rape go hand in hand in everyday life and in dreams.

> **People usually fail to apprehend the hidden dynamics when they dream about rape. They fail to see the dramatization.**

People usually fail to apprehend the hidden dynamics when they dream about rape. They fail to see the dramatization. The truth fits the same as when metaphors make spot-on comparisons that reveal what's hidden, unknown, repressed, and overlooked.

The hidden dynamics may be cultural and societal. In the above instance, the young man's culture expects males to be tough and tolerant, especially around their females. For another man, his recurring rape dreams feature men he doesn't know, who appear and behave like the "man's man." They are dominant in his dreams, and while he's not exactly submissive, he "takes it like a man." He's neither effeminate nor gay but is starting to wonder about his sexuality; why else would he dream recurrently about gay rape unless it's a secret fantasy?

But his feelings about conforming to cultural expectations of masculinity are behind the dreams. He's expected to act macho and distant as a male and feels inadequate in comparison to tough guys. And because the coercion and shame messages are coming from social forces, it's difficult for him to apprehend the source.

Females also live under a cloud of cultural expectations about how they should appear and behave, and when it feels coercive, abusive, and involuntary, the dynamics are ripe for expressing through rape dreams. And it's true even for the women (and men) who live up to the prototype of their gender. Yes, she may wear uncomfortable shoes and spend hours waxing and doing her makeup and hair, then walk into public and make the right impression, but is it truly voluntary?

To answer the question, let's think like the dream author. Voluntary sex is not rape, but involuntary sex is. So where is the line? And how does the association with gender expectations carry over as a metaphor in rape dreams? Answer: sex appeal. Males and females conform to gender expectations because it makes them more attractive as lovers and mates and gives them power. Sex appeal is a background idea that the dream author notes and expresses as rape if the behavior is involuntary, inauthentic, or power motivated, and the pressure to conform feels coercive.

A similar dynamic comes into play when a person feels like a sex object. They may draw sexual attention, then dream about it as rape. Take, for instance, the nightmare a woman had where she's at a gas station when a creepy man grabs her, pulls her behind the building, and rapes her. Afterward, she calls her boyfriend and chews him out for not protecting her. Note that reaction; it reveals the hidden dynamics.

An incident earlier that day brought on the nightmare. She was at a gas station, and a creepy man walked by and gave her a lewd look. It made her feel like a sex object, and her vulnerability sent a shockwave of fear through her. Her dream processed the memories and emotions and translated them into a scenario where the fear came true.

Rape dreams might originate from feelings of having been made into a sex object by another person in one's life.

But why call her boyfriend afterward and chew him out? Her reaction doesn't fit the scene, but oh, does it tell a story. See, usually she feels safe around her boyfriend and can depend on him to protect her from bad men—but he must be paying attention. At the gas station earlier that day, he was completely oblivious to what happened to his woman. She's pissed at him for that and at herself for relying on men to defend her from predatory men.

Her dream is unusual for how closely it replicates the incident from memory, but doing so also makes interpreting it easier. Clearly, the dream is a response to the incident because it occurred soon afterward. Plus, the gas station setting and the creepy rapist character are almost identical to her memory.

Some schools of thought about dream interpretation claim that all dreams can be traced to memories from the past day or two, and while incorrect (some dreams are not based on recent memory), it does provide a starting point for reflecting on your life and searching for correlations with recent events. On the literal side, a brush with danger or an assault may spark a rape dream, and on the figurative side are a variety of situations and conditions: humiliation, violation, domination, coercion, fear, abuse, and so forth.

But many of the examples provided already were not caused by recent incidents. Instead, they are ongoing situations and conditions, and the correlations are found in the person's patterns of thought and feeling, relationships with people, relationships with deeper aspects of the psyche, and attitudes. Reflecting on your recent life may provide an avenue to the meaning, or it may not.

Think back to the revenge dream where the woman shoots her rapist. She could ask herself if she'd thought about revenge and her rapist during the day or two before the dream and answer yes—but the rape itself occurred *years* prior to the dream. She is not processing recent memories of it, but the memories, and especially the feelings, are ever present below the surface, and she may not be consciously aware of them—not enough to use them to guide her to the meaning of the dream. She is better off widening her scope of retrospection and correlating with patterns she sees in herself and her life—and in her dreams.

In one woman's recurring nightmares about being gang raped, the men are never ones she knows or recognizes, and the scenarios vary. Usually, she's doing something ordinary when suddenly, men surround her. Also, the people nearby don't help her, and the reason is because her nightmares about gang rape are about her fear of men in general, and no one helps her because she thinks that no one understands her fear. Like in her nightmares, they just stare at her dumbly.

> **For some women—and men, too—gang rape reflects their issues with males in general and patriarchal authority structures.**

She hasn't been raped, and she is hypervigilant about avoiding dangerous situations. Seemingly, she has little to fear. But she has experienced being treated like a sex object, has felt helpless and vulnerable, and has been violated by unwelcome sexual attention and advances. Most of all, she knows the dangers that a gang of men present to a woman who is a rabbit among wolves. Her own weakness is what she really fears. The environment *inside of her* that her patterns of thought and feeling create is the source of her nightmares about gang rape. The men who rape her in her nightmares physically penetrate her, and she feels it vividly. It's a visual metaphor.

For some women—and men, too—gang rape reflects their issues with males in general and patriarchal authority structures. They may have no recent incidents in their life that provide a correlation with their nightmares and may not recognize the source because it's too psychologically distant, but a good starting point for any nightmare about gang rape is to explore how the dreamer feels about the gender of the rapists. Dig into their social interactions and encounters with groups of that gender and explore their personal patterns of thought and feeling.

You'd think that rape is always about actual violence inflicted on the person, but the real violence is usually happening inside of them. When rape is forced sexual penetration, the dream author may mean simply that something is forced on you and it gets inside of you. The metaphor is expressed visually. For one woman, her nightmare creates a scenario where she's forced to give oral sex, and the penis of her rapist grows so big that it gags her. It's a visual metaphor for the idea of "forced down your throat." In her waking life, she was being forced to accept a situation that sickened her emotionally. For a man who is anally raped by Satan, the nightmare is a symbolic expression of a situation where he's in a flame war with a classmate. Anal rape symbolizes the humiliation and anger of the situation. It's "inside" of him. When something gets inside of you in a bad way and carries with it feelings of humiliation, shame, violation, pain, and others associated with rape, dreams show the idea as a visual metaphor.

An exception to the rule is provided by the nightmare a high school girl had about a group of female classmates raping her by shoving objects inside her vagina and rectum and forcing her to perform oral sex. In her waking life, the violence is real and pervasive, and her violators really are the "mean girls" that her nightmare uses as characters. They bully and harass her and can get physical but stop short of rape. Psychological violence is what her nightmare means by rape, and humiliation is what it means by forced oral sex, and it chooses the mean girls from her school as characters because they are the source. Her fear of them never goes away.

> **When something gets inside of you in a bad way and carries with it feelings of humiliation, shame, violation, pain, and others associated with rape, dreams show the idea as a visual metaphor.**

Rape dreams can continue years after a person leaves the environment where the violence—whether physical or psychological—occurred. It's a symptom of PTSD. The pattern is especially prevalent in the dream lives of people who suffered chronic abuse. In one example, a woman went into hiding to escape her violently abusive ex-boyfriend, but he appears nightly in her nightmares and rapes and murders her. The nightmares bring to life the very real possibility that one day he'll find her, and on a more figurative level, they speak to her role as the victim, and that's where she can be helped. A victim is powerless but she's not, and her dreams are a space where she can learn to fight back—safely—and change the script behind her nightmares. She can rehearse the threat and respond, even if it's to say that she'll go down fighting.

The dynamics behind rape dreams may be entirely internal in cases where rape is the best way to describe how the person's ego interacts with the rest of the psyche. Rape is a mindset of doing violence to oneself, often seen in people who were raised to hate who they are and think they must take what they want by force. Rape is a way of crushing and humiliating anything in themselves that speaks to the contrary—that's what the rape victims in their dreams represent. The person crushes their sensitivity and loathes their vulnerability. Their ego is trapped in a bipolar "sadist–masochist" dynamic—the two always travel together.

And the more extreme the imbalance, the more it shows in the extremes of their dream life. One extreme manifests as committing rape in their dreams,

Contrary to what one might think, rape is not an act of sexual desire so much as it is an act of violence and hatred. Dreams of rape, therefore, are a reflection of this violence and not of desire.

then the tables turn, and they are raped, a flipping of polarity from one extreme to the other. In this sense, the rapist is a personality type that flips back and forth between extremes and treats everything, including themselves, as worthless objects to be dominated, despised, and discarded. By expressing the psychological dynamics as rape, the dream author is merely pointing out the obvious. It's a form of psychological possession.

Rape nightmares are especially confusing for people who dream about being the rapist. If the person is not pathological, their usual reaction is to think, *How could I do that?* Intense feelings, situations, and conditions may drive the action from behind the scenes, but rape is symbolism whether the dreamer commits the act or it's done to them. The following example is very intense and dark.

A man dreams that he's outside the grocery store where he works. He intently watches the front of the store from the shadows. His pretty, female coworker leaves the store and walks to her car. He sneaks up, abducts her, shoves her into her car, drives to a secluded area, and pulls over. She frees herself and flees from the car, only to fall into a ditch on the side of the road. The dreamer corners his prey and bears down, saying, "I've just got to have it!" The dream fades out as he's about to rape her.

He shared his dream publicly, and as you might expect, most of the reactions were of the "Dude, you're sick!" variety. Some people suggested that he seek psychiatric help before he hurts someone by carrying out his rape fantasy. They completely misunderstood the dream. Let's look at the personal context—it's always the place to begin.

He really does work at the grocery store in the dream's opening scene, and the coworker really is someone he works with. No, he's never fantasized about raping her or anyone else, but ... he has intense sexual feelings for her. He says he'll look at her while they're working and want her so badly, but he has no chance with her because she's out of his league, and the one hope he had was crushed recently when their employer passed him over for a promotion into a management position. It may take years for another position to open up.

The context explains the symbolism of the dream's opening scene. He really does have his eye on his coworker, depicted in that scene as watching her leave the store, and really is waiting intently for something to happen at work—a promotion. It doesn't happen, so then what? He takes what he wants—her! And he does it by using her car to abduct her, a symbol meaning that having a girlfriend like her will take him to where he wants to be in life, with a second layer of meaning that force is the only option left for him to get what he wants. He tried doing things the right way, and it got him nowhere.

In ordinary reality, he's a lonely man working a dead-end job and lacks the charisma to attract a pretty girlfriend like his coworker. But in his mind, if he's a manager, well, now, of course, she's going to want him! And if she wants him, it *validates* him. Scenarios in dreams that involve violence can show that the person needs something to feel validated, but they lack the means to get it.

"I've just got to have it" is a statement that sounds like what a rapist would say, but he really means that he's got to have the girl to validate him and have the important job to get the girl. The seclusion of the final scene is the dream's way of reflecting his most private thoughts and feelings, and the ditch is a graphic representation of where his mind went after his hopes were crushed by getting passed over for a promotion. He's feeling lowly and desperate.

His dream is not a rape fantasy; it's a symbolic expression of his situation and feelings about it. But the next example is a rape fantasy.

A man dreams that he's dating a woman and they have sex. It's nice but lacks stimulation. The next night, he dreams that he spots a woman he wants, stalks and rapes her, and it's highly stimulating. That's enough information—personal context will explain the rest.

The second dream is a rape fantasy, and he really does have one—he's obsessed with it to the point of badly wanting to carry it out. The first dream sets up a contrast with the second one that reveals the hidden personal dynamics. He's a good-looking, socially desirable man. Getting girlfriends and sex partners is easy—maybe too easy because it no longer stimulates him. No challenge exists. But raping someone and getting away with it—that's stimulating and challenging.

The contrast between the two dreams is a message. To have a normal sex life, he must give up his rape fantasy, but if he carries out his fantasy, he'll cross a line that can never be uncrossed. He can have one or the other but not both. Maybe knowing the damage that rape does to the people who survive it would puncture a hole in his fantasy, but it's impossible to know. He disappeared after discussing the two dreams.

Three decades after a woman was raped as a virgin, she continued having nightmares about being in the clutches of a psychologically overpowering sadist—a fair description of the rapist but also of the psychological complex that developed out of the experience with him. The fear and humiliation never left her, festering in the background and feeding like a parasite on her feelings. In another case, a person who was molested as a child dreamed about being paralyzed as the act is repeated almost verbatim to how it happened (see the end of the discussion in the Paralysis entry).

The horror of the experiences is beyond words to describe, and it's a sticking point for understanding rape dreams when people say it's not right under any circumstances to toy with something so despicable by using rape as metaphor and symbolism and resubjecting the survivors to their trauma. But the dream author sees things differently. It wants to tell a story that matches well with personal and situational dynamics and, by doing so, provide opportunities to heal and grow. Social conventions are immaterial.

See also: Incest, Molestation, Murder, Paralysis, Possession, Imprisonment/Entrapment

SERIAL KILLERS

To understand what a dream means by presenting a serial killer, begin with common associations. First of all, serial killers are methodical. They plan their deeds and are deliberate. They also repeat their crimes—it differentiates them from ordinary killers and murderers. Now, put yourself in the shoes of the dream author and imagine how you could use a serial killer as a symbol for ideas related to things that are methodical, deliberate, and repetitive.

Dreams use the symbol in stories to parallel situations in life such as gaslighting—the methodical, deliberate, and repetitive effort to erode someone's sanity. It's an extreme end of the spectrum and an obvious parallel, but keep in mind that dreams dramatize and exaggerate, opening possibilities for using a serial killer as a symbol for situations and conditions where a person questions their mental health and grasp of reality. Dealings with serial killers are unreal in the sense that they are extreme and extremely rare, making them fantastic symbols for a situation when a person says, "This can't be happening; it's not real."

A repetitive situation that threatens or erodes a person's well-being is also ripe for being symbolized as a serial killer. A serial killer can be thought of as simply a threat, but dreams use it specifically for repetitive threats. On one end of the spectrum, the threat could be the monthly mortgage payment or other cyclical struggles with finances and money. Missing a payment could lead to Armageddon, figuratively, and a serial killer is a great symbol for big threats and imminent dangers. On the other end are threats that come from within a person. If a person can be said to be a danger to oneself and others and the danger is existential, a serial killer tops the list of symbols that can capture the dynamics of the situation. Serial killers wipe people out of existence, and dreams can run far with such ideas when something about a person's existence feels threatened.

The methodical nature of serial killers is also an idea that dreams can run with. In one such dream, a business owner is inside the warehouse where he conducts his business. He gets a text message: *A serial killer is inside the warehouse.* He looks around, sees no threat, and goes about his business. He gets another text: *Watch out, the serial killer is right behind you!* Again, he sees no threat and continues like normal, but the dream lingers with him, and he seeks help in understanding it. Since it occurs in the warehouse where he works and the setting is re-created true to ordinary reality, he focuses on that area of his life and looks for threats to his business. To understand the serial killer, he thinks in terms of being set up for the kill. And since the serial killer is said to be right behind him, he is wise to look for something that's hidden or unknown and creeping up on him.

Real serial killers such as Ted Bundy (pictured) are fairly rare in real life, so to have a dream of such an evil predator can represent some sort of repetitive threat in the dreamer's life.

It's a tall order, but he takes the dream seriously and thinks long and hard about it. Then, a realization blows his blinders off. His main supplier is also a business rival! He put his trust in the person and has been maneuvered into a position of vulnerability. If the rival turns on him, his business is dead, and that's exactly what's happening. The rival appears trustworthy, but something is beneath the surface that the business owner hadn't been able to put his finger on, and with the help of his dream, he realizes just in time that he's being played.

The dream sums up the situation perfectly with the scenario where a serial killer is inside his warehouse and he isn't aware of it. First of all, the rival is methodical. Second of all, the intent is to kill the man's business and strike at a moment of maximum vulnerability. And third of all, the rival presents himself one way, but beneath the surface lurks a cold and calculating killer.

The dream also demonstrates that a serial killer is a hidden danger that's sensed intuitively. The subconscious mind is the sender of the text messages warning about the killer. It picked up on the nefarious intentions of the rival and communicated the information. We often ask ourselves how the worst sorts of killers can live among us without our knowing, and it's because we believe surface appearances. Serial killers act and appear ordinary and live among us, usually, and those facts give the dreaming mind a great symbol to use anytime we sense something dark lurking beneath the surface but can't identify it. In this sense, the serial killer is a symbol for the wrong we fail to recognize for what it really is.

Those associations open the possibility for a dream to use a serial killer as a symbol for the wrong that could catch up with you. It can symbolize situations where a person knows deep down that they've done, are doing, or are considering doing something terrible or wrong or they fear ostracism. Serial killers, when caught, are harshly punished and cast out of society. A situation, condition, or circumstance that can be described as beyond bad is ripe for comparison to a serial killer.

Behind a "serial killer dream" may be a plea for help because the dreamer can't stop themself from doing what they know is wrong and destructive. It's another association with serial killers that dreams can run with. Serial killers can't stop themselves from killing. It gratifies a beast within them. Now, imagine what a dream could compare a serial killer to: an addiction, a destructive cycle, a consuming darkness. Or, literally, picture the diabetic who can't stop eating sweets or the thrill seeker who can't stop pushing the limits. It will kill them one day.

> **Behind a "serial killer dream" may be a plea for help because the dreamer can't stop themself from doing what they know is wrong and destructive.**

Serial killers are obsessed, or, maybe, possessed is the better word. Something evil compels them. The dream author observes those associations and creates a serial killer character or puts you in that role when the comparison makes a good metaphor. The discussions in the entries on Vampires and Possession offer a wealth of insights about the seduction of the ego. The serial killer puts a twist on the idea, especially when power and dominance possess the ego and its mindset is predatory. A dream could project the idea onto a serial killer character, but when it wants to mirror your ego, it puts *you* in the role. Then, the spotlight of dream analysis shines on your inner life and personality—especially your attitudes, behaviors, and projections. Find what the serial killer illustrates about internal dynamics by asking, what do I see about myself in the character? It may be difficult to personally identify with it, but step back from the implications and look for the metaphor, the comparison, the exaggeration, the dramatization, and your patterns of behavior, thought, feeling, and perception.

Acting like a serial killer in a dream can symbolize doing something despite the harm it can cause to oneself or others. Some serial killers commit murder simply because it gives them a thrill or they feel like doing it, and those associations lend extra layers of meaning to the symbol when a person does something they shouldn't despite knowing better. They do it anyway, like a serial killer. And doing it repetitively differentiates the behavior from the symbolism of killing or murder.

On the milder side, a dream can use a serial killer to symbolize the idea of something that sets a person or situation apart. Serial killers are rare, and their

Taking on the role of a serial killer in a dream could suggest a desire to do things even though you know they will cause a lot of harm to others.

actions set them apart from ordinary people. They see things differently and can think that they are justified. This idea is at the heart of a dream where a woman's neighbors accuse her of being a serial killer after a rash of unexplained deaths in her community. She knows she's not to blame and defends herself vigorously. The dream dramatizes a situation where she feels different from her neighbors and ostracized because of it. She has different viewpoints and beliefs and feels like her neighbors talk about her behind her back like she's a criminal.

To dream about catching a serial killer or murderer can mean taking control of a bad situation or condition, especially an internal one, or mastering an impulse or compulsion. Or it may simply be a role the dream creates to cast the dreamer as a hero. If the killer is not caught, it may mean that the person has more work to do or more to understand about a situation or condition.

To dream about dating a serial killer may point toward trouble coming in a relationship. Nothing says "I picked the wrong person" like dating a serial killer! It can also symbolize toying with an idea that's likely to lead to trouble. Dating is a preliminary stage before making a commitment, and when a dream uses dating as a theme as opposed to a stronger commitment like marriage, it's done deliberately to illustrate a dynamic.

Take, for instance, the dream where a woman is dating another woman who is rough and manly, then finds out her lover is a serial killer. During the dream, she asks herself if she can accept the trade-off between dating someone who is dangerous and the feeling of protection she enjoys when they are together. The dream illustrates an internal dynamic where the dreamer has been test-driving a change in her personality by becoming more acerbic and confrontational and projecting a tougher image. Her dream presents the scenario as dating because the changes in her personality are not yet a permanent part of who she is and specifically as dating a female serial killer because first of all, she's female, and second of all, it sums up the idea that she's changing her personality to protect herself. A serial killer is no one to mess with.

The dream is also about power. Serial killers take it despite the harm they cause, and dreams use that association to create meaning that highlights power dynamics. It's a dramatization of what the desire for and use of power does to them and to the people close to them. On the other hand, the serial killer may be a compensatory figure to balance a person who is too passive. The killer is the opposite extreme of passivity, and its purpose as a dream character may be to nudge the person to be more aggressive. The psyche is always seeking balance.

People who study serial killers and are otherwise fascinated by them are known to dream about intense situations involving them. These "what if?" dreams create virtual reality simulations to explore the subject. Take, for instance, the dream a woman had about being a detective who interviews a serial killer face-to-face, with nothing to protect her except her wits. The scene is super intense and movielike, and much of it involves her internal dialogue in response to being in the presence of an uber predator—does she have the fortitude? Her dream is a test run to see if she can handle a career in criminology specializing in serial killers. She's an undergraduate and wants to get a graduate degree and work for the FBI. If she gets the job, she'll come face-to-face with serial killers

> **People who study serial killers and are otherwise fascinated by them are known to dream about intense situations involving them.**

and their crimes. But deeper down, the dream is really asking her if she can handle being so close to such a morbid subject.

A dream could create such a scenario simply to test one's courage, not in response to a specific situation or fascination. Fear is what the serial killer symbolizes, and the dream is an opportunity to face it head-on.

A final consideration to highlight is the rarest of all dreams about serial killers and murder: ones that replay or foretell actual events. Call it a gift or a curse; some people dream about actual events that create big ripples in the collective psyche, and death by violence is one of the biggest. The realism sets the dreams apart from ordinary symbolic ones; the dreamer sees events as they happened or even as they are happening or are about to happen.

The Red Barn Murder is a famous historical case where a dream led to solving a heinous murder. In 1827, a man lured his lover, Maria Marten, to the Red Barn, a famous landmark in Suffolk, England; murdered her and buried her body there; then claimed that they eloped. Maria's stepmother had several nightmares that her stepdaughter was murdered and buried at the Red Barn. She spoke openly about them, eventually leading to the discovery of Maria's body and the arrest, conviction, and execution of her murderer.

The entries below offer more discussions of subjects that relate to serial killers and the meaning and psychology behind dreams that feature them.

See also: Evil, Killing, Murder, Possession, Rape, Vampires

SUICIDE

Among the scariest and most misunderstood dreams are those that feature suicide. A person dreams about it and wakes up wondering about the message—is something sinister trying to lead them to self-destruction? Maybe, but as in the case with murder and other dark dream themes, more is happening than meets the eye.

Simplifying the idea and looking for metaphors are two of the best initial approaches to interpreting suicide dreams. The simple idea is that suicide

Clearly, dreams of suicide concern self-harm, but it might not mean bodily harm. For example, one can commit "career suicide" by deliberately doing something that gets them fired.

means doing something that causes oneself harm. Parallels with ordinary life include destructive patterns and thought processes and taking actions that harm or could harm one's life and prospects.

Now we can look for metaphors. A metaphor is a colorful way of expressing something that end-runs around our ego barriers and filters. So not only does the dream author love metaphors for how they tell a story but also for the ability to get a point or message across, taking note of the situations and conditions where we use suicide as a metaphor and including it as part of a story when the dynamics of outer and inner life call for it.

Career suicide is the meaning behind a man's dream that shows him standing at the edge of a cliff and telling family members that he's going to jump. They say it's suicide. He jumps anyway and lands in a pool of water, climbs out, and says, "See, I told you I'd be all right." The dream dramatizes a situation where he left his salaried job to start his own business. His family says it's a huge mistake—career suicide—but he's confident that he'll succeed, and indeed, that's how things turned out. Making the leap of faith is the metaphor enacted when he jumps off the cliff, and his statement afterward about being all right is how things turned out. His career suicide turned out to be a great move!

Royally screwing up a relationship is relationship suicide, and in one man's dream, it plays out as a scenario where he returns home, where he lives with his mom, and finds her hanging from a rope in the basement. She committed suicide. Despondent, he runs outside looking for help, finds none, then returns to the basement, and his mom is standing there as if nothing happened.

Looking in from the outside, you might think that his mom is suicidal and that's why he had the dream, but the truth is, he's been dealing drugs and is caught up in the lifestyle, and his greatest fear is his mom finding out. It would kill their relationship. Things would never be the same between them. She has no idea what he's like and what he does when he's away from their home.

The dream dramatically encapsulates the situation in the image of her hanging from a rope. He looks for help and can't find any because he's the only one who can help himself in this situation. When he returns to find her alive in the basement, the dream reflects the current conditions. He hasn't been busted dealing, and his mom doesn't know what he's been doing. Suicide reflects his fear and is forward-looking by showing the consequences if she finds out. The dream uses their basement as the setting where the suicide takes place as a way of saying symbolically, "I don't want to think about it." The basement represents his subconscious mind, where his fears dwell.

Also, a layer to the dream may express fear for his mom's physical safety. He's caught up in a criminal enterprise where innocent people are known to get hurt, and he does live with his mom. The dream mixes reality with fiction in a way that's uncomfortably close to the truth.

Another "suicide dream" features a man declaring to his family and close friends that he's going to hang himself, and they can't do anything to stop him. They protest and plead as he puts the rope around his neck and carries through on his threat. The dream creates a scenario for him to observe something about himself. He has an attitude problem and won't listen to anyone but himself or heed anyone's advice or wishes but his own. And in the end, he's the only one who is really hurt by it. It's his neck in the noose, and he's the one who put it there. Suicide by hanging is a satirical metaphor that says, "Nothing gets through to your head."

A young man experienced a dream where he's hanging out at the home of a friend where a large group socializes. It's their usual place to party. He suddenly can't stand it anymore and goes to his mom's car parked nearby, reaches under the passenger seat, pulls out a gun, puts it to his head, and pulls the trigger.

Bang! Fade to black.

That dream is another example where the dreamer's personal context explains what it means and why he created the experience for himself. The opening scene at the home of his friend is where he spends most of his time. His reaction of suddenly not being able to take it anymore is the outward manifestation of what's happening internally as he's dreaming, bringing forward his subconscious thoughts and feelings. What he really can't stand anymore is the fact that he's wasting his life. He has big ideas about what he wants to do and be but can't figure out how to make them happen, so he hangs out and parties and wastes time. His dream translates the idea as wasting his life by committing suicide.

When mom's car suddenly appears in the scene and the dreamer goes right for the gun beneath the passenger seat, the imagery is in response to the previous scene where the desperation of the young man's situation hits him full force. It's valuable background information because his mother's influence is the reason why he has big dreams for his life. Plenty of people waste their lives and don't think twice about it because they don't want to do anything else and no one is suggesting otherwise, but not so in his case. That's why the car suddenly appears and the gun is inside it.

But more is going on here. The gun in her car is a big discrepancy with reality because first of all, his mom doesn't carry a gun, and second of all, her car would never be parked at his friend's house. In other words, the scene is "staged" for him to play out the drama. The gun is under her passenger seat because both figuratively and literally, that's his place in her life. He's a passenger for the ride of life with his mom, and he's a passenger when they drive together in her car. He is experiencing a huge inner conflict, and huge conflicts are known for leading to suicide. It's the perfect story theme to match with the dynamics of his situation.

The above example provides two common parallels with suicide: a wasted life and a major conflict. Suicide is a dramatized way of telling the story. But what about when suicide is meant literally? When a person is contemplating or planning suicide, their dreams will respond, and a common way is by providing a "what if?" simulation to explore questions such as:

- What if the person's problems only continue in the next life?

- What if they botch the suicide and only make matters worse?

- What will happen to the people they leave behind?

- What happens next—are they truly dead and gone, or does their existence continue?

The dreams realistically explore the possibilities, usually by highlighting the dreamer's own beliefs and expectations. However, some "what if?" suicide dreams sure do appear to tap into a larger field of information and consciousness. In one case, the person dreamed about seeing themselves commit suicide in another life, then woke up feeling as sure as the sun rises that committing suicide again would lead to the same result of being reborn to face the same problems. It's impossible to know for sure if the dream is a glimpse of a past life and a pattern that's continued into the present one or a dramatized *Groundhog Day* scenario where each day repeats the patterns of the last one. The person took it as a message to face their problems but could have just as easily decided to put off facing those problems until the next life. If they're sure they'll live again, why not?

A teenager who'd planned to commit suicide by overdosing on pills dreams about asking God to stop her. Getting no reply, she opens the bottle of pills and sees a ring inside; she recognizes it as her grandma's—the grandma she adored but who died when she was young, and ever since then, she has felt alone in the world. She was sure that the ring was a message that her grandma is still alive in another life and wants her to live, especially considering how she found it inside the bottle of pills she was going to use to kill herself.

However, in other cases, suicide dreams appear to confirm a person's darkest thoughts and wishes—for example, by doing nothing to stop them from killing themselves or showing them in an afterlife of black nothingness. It's impossible to know whether the experiences are subjective or something more, and it's a loaded subject because while some people appear to receive divine intervention through their dreams, others don't. How many in the latter category end up as a statistic?

In some dreams of suicide, God or some benign spirit intervenes to prevent the act; in others, there is no intervention, and what could be a lonelier dream than that?

Or, worse, a person can feel driven to suicide by their dreams either because of the relentless replay of their worst fears and troubles or because of an active presence pushing them over the edge. In one such case, a man is plagued by an evil presence in his nightmares that wants him to kill himself. It says that his life is worthless, no one loves him, and things will never get better. He thinks that the presence is a real spiritual entity, but it says to him the same messages he repeats to himself: he's worthless, no one loves him, life is meaningless, and so on. The entity is very likely to be a personification of the negative voices in his head, and his dreams are giving him a target to aim at to help himself. By facing the entity, he faces what it represents. It's bitter medicine, for sure, the equivalent of a defibrillator to shock a stopped heart into beating again.

A man dreams that he's at work, in the loading dock area at Walmart, when a semi pulls in and three men jump out. The scene is typical of an ordinary day at work until one of the men sits down on a chair and the other two men stand behind him. Employees gather to watch a spectacle. One of the men behind the man in the chair pulls out a big knife and cuts his throat. The man accepts his fate like a human sacrifice. No struggle. No final words. Just grim determination and a lot of blood. It's the equivalent of suicide through voluntary human sacrifice. The dreamer looks around and sees on the faces of his coworkers that they aren't shocked by what they see; it's just part of the job. He spots a manager nearby and catches his eye, and the manager shrugs. *Just another day working at Walmart! Show's over, get back to work.*

The human sacrifice character is a projection of something about the dreamer—that's the place to begin interpreting the dream because it's a guideline that's almost always true. It leads to the question, what does he see about himself in the character? The implication of being like a human sacrifice because his job is sucking the life out of him meets strong resistance. He insists that working at Walmart isn't that bad, and besides, it's the best he can do for the time being and he's got bills to pay. But the more he thinks about it, the more he realizes that the man in the chair is the image of how he really feels. He minimizes to himself the personal costs of working long hours in a grim environment that extracts big sacrifices in return for meager pay, so in response, his dream maximizes. The metaphor of being a human sacrifice is exaggerated but true. And, furthermore, he's growing complacent. It's easier to just report to work and get it over with rather than plan for life after Walmart. He's a young guy with a lot of life ahead—when is he going to start working toward a better future? That's the real question behind the dream.

What are you trying to tell yourself? That's another question to help you penetrate the meaning and *purpose* of a dream as a self-created experience. In the above example, the purpose is to give the man a jolt and help him break out of his complacency, and it's a big reason why dreams amplify—so you hear the internal messages that are being ignored or drowned out. His justifications are drowning out the little voice that's asking him to start doing something now so he doesn't wake up years later and face another dreary day at the Walmart loading dock.

> **A meaningful dream shows the ego what it does not know or understand—or doesn't want to know!**

A meaningful dream shows the ego what it does not know or understand—or doesn't want to know! With suicide, the message may boil down to the need to make room for personal growth. The ego knows what it knows and doesn't care to know anything else, and when the situation turns chronic and impedes growth, the unconscious mind responds forcefully. Many of the most dramatic dreams that push the idea of suicide are you—the unconscious part of you— telling your ego to get the hell out of the way. Your "death" will lead to rebirth. It's a mythological story—the Phoenix rising from the ashes is a variation of it—and it's based on a truth that's been observed millions of times. People are sometimes their own worst enemies. A normal part of the individuation process of personal development is for the ego to give way for something greater than itself to emerge in the person. It voluntarily gives up its struggle. But it feels like death, and it's hard to do.

See also: Dark Magicians, Entities, Falling, Ghosts/Poltergeists/Spirits, God, Killing, Possession, Terrorism

TERRORISM

The dream author takes its cues from how we use language to communicate. Humans communicate mainly through words, and dreams do it mainly through symbols. In the word "terrorist" is a root idea: terror. It's what a dream can mean when it uses a terrorist as a symbol. Something is terrifying. It's terrible. It's a terror.

Now add to the mix the fact that a terrorist uses terror for an agenda or to wreak havoc, and it hands the author a combination of ideas that match well with certain dynamics. Think figuratively, not literally, and the terrorist in a dream can symbolize a person who uses intimidation, threat, or force to advance their agenda. A person who cows others into submission. The comparison between such a person and a terrorist is not a big stretch—when making a metaphor, we can stretch the idea further and compare it to, say, a teacher who uses the threat of a bad grade to force compliance or a parent who uses punishment or the threat of it to change behavior. Think of the scary boss who uses such tactics—are they a terrorist? Metaphorically, yes, if they use fear or force to advance an agenda or wreak havoc.

The objective accuracy of the comparison doesn't matter to the author of dreams. Subjective feelings and perceptions are what matter—the feeling or perception of being coerced, intimidated, frightened, threatened, or terrorized. A dream could use a different symbol to express the idea, but for some reason, it thinks that a terrorist is a better match. Figuring out why gives you a way to decipher the dream's symbolic code.

You can bet that the dream chooses a terrorist as a symbol for strong situations and feelings because terror is a strong word that we use to convey ideas that are stronger than merely feeling a bit frightened. The terrorist is a level or two or three above that, depending on how a dream presents it as part of a story and how the dreamer reacts. The symbol is especially useful when the feelings combine with other dynamics that involve advancing an agenda—then, it's easier to see why a dream chooses a terrorist over other symbols that convey the same basic idea.

Expand your horizons beyond a terrorist meaning a person—think of it in terms of a *thing*. The terrorist as a character looks like a person, so it's natural to assume it symbolizes one, but appearances can be deceiving, and beneath the mask is an idea the character personifies.

Take, for instance, the following dream where the dreamer is out in public and a woman with a baby asks if she's heard the rumor that terrorists are going to attack. The dreamer understands it to mean their location. Suddenly worried, she scans the sea of faces and spots people acting suspiciously. The dreamer tells the

Often masked, terrorists in a dream can stand for an undefined threat of unknown origin. Of course, it can often also represent the feeling of being "terrorized" by someone such as a boss or other authority figure.

woman to flee—to save her own life and her baby's. She catches sight of the terrorists moving closer to her, as if they're aware that she knows who they really are. She wants to run, but suddenly, the crowd wedges her in. Her panic skyrockets. She sees a terrorist move within feet of her and reach a hand inside his bulky jacket. Frozen in terror, she hears a boom and jolts awake.

The opening scene of the dream announces the subject of the story by showing the dreamer in public. It's the central idea, and everything else relates to it either symbolically or as part of the story. Analyze how the scenario plays out, and it makes you wonder if it dramatizes what happens to the dreamer when she's in public. Does the idea of terror come into the picture? It would certainly seem so. The next scene expands on the idea when the woman with the baby tells her about the rumor of a terrorist attack, then she sees terrorists in the crowd. It suggests the idea that you never know what dangers lurk when you're out in public. All these observations gel together when understood as dramatizations of the dreamer's social anxiety.

> **A dream can use the same basic scenario to dramatize the experience of bullying, ridicule, and rejection.**

"Terror" is the word that captures her feelings when she's in a crowd, the anxiety clamps down, and she's unable to function, frozen in terror, which the dream's final scene dramatizes as being unable to move, with a terrorist about to set off a bomb. When her social anxiety turns into a panic attack, it's like a bomb goes off in her nervous system. Knowing that the dream dramatizes her social anxiety, the meaning of the terrorists becomes obvious, but not the meaning of the woman with the baby. But if you understand that by telling them to get away and save themselves, she really means that she senses a panic attack coming on, you can trace the statement back to its source in her inner life. She speaks from an inner space of vulnerability and inability to protect herself that, beginning at a very young age, are the root sources of her social anxiety. The woman and baby are the healthy aspects of her ego and inner child, respectively, that she wants to protect.

A dream can use the same basic scenario to dramatize the experience of bullying, ridicule, and rejection. Who commits the act? People do, sometimes randomly while in public. How does it make the target feel? Terrible. How does a dream express the idea? With terrorists who "target" the dreamer.

Picture a terrorist and note what comes to mind. Those associations are what a terrorist can mean personally to you and how your dreams use the symbol. Typically, the terrorist is the image of terror, chaos, fear, danger, and loathing, but one person's terrorist is another person's freedom fighter, and it makes a big difference in how dreams use the symbol.

While many dreams featuring terrorists pull associations from our common perceptions to create symbolism, the enigma of terrorists and terrorism is a blank canvas on which to project any number of ideas. Take, for instance, the nightmare a man experienced that features him in a shopping mall, trying to decide which store to visit. Next thing he knows, a car screams down the middle of the mall, screeches to a halt, and out of it jumps a band of terrorists. They open fire on the crowd, and the dreamer sees people dropping left and right. He stampedes into a store, squeezes into the back with other terrified shoppers, and waits for someone to do something to save them. A terrorist appears at the front of the store, levels his rifle on the pack of people, and is about to squeeze the trigger when the nightmare ends.

The nightmare's main idea is about fear of making decisions. The opening scene shows it as the man trying to decide which store to shop in. A shopping mall is the perfect setting because it features many stores to choose from. The terrorists symbolize the idea of fear, and their decisiveness stands out in contrast to the dreamer's indecisiveness. They are on a mission.

The next scene, where he's crammed into the back of the store, enacts the idea of the metaphor "backed into a corner." It's his habitual response when he must make a decision and won't do it unless forced to. That's the simple idea of the final scene where the terrorist levels the rifle at the shoppers. What began as a bad situation requiring decisive action just got worse, and it shows his habitual response in such situations to wait for others to decide what to do, then "go along with the crowd."

> **Dreams are more than a collection of symbols; they present symbols as part of a story, and action drives the story.**

That example packs many ideas into a few scenes and creates layers of personal meaning. It highlights habitual responses and patterns, and it demonstrates co-creative dream theory by creating an outline of a story, then playing it out like a *Choose Your Own Adventure* book. If the dreamer makes a choice in the opening scene about which store to shop in, the story unfolds differently. It would be unnecessary to bring in the terrorists to symbolize the idea of the fear of making decisions.

The nightmare uses fear as a basis for the symbolism of the terrorists, a common association, but then it paints more ideas onto the canvas that do not obviously relate to terrorists. It tells the story mostly through symbolic actions—take note because dreams are full of actions that express ideas the same as symbols do. Dreams are more than a collection of symbols; they present symbols as part of a story, and action drives the story.

Another uncommon idea for the meaning of terrorists in a dream is that they are people who buck society and rebel against its norms. For example, a dream where a young man joins a terrorist group tells a story about his ego aligning with counterculture beliefs. The terrorists represent those voices in his head, and joining their group means that internally, he agrees with what they represent. They don't commit acts of terror, an indicator that the meaning doesn't have anything to do with terror or terrorism.

Terrorist groups could be representative of something negative happening in a group dynamic situation.

In a similar dream, the dreamer joins a terrorist group along with his best friend and commits minor criminal acts. Their displays of rebellion symbolize their embrace of being outcasts. They are unpopular socially and display their weirdness like a badge of honor. They think of themselves as unsung heroes with the courage to stand up against conformity, an uncommon association with terrorists but one that underlies the symbolism in this case.

The word "group" often follows the word "terrorist," opening possibilities for dreams to speak to group dynamics and situations ranging from rebellion and quirkiness on one end of the spectrum to hate, violence, and criminality on the other. "Suicide" is another word closely associated with terrorists, and the dream author could get some mileage from it by speaking to that subject and ideas related to it, such as "career suicide" and "waste of a life." Becoming a terrorist is commonly thought of as suicide and a waste of a life.

Playing the role of a terrorist in a dream carries with it ideas such as assuming a counterculture role or identity in society or embracing unpopular beliefs, but it might highlight internal dynamics, too, such as chaos and rage. Terrorists cause chaos, and you can imagine how a storyteller can run with that association to speak to the internal conditions of a person that cause them chaos. Playing a role in a dream suggests personal closeness with the idea behind it, such as being the source of the chaos in one's life or possessed by rage or morbid fascination with death and killing. By contrast, a dream is more likely to present chaos caused by outside sources and conditions in one's life as characters beyond the dreamer's control.

A woman dreams about terrorists strapping her down and injecting neon-yellow fluid into her spine. The fluid symbolizes the inflammation in her body caused by an autoimmune disorder, and her spine is the injection site because the source of the disorder is in her nervous system. It causes chaos in her body. The dream shows her strapped down because she feels helpless against the disorder, with a second layer of meaning related to how it restricts her life. It's as if terrorists have taken control of her body and life. Plus, she's terrified that the disorder will kill her.

A dream can use terrorists to symbolize the idea of unknown reasons, sources, and causes, building atop the impression that terrorists come out of nowhere and are driven by mysterious motives. One moment, life is normal, and the next, it's blowing up, an association the dream storyteller can use to tell a story about a sudden change for the worse, like in the above example.

"Deteriorating conditions" may be the simple idea behind the image of a terrorist or terrorist attack, and such conditions include one's life, health, and even sanity. Terrorists must be insane, according to popular belief. Then again, a terrorist can just as well symbolize a hidden motive or agenda.

See also: Cancer/Disease, Killing, Murder, Suicide, War

WAR

Dreams use violence and violent themes to symbolize conflict, and war is a group conflict. It's organized, deliberate violence. Those associations are the building blocks of what war means in a dream. Find out why the dream author uses war over other options to symbolize conflict, and it's the first big step to interpreting it.

War isn't a squabble or skirmish or even a fight; it's a protracted and intense conflict, and as a dream symbol, it matches well with situations such as a dysfunctional environment at home, work, or school or a dysfunctional relationship. In those situations, people can divide into camps or sides, adding another layer of meaning that matches well with war. Picture when a couple breaks up and their friends align with one or the other. Or look inward by imagining a situation where a person is said to be divided against themself. The situations are ripe to symbolize not just a war but a civil war because the conflict is between two sides that used to be on the same side. The worse the conflict, the worse its portrayal as war in a dream.

Dreams reflect the nature and level of conflict in their content. Take, for example, one man's dream about the news reporting rumors of the United States starting a war with China. He's an American and thinks to himself that it's a bad idea to go to war with China; the government should make them an ally instead. The dream illustrates a division within himself between allopathic and holistic medicine. He asked his physician's opinion about adding holistic treatments to his health routine, and the physician railed against it. It influenced the dreamer against holistic medicine, shown in the dream as rumors of war between the United States (Western-based medicine) and China (Eastern-based medicine). But after thinking about it more, he formed the opinion that the two styles of medicine can complement each other, which the dream reflects in his thoughts about making China an ally instead of an adversary. The dream

Representing conflict, war dreams are indicative of some kind of fight that has escalated into a protracted and dysfunctional situation such as a marriage that might be heading toward divorce.

portrays the nature of the conflict and its low level of intensity by creating a scenario where war between the United States and China is only a rumor.

In a dream about a never-ending war between humans and aliens, the enemy is only seen from a distance. The situation the dream depicts is her never-ending battle to keep up with wave after wave of intense work. Figuratively, it's a war, but she doesn't take it personally, and her dream reflects that personal dynamic by showing the war at a distance.

On the other hand, in one man's dream, the war is up close and personal as he fights for his life against enemy soldiers. They are close enough to see eye to eye during combat, and their attacks are clever, the same as the subtle ways he undermines himself by repeating the personal narrative that formed around the belief that nothing he does is ever good enough. In the dream, he fights hard, but it's never good enough to stop the enemy. His inner conflict is intense and personal, and so is the war. He is at war with himself.

In a dream that features Nazis as the enemy soldiers, they are symbols for an attitude of callous indifference. The dream author may choose Nazis to symbolize the idea of "the worst of the worst."

A man dreamed about a battle to the death with a clone of himself, with the only difference being that his enemy self is clean and angelic and his dream self is dirty and grimy. The battle is within himself over his perception that as a physician, he needs to maintain a clean and angelic image, but he knows himself as a "down in the trenches" kind of guy who is neither clean nor angelic.

War and war-related themes are popular metaphors, and the dreaming mind loves to enact them. The "big game" is a war and an apt metaphor because it's organized between sides and has winners and losers. A lawyer "goes to war" against the opposing side, or the politician goes to war in a "legislative battle." When you want to express the idea of intense competition or conflict, war is your metaphor.

The dream author takes its cues from how, when, and why we use such metaphors and tells war stories when the dynamics of one's life match up. At work, you want to advance a proposal and are expecting intense resistance, and you prepare by making alliances with coworkers and lining up your arguments—you are preparing for war. You see something very different from your spouse and the atmosphere is tense, ready to explode—the author makes the comparison with war.

The atmosphere of war is in popular use as a metaphor and as a dream theme. Things are so tense, it's like a bomb is about to go off, and to re-create the atmosphere, a dream uses war as a theme. The atmosphere in your mind and heart is gloomy and dreadful, and war is a dream theme that reflects it. You are devastated. Your life is in ruins, and your dreams illustrate the idea as the aftermath of war: blasted landscapes, dead soldiers, shell-shocked citizens. Or your life is in chaos, and your dreams show scenes of chaotic battlefields and incompetent commanders. The story can be told in many ways, and life can be and feel like a war in many ways.

> **Battling a disease or other sort of health condition is the sort of situation that dreams portray as war.**

Battling a disease or other sort of health condition is the sort of situation that dreams portray as war. Diseases damage the body; they invade and kill. Also, figures of speech such as "the war against cancer" express a set of ideas in war terminology. It's no wonder that dreams turn the terminology into imagery.

Take, for instance, the dream a woman experienced where she's a soldier near the front lines of a battle outside her hometown. The commander of the army defending the town calls in an air strike, and the bombs miss their target and instead strike the town, obliterating the home where she was born. The landscape of the dream symbolizes the inside of her body, and the war symbolizes her battle against a severe disease. The air strike symbolizes the medical treatment ordered by her doctors, and missing the target expresses her fear that the treatment is making her condition worse. That's the idea behind the bombs obliterating the home she was born in. The treatment could kill her.

Dreams can use war to reflect a state of mind or attitude. For example, a "war footing" is belligerent and confrontational. A dream may tell the story of a defensive footing as defending against enemies or fortifying a defensive position and an offensive footing as advancing on an enemy position. If you think everyone is out to get you, it's a war state of mind. See how the dream imagery reflects what's happening in your head and heart, and it leads you to the meaning.

War is perceived as a last resort after other efforts fail to resolve a situation, and dreams can run with that idea. Some wars, though, are about ambition and greed. Some are driven by psychosis, by desperation, by brutality, by arrogance, and some just for the hell of it. War dreams are similarly driven. What happens next when a negotiation fails, one's personal territory is invaded, or a weakness is noticed and presents the opportunity for exploitation and personal gain? It means war.

In this way, dreams can be forward-looking by using war as a theme for what could happen next or even for what needs to happen. Forecasts and foreshadowing of war are common ways of saying that something big is building and likely to lead to a dramatic climax. It gives the dream author a smorgasbord of themes and ideas to work with.

Dreams are also inward-looking and create scenarios to help the ego know and understand itself better. Take, for example, a young man's graphic war dreams. He plays the role of a soldier who terrorizes, plunders, and kills. He knows that what he's doing is wrong but says to himself, *War is Hell, and no one is going to stop me.* The dream creates a scenario where the normal rules and restrictions of civilized life and consequences for breaking them are absent, and it allows him to see deeper into himself. It's not to say that he'd plunder and kill; it's showing him that he'll take advantage of a situation if he thinks he can get away with it. His dark side comes out when he thinks no one is

Wars are not fought only with guns and bombs; a family at war can be nearly as dramatic and damaging to those it affects.

watching. But then, he'll moralize and condemn other people who do the same thing, failing to see that what he condemns in others is exactly the weakness he sees in himself but justifies.

War is a situation where the usual rules of society don't apply. Dreams use those associations in relation to situations when a person takes the opportunity to get away with something they normally wouldn't do, such as cheat, break a law, or even express a suppressed thought or feeling. "Nothing to lose" may be what a dream means by war.

For people whose daily life is like a war, the theme is likely to recur in their dreams. However, war imagery recurs regardless of the conditions of one's life because it's popular in media and culture. Most of us have thousands of war-related memories the dreaming mind can tap into, so it's no wonder that war imagery appears in our dreams. If a war dream reminds you of a war movie, game, or other form of media, explore those memories and what you remember about the story and your experience; your dreaming mind may have picked up on something about it, such as the idea of sacrifice in *Saving Private Ryan*, camaraderie in *Band of Brothers*, or carrying out missions and meeting objectives in *Call of Duty*. War in a dream may be a way to set the scene to tell a story about ideas that relate to it: patriotism, heroics, distraction, focus, taking aim, taking sides, strategizing, and so forth.

For people who've been in combat or lived in a war zone, the memories are personal, vivid, and extensive. They dream about war as it really is, and recurring dreams about war are a feature of PTSD in soldiers, veterans, and survivors. War is a searing experience, and naturally, it's a recurring subject in the dreams of people who live through it. They say that the dreams are ultrarealistic and unwelcome, even tormenting. Advanced therapeutic tools of dreamwork can be helpful in such cases to work through the dreams and address what's driving them. Healing trauma is a high priority for dreams, and for people who have been traumatized, it's impossible to avoid.

Finally, research into reincarnation has noted a trend where people remember past lives as soldiers who died in war. Some of the most compelling cases involve young children remembering verifiable details: names, dates, places, battles. Dreams—particularly recurring dreams—are a common way for people to become aware of past-life memories. Your first step is to search for parallels between the dream content and your life—war dreams are commonly confused as past-life dreams. But when the dreams stand out for their intensity and vividness and you see from the perspective of someone who is you but is not who you are in your current life, it's an indicator of past-life memories. Dying in combat cuts short a life, and the reincarnated person may return to finish what they started; that's why their dreams make them aware of their past life.

See also: Apocalypses, Armageddon, Cancer/Disease, Killing, Nuclear War, Storms/Blizzards/Hurricanes/Tornadoes, Terrorism

Disasters and Afflictions

D isasters and afflictions are bad things that happen, and that definition fits most nightmares. Defined loosely, you could say that all night-mares are disasters. They barrel through your interior landscape and make a mess. They leave you shaken. You avoid them if you can.

Disasters and afflictions are thought of as mostly unavoidable events: the hurricane or tornado that destroys; the fire or blast that sweeps through; the disease that strikes out of the blue. Even when you are the cause of a dis-aster in a nightmare, such as when you set the fire that destroys or drive the car that crashes, you act from impulse as if following a script written subcon-sciously. And the truth is that you are following a script, but *you* are the coau-thor of it. Dreams and nightmares are co-created experiences, and you won't get far with resolving a nightmare if you don't first accept responsibility for it.

The logic behind accepting responsibility even when you don't see your role in creating a disaster or bringing on an affliction is that it enables you to respond by saying to yourself, *I may not have created this mess, but I'm going to own it.* That's step one before anything good can happen. Nightmares often stem from the inability or refusal to respond to chronic conditions in waking life. They stem from being and feeling resistant, unwilling, and powerless to own up to your role. You may not have created the mess, but you are living with it, and the sooner you realize that and respond, the sooner the cleanup and re-building can begin.

Some disasters and afflictions and their ensuing messes and calamities are truly beyond your control. But when they enter your dream space, they are in your space, your zone of control, because it's *your* dream. By owning it, you can respond to it. Some people develop dream powers to stop disasters or, at least, escape them, whereas other people without those powers feel helpless.

Ownership is the first word that's essential for staring your nightmares in the eye from a position of strength, and the second word is responsibility. You are *response-able*, and the ability to respond means that you are certainly *not* helpless—by God, it's your dream, and your powers are only limited by your beliefs! The ability to respond by taking responsibility and assuming power so that you are not helpless are what separate the people who are beaten down by their nightmares from the ones who are lifted up by them. Nightmares are a kind of boot camp, and you either gain the strength to fight or you don't. You are the only one who can do something about the drill sergeant—the nightmare—screaming in your face. It's only later that you realize the huge favor it does for you by getting your butt moving and forcing you past your limits.

Disasters and afflictions in nightmares are symbols or symbolic actions, and they are defined largely by the story's context and by you and your life. The same formula applies to all conventional dreams and nightmares and ditto for the approach to interpreting them. Begin with the question, "What am I trying to tell myself?" Then, decode the symbolism and analyze the story, looking for your hand in creating the experience.

Take responsibility. You are not helpless.

CANCER/DISEASE

Oh, my God, do I have cancer? It's a natural reaction to a "cancer dream," and the short answer is no, probably not. The body has an early warning system for the development of disease and illness and uses dreams to send the alert, but cancer is a symbol that matches up well with situations and conditions that have nothing to do with actual disease, and that's why you dream about it. Cancer and disease, like almost everything else in dreams, are metaphors and story pieces.

The number-one reason why the dream author chooses cancer and disease as symbols is because they slowly eat at you, so the first question to ask is, what's eating at me? Fear, stress, anxiety, and worry top the list. They're also

Because cancer is a disease that can take a long time to develop before it is lethal, having a dream about a cancer diagnosis could mean that there is something that has bothered you for a long time and is slowly eating away at you.

things that cause disease and illness in the long run, giving the dream author an extra reason to use cancer as a symbol for something eating at you. Doubt, anger, pessimism, and negativity are also strong candidates.

On top of that, cancer and other diseases lurk unseen in the body until making themselves known through symptoms and pain, and so do other things that eat at you. Cancer and disease usually develop out of sight, and in dream-speak, it can mean outside of conscious awareness. The tendency is to ignore or deny what's wrong until it's too late. The dream author needs to deliver a stronger message and grab your attention, so it uses disease.

Something is wrong and needs your attention—that's a simple way of understanding what a dream means by cancer and disease. The dream author chooses cancer specifically as a symbol to say "urgent!" It may be the jolt you need to take action on something. "Danger!" is another message that such a dream delivers. "Look deeper," it says.

A terrific example is the dream a mother had that tells a story about her 4-year-old child having cancer. A doctor delivers the news and says that a treatment plan is being devised. She wakes up with the terrifying thought: *What if my daughter really has cancer?* But an exploration of the context of her life reveals the symbolic meaning. Her husband, a soldier, is at home and under her care after suffering severe injuries in combat. Plus, she has a newborn baby to care for. The time she used to have to give to her 4-year-old vanished almost overnight, and she's observing that her daughter is suffering from lack of attention. It's a hard situation. Something is wrong—that's what the dream means by cancer—and she's aware of it, and the "treatment plan" is to make time for her daughter.

Cancer is a flaw, and one man's dream tells the story as meeting three wise men and asking them who they are.

"Your intellect," answers one.

"Your spirit," answers another.

"Your cancer," answers the third.

The last answer is an odd one, wouldn't you say? To understand the dream, begin with how the dreamer identifies with the dream characters. The first two are easy. He possesses great intellect and spirit and endeavors to be wise and enlightened like they are. He thinks that to be wise, he must eradicate his personal flaws. But the third wise man, the cancer, has an equal place with the first two, and the message of the dream is to embrace his flaws.

We use words like "eradicate" and "fight" when speaking of cancer and disease, and those words imply struggle and conflict. But nearly everything you dream about—even disease—is part of yourself, and to struggle with it implies an antagonistic relationship. The psyche, however, views such antagonism with oneself as a civil war. The solution is to make peace with yourself and allies of your internal enemies. They did not start the fight—the cause is the ego's stance in relation to other aspects of the psyche. The more rigid the ego's stance, the more it invites a harsh lesson in the realities of its situation as a small part of a self-regulating system, the psyche.

Now the door opens to a discussion of dreams about cancer and disease that are literal. They happen, and case studies and anecdotes abound. Dr. Larry Burke collects them. He coauthored the book *Dreams That Can Save Your Life* along with Kat Kanavos, who survived breast cancer in large part because of a super-vivid dream that told her straight up, "You have cancer and need to see your doctor now!" The dream showed her exactly where the cancer was, and her doctor found it and surgically removed it. Dr. Burke is pioneering the use of dreams to aid medical diagnoses, and the core idea of his approach is that cancer and disease are somatic metaphors. Soma means "body," and a somatic metaphor is the body's expression of an underlying condition through symptoms that are metaphors for it. Angina, for example, is a heart condition, and for one woman, her angina expresses the pain of a broken heart from her loveless marriage. It's slowly killing her like a disease, and now, she has a disease that can kill her. The metaphor is becoming reality.

It's a harsh lesson, and the flip side of it is that you have the power to affect your body with your mind and spirit. A somatic metaphor is an unconscious expression of the body through physical symptoms and conditions. Well, what about a conscious expression? The body should be able to express itself through health and vitality, too. This way of looking at it leads us back to the ego's relationship with the rest of the psyche and with the body. An antagonistic and fearful relationship is expressed one way; a cooperative and hopeful relationship is expressed another way. The logic is simple: respond to a dream about cancer and disease by searching for the metaphorical expression of underlying personal and situational dynamics and improving the ego's relationship with the psyche and the body.

> **A somatic metaphor is an unconscious expression of the body through physical symptoms and conditions.**

It's a starting point and no guarantee of a cure for whatever the body is expressing through somatic metaphor, but it's a power available to you. The old saying that "dis-ease is the root of disease" is true. It's a complicated relationship, though, and environmental factors are not so easy to diagnose and address.

However, dream symbols are doorways to the parts of the body, mind, and spirit they represent, and you can use the dream imagery like an electrical circuit to deliver energy wherever a dream points to. If it's heart disease, send positivity and hope to the heart. If it's brain disease, send it there. When dreams are specific about the parts or systems of the body affected by disease, focus attention there. The ancient Hawaiian "Huna" philosophy asserts that where attention goes, energy flows. That attention begins with dream interpretation and continues with dreamwork techniques such as Embodied Dreamwork, Active Imagination, and Gestalt, and it can continue further with energy medicine and other techniques.

A woman who had late-stage brain cancer dreamed about a serpent saying that it was going to kill her, and she couldn't stop it. The serpent is a symbol for her cancer. Soon afterward, she dreamed about a majestic black panther protecting her, and miraculously, her cancer went into remission. The panther is a symbol for her fighting spirit. War imagery is common in dreams about battling a disease or illness within one's body.

Chronic situations cause nightmares, and cancer and disease are chronic situations. After a cancer dream, it's wise to ask yourself questions like what's been going on for too long and what's bothering you that's being ignored.

The clock is ticking—that may be what a dream means by cancer. Cancer is generally slow-acting, and while it may have a deadline associated with it—a "prognosis"—the implication is that you still have time but better get moving. For example, yes, your health is slowly declining, but you aren't dead yet, right?

> After a cancer dream, it's wise to ask yourself questions like what's been going on for too long and what's bothering you that's being ignored.

Respond now, and it may be fixable. Continue as you are and, well, your deadline is coming.

In many cases, dreams about death are really about life. They are a powerfully effective message that you only have so much time, so get busy living!

Cancer is a harsh message, that's for sure, and in dreams, it's the bitter medicine that delivers a needed jolt. Keep in mind that you create your dreams subconsciously along with the primary archetype in the unconscious mind called the Self. Start with the assumption that you choose the experience of a dream for yourself or, at least, play a role in creating it. First of all, it helps you answer the "why" questions behind the experience, but it also helps you take responsibility, and that may be the core idea behind a cancer dream. You are able to respond.

See also: God, The Grim Reaper, Haunted Dolls, Jesus, Killing, Suicide, War

CRASHES

Plane crash, car crash, train crash, boat crash—the basic idea is the same. A moving object stops moving in a big, dramatic way. It's one of countless ways for a dream to create a metaphor for disaster and destruction. And as far as interpreting it, the devil is in the details.

Take a plane crash, for example. If a crash means disaster, why choose a plane over a car or train to tell the story? It's because a plane as a symbol carries specific associations that match well with the dynamics of whatever the dream spotlights. First of all, plane crashes are generally more explosive and destructive. Also, planes carry large groups of people, and the dynamics a dream highlights may involve a group of people. Think of the passengers on the plane as your fellow travelers in a domain of life, such as family and occupation, or think of the passengers as a grouping of your interior parts, and they are on a plane together because they have something in common. For example, your "high-flying career" is going places because of the combined efforts of your intellect, ego, and willpower. Understood that way, you now have a good place to begin searching your life for parallels with the idea of a crash.

Next, add on the idea of not just movement but moving quickly—you're in a plane, after all, and the author may use a plane as a symbol because of its speed. Movement in dreams often means "going places in life." Your life "moves," and dreams visualize that idea.

But the most common reason why the dream author chooses an airplane over other forms of transportation is because a plane takes flight, and flight is

Dreams of a plane crash might stem from fears of something extremely dramatic happening that affects groups of people and not just one or two passengers.

one heck of a metaphor. You were "flying high" before disaster struck. Your high hopes and aspirations were dashed. Your lofty plan—add an "e," and you have "plane"—came crashing down. The dream author wants to visualize those ideas, and if it sees "up in the air," "off the ground," or any of the other countless ways that language uses flight, air, and aircraft metaphors, it uses them to tell the story in the best way that captures the personal and situational dynamics.

A romantic or sexual relationship that was flying high before taking a dramatic downturn is exactly the sort of situation a dream describes in terms of a plane crash. Love and sex are uplifting, the "air beneath the wings." They are euphoric. They "take us away" and spark thoughts and hopes for the future. The future is a distant place that seems to be coming quickly when a person is propelled by love and euphoria, and the parallel with flying is easy to make because it's the fastest conventional means of getting to distant places. In dream-speak, distance means *personal* distance, like when someone says, "I'll never get to the place I want to be in life." It's too far away.

A man dreams that he's on a plane with his new lover as it's taking off. He feels the rush and exhilaration of the engines roaring to life and launching the plane—10/10 on the excitement scale. But suddenly, the plane splits in half, leaving him on one side and his lover on the other, and it crashes back to Earth. His half of the plane remains intact after the impact, but it obliterates his lover's half. A few days after the dream, she suddenly ends the relationship—you could say that the takeoff was aborted—and it wasn't the first time a new relationship ended like that for him, so he wasn't completely surprised when it happened again. It's impossible to know for sure whether his dream reflects his expectation—a common reason for writing off dreams that seem to predict the future—or foretells the breakup.

The dream clearly says that a breakup is coming—the plane breaks in half. It puts him in one half and his lover in the other, showing a divide. The takeoff symbolizes the newness and exhilaration of the relationship. How it predicted the breakup coming isn't clear, but dreams are known for foreseeing the end coming even when the dreamer is clueless. People have an inborn radar for detecting signs of trouble in important relationships and dreaming about information "out of the blue" and just in time is often a person's first introduction to intuitive and precognitive abilities.

When something comes out of the blue sky and throws you for a loop, when your hopes come crashing down, when reality hits hard, when the bottom drops out, when you experience a huge letdown, it's like a plane crash.

For one young man, the nightmare of seeing his father come back to life and reunite with his family only to board a plane, promising he'll be back soon, that crashes with a big explosion before his eyes was like seeing his father die again. You can imagine how hard it hit him and why it made him question his beliefs. He wants to believe that his dad is in heaven, but he's not sure that such a thing exists. It's a big inner struggle, and his nightmare shows it. The plane crash symbolizes a strong doubt that shattered his belief that his father was alive in the next life.

We've all heard the stories about dreams that predict disasters, and some of us know that they can come true. Naturally, you're going to wonder if it's a warning, but the odds are way against it and heavily in favor of a crash being symbolic. A crash may be part of a larger story about apocalypse, or it's a means of creating the atmosphere of disaster and calamity.

> **A crash may be part of a larger story about apocalypse, or it's a means of creating the atmosphere of disaster and calamity.**

A businessman with a long flight coming up dreamed about a plane crash and got a sinking feeling. To tell what the dream really meant, he searched its contents for details that matched up with ordinary life, such as the plane being the same type that he was going to fly in. Other than the crash, does the dream have discrepancies with a normal flying experience? And since the flight was for his job, he looked for parallels between the symbolism of a crash and how it might describe something about his work life and found it. Recently, a big hope he had for his career came crashing down. The realization pinged his brain, and he felt comfortable when he boarded his flight because he understood the personal symbolism of his dream.

"Crash landing" is another metaphor that dreams may symbolize as a plane crash. It can mean a sinking feeling, a sudden stop, or a sudden loss. It can mean "crushed," "coming down," or a letdown after a thrill fades or the adrenaline wears off. The higher you go and the longer you stay up there, the harder you crash.

A car crash can be a metaphor of choice to symbolize the above situations when their dynamics involve slower movement, closer objectives, and daily activities—the going from point A to point B in everyday life. Plus, a big factor for the dream author choosing a car crash over other types of crashes is that it can put the dreamer in the driver's seat. It brings in the idea of control. Planes usually have pilots, and it's not to say that a dream can't put you in the cockpit, but driving a car is a more common experience, and the storehouse of memory for most adults is chock full of driving cars themselves.

The symbolism of a car crash runs the gamut of meaning from a simple idea such as a scheduling conflict or collision between opposing priorities to a complex one such as a spectacular failure or a sudden setback. In one woman's dream, she's barreling down the highway with her partner in the passenger seat, and she can't help herself from pressing harder on the gas pedal. The car shoots up to 100 miles per hour. A wall looms. She presses the brake, but the car keeps steaming ahead. Her partner pulls the emergency brake. The car plows straight into the wall. She then realizes that she's dead, and nothing exists but black emptiness.

A car crash can symbolize everything from the minor (trouble with scheduling conflicts at work) to the more major (a dramatic setback in one's life).

Simplify the dream's imagery, and it leads to questions that help trace it to its source. In what way are you going too fast in your life and can't slow down, and do you see a sudden, dramatic breaking point coming? Phrased that way, the imagery's meaning and how it parallels her life become clear. In life, the woman is barreling forward with too much to do and not enough time to do it. That's the idea expressed in the imagery of her speeding on the highway. Then, her life gets busier, and the circumstances are beyond her control. In other words, she's pressing even harder on the gas and can't help herself. She senses a breaking point coming—she can't sustain the frantic pace, but it's impossible to stop now, symbolized as the car's brakes failing. Her partner sees the emergency coming and is trying to help, symbolized as pulling the emergency brake.

Now we get a clear picture of what smashing her car into the wall symbolizes. A person can go no further after hitting the proverbial wall. Parallels with life include going no further with a plan, idea, or relationship or that the mind and body just can't take it anymore. The woman's dream correctly predicted a breaking point coming. She managed to do everything she needed to do, and as soon as the pace slackened, she took to her bed, physically and mentally "out of gas," and stayed there for weeks. She "crashed."

The black emptiness of the dream's ending haunted her for years afterward. It seemed to confirm her fear that no life exists after death, but it may have foreshadowed the dark personal place she was in following her crash and alluded to a fear that she was killing herself by pushing too hard. An idea also exists of succumbing to darkness and being completely alone in it.

That dream is rich with metaphorical imagery: the speed of the car, the highway, the dreamer behind the wheel, the brakes failing, the emergency brake, the wall, and the black void. Each detail expresses a dynamic of her situation. No wonder her dream author chose to tell the story as a car crash over another type of crash.

Next, we explore a similar dream with richly meaningful imagery. In it, the dreamer, a teenager, is riding in the passenger's seat of his mom's truck. She's driving on a snowy road and is barely in control, weaving and going too fast. They come to a bridge over a frozen lake, and she misses it. The truck slides. The ice breaks. The truck sinks. The dreamer rescues his mom and gets her to shore, then lectures her about how her bad driving almost got them killed.

Simplify the dream, and an idea jumps out from it: bad decision making. Driving too fast on a snowy road is a bad decision. Mom is behind the wheel, and her decisions propel the actions of the story. It makes you wonder, what is her son, the dreamer, observing about her decision making if anything? You can't say automatically that the dream is about his mom as she is in ordinary waking life—that assumption is the number-one mistake that people make when trying to interpret a dream that features someone they know. They confuse the person with the dream character, but the character is actually an actor playing a role.

But in this case, the dream really is about his mom, her bad decisions, and their impact on her son. It summarizes his life with his mom by putting him in the passenger seat as she drives her truck—her actual truck, not an imaginary vehicle, creating a closer symbolic connection with everyday life. Mom is the decision maker, and she habitually makes bad decisions. The dream doesn't speak to a specific incident but instead to a pattern, and part of the pattern is that he rescues her from the messes resulting from her bad decisions. The dream tells the story as him rescuing her from her sinking truck. Lecturing her about her bad driving refers to her bad decisions.

The snowy road, the reckless driving, the ice breaking, the rescue, and the lecture are details that concisely and dramatically sum up the situation. Understand them as part of a big picture. Their interrelationship within the picture defines what they mean. The snowy road, for example, can symbolize moving through life with depression or sadness, but in this dream's context, it means treacherous conditions and, more importantly, the potential for disaster at any moment. Put Mom behind the wheel of her truck as she drives too fast, combined with the context of her history of bad decision making, and it defines what the snowy road means.

> **A train as a symbol gives the author the option to speak to dynamics involving tracks, such as being "on track," and a crash meaning being "off track."**

Airplanes and cars are symbols in dreams that the dream author has at their disposal. A train as a symbol gives the author the option to speak to dynamics involving tracks, such as being "on track," and a crash meaning being "off track." Also, tracks define a train's direction, and the author can use that association to poke at a tendency for a person to be set in their ways, single-minded, and relentless, and to speak to one's course in life or the course of a relationship or endeavor. Plus, train cars interconnect, and as one moves, the others move in the same direction and with the same speed. What a great metaphor for closely interrelated ideas and qualities and for people who march in lockstep.

For one young woman, her dream about a train crash dramatically summarizes a situation where the coach of her track team led them into a disaster, and it left the team in disarray. The situation was a "train wreck," and the imagery perfectly matches it. Symbolically, the coach is the locomotive, and in the dream, the train wreck starts with the locomotive jumping the tracks. The train cars following the locomotive symbolize the team members—they follow the coach off track. The resulting mess of mangled train cars and smoking ruins is a great metaphor for describing the state of things after the disaster. Plus, it's a track team that got off track!

A boat as a symbol gives the author a good option for the longer, slower journeys in life. Family life is among the most common dynamics that dreams symbolize as a boat journey. It's an image that captures the ebb and flow of life and the dynamics of a slow pace and a special destination. Journeys by boat carry romantic notions and ideas, too, making them great metaphors for special relationships and events.

Now imagine a relationship that's in "troubled waters." A relationship that's headed for disaster. Imagine how the author visualizes ideas like "the ship is sinking." Yep, you guessed it, it uses a boat as a symbol and a disaster as symbolism that matches with the personal and situational dynamics.

More associations come into play when dreams use water to symbolize emotions. The boat represents the idea of navigating emotions, and when emotions are overwhelming, the boat takes in water and may sink. Again, what a metaphor!

The conditions of the water can further illustrate dynamics, such as frozen water and icebergs being symbols for frozen emotions and emotional obstacles. Hot, steaming, and boiling water are common metaphors for anger, resentment, and rage. And nothing says "overwhelmed" like a tidal wave or a sinking ship. You, as the ego who navigates your emotions, are like a boat on

Many metaphors can be found in ship symbolism, such as navigating rough waters, stormy seas, the highs and lows of waves, and, of course, the threat of sinking.

an ocean, and the dream author can begin there to tell a great variety of stories that match up with a great variety of dynamics in life.

"The boat on an ocean" is also a metaphor that captures the dynamics of the ego's relationship with its counterpart, the unconscious. The ego is small in comparison, and it floats atop the psyche, a much vaster and deeper structure. Everything above the water line represents the conscious aspects of a person, and below the water represents the unconscious aspects. The comparison gives the author a story motif for the ego's relationship with the rest of the psyche, and the long-term goal is to harmonize the conscious mind with the unconscious. Nightmares—chronic ones, especially—involving storylines where a person's ship is in troubled waters are known to illustrate the dynamics of the relationship. Plus, the "sinking ship" is a common metaphor for describing life's perilous situations, conditions, and circumstances.

A woman has a dream that her friend's sister is on a boat that she sees from shore and helplessly watches as it sinks and the sister perishes. Soon afterward, she receives news that the sister died—she was murdered. The last the woman had heard, her friend's sister lived normally, the mother of young children. But in the meantime, her life took a sharp downward turn when she got involved in a drug scene. The woman sensed strongly that her dream foretold death through the metaphor of the ship sinking.

It wasn't the first time she'd had such dreams. She learned to recognize when they made predictions and ventured into ESP territory because they'd abruptly yank her from one dream space into another without explanation or transition and show her scenes that later came true. The truth was metaphorical in some of her predictive dreams, such as the metaphor of the boat sinking. Other times, the truth was literal, such as her recurring dreams that plopped her square in the middle of an old friend's life and showed her exactly what was happening in it despite being out of contact for many years. Her story is told in episode 2 of my podcast, *The Dreams That Shape Us*.

Ian Wilson, who teaches lucid dreaming and studies precognition, dreamed about driving his car on a snowy road with his daughter in the back as they approach an intersection with a stop sign. He steps on the brake pedal. The car hits a patch of black ice and slides into the intersection. He looks to his left and sees a big truck about to smash into the driver's side door, and his last thought is that his daughter is going to grow up without her father. The goosebumps Ian's dream gave him compelled him to buy studded snow tires, something he'd never done previously despite living through many Canadian winters. A couple of months later, he was driving with his daughter on a snow-covered road, approached the same intersection as the one in his dream, stepped on the brakes, and hit a patch of black ice. The car slid and, true to the dream, he looked to his left and saw a big truck barreling into the intersection. At the last moment, the studded snow tires gripped just enough to slow him down, allowing the barreling truck to pass through before his car slid into the intersection.

Ian said that his dream saved his life and, perhaps, his daughter's, too. But it wasn't just the dream that saved them, it was his response by taking precaution, and his precaution stemmed from knowing his dream life and its patterns and recognizing the unusual vividness of his precognitive dream.

A spectacular crash dream that came true began with the dreamer seeing through the eyes of a man driving a car with a female passenger in a high-speed chase that was eluding the police. The driver tries to cut across the highway median, and the mistake launches the car airborne; it rolls over and is demolished, killing the driver and passenger. A week later, the man who had the dream is driving on a highway, his wife in the passenger seat. A swarm of police cars with lights flashing fast approaching behind them. He pulls over, and the exact make, model, and color car as the one in his dream zooms past him with a man driving and a female passenger. He knows what's about to happen. The driver tries to cut across the median but is going way too fast, and it launches the car airborne. It hits the ground, rolls multiple times, and is demolished. The driver and passenger die.

> **Crash dreams are dramatic enough without adding the X factor of whether they could come true. Precognitive crash dreams are much less common than standard symbolic ones....**

He felt an odd connection with the couple in the car, and he thinks that's why his dream previewed their destiny. He was a husband driving with his wife, and they were a couple in a high-speed chase on the same stretch of highway. With a twist of fate, it could have been him and his wife in that car. He doesn't know anything about the other couple or the circumstances that led to crossing paths with them during their final moments, but in the instant when he dreamed about being the driver and making the final, desperate, fatal decision, he understood everything and sensed a connection that words cannot describe.

Crash dreams are dramatic enough without adding the X factor of whether they could come true. Precognitive crash dreams are much less common than standard symbolic ones, and that's the place to begin. Interpret the dream the same way as you would any other, and if you don't find personal meaning and after deep consideration you still feel like it's predictive, act on it. Err on the side of caution, and for heaven's sake, don't let doubt prevent you. It's the most common reason for why people ignore dreams that warn them of disasters that can be avoided or mitigated.

Another X factor is dreams that predict something bad happening to someone you know or know of—should you tell them? Follow the same process by first looking for the personal meaning. You may resonate with the person in ways that explain why your dream uses them as a character, but if not, the best course of action is to bring up the subject and ask if they want to hear about the dream. But make sure you do your diligence first.

For one man, his dream about NBA legend Kobe Bryant dying in a helicopter crash felt so real, he wanted to reach out and warn him—the man was a big fan of Kobe. But instead of risking the likelihood that he'd just end up looking like a fool or worse, he recorded his dream and shared it online. The dense fog and the helicopter crash into a mountainside matched up exactly with the incident, and the timestamp of the post proved that he dreamed ahead of time about the fatal crash.

Jo Jo Billingsley was the lead vocalist of the Honkettes, the backing singers for Lynyrd Skynyrd. Frontman Ronnie Van Zant called her up and asked if she'd join the band's tour in a couple of days, and she happily agreed. They'd all known each other for years. That night, she had the most vivid nightmare that the band's plane crashed and caught fire. She heard the screams and cries of pain and woke up terrified. Her momma came to help after the nightmare and assured her that it was just a dream. Jo Jo quotes herself as replying, "No, Mom, it's too real."

She tried frantically to reach the band by phone and warn them and finally succeeded. The band members got the message, took a vote, and decided to fly one last time in that plane, then they'd get a new plane. The crash that night killed six people aboard.

See also: Apocalypses, Falling, Fire, Killing, Storms/Blizzards/Hurricanes/Tornadoes, Terrorism

FALLING

The man's nightmares about falling recurred almost nightly. He'd be dreaming when suddenly, he'd be in midair and starting to drop, then feeling the acceleration and seeing nothing but black emptiness all around him. In seconds, he's falling too fast to survive the impact. The terror of imminent death snaps him awake. Then, one night, he falls and falls and smashes into the ground. Ouch! He wakes up feeling sore, then looks around and sees the mess of empty beer bottles surrounding him on the floor where he'd passed out and says to himself, enough is enough. He quit drinking from that day forward and never again had another nightmare about falling.

Often in falling dreams the dreamer doesn't hit the ground; the act of falling itself is the important symbol and can indicate you feel as if you have lost support from friends and family in your life.

The context of his situation explains his "falling nightmares." When describing addiction, we often use words like slip, plummet, collapse, tumble, crumble, plunge, and sink; the dream author observes our use of language, and instead of saying what falling means, it shows it symbolically, and the dreamer may even feel it physically. A terrific array of synonyms gives the author the means to precisely express the situational and personal dynamics. A plunge into addiction is sudden and forceful, for example, and a descent is slow and insidious. For the man who had chronic nightmares about falling, his addiction accelerated, and in his nightmares, his fall accelerated. He finally "hit bottom" in his life, and in the last nightmare, that idea played out when he smashed into the ground. You could say that he was in a fallen state of being.

The dream expresses the meaning in the symbolism of the imagery, efficiently summarizing the man's addiction as a metaphor about falling. For a woman whose recurring dreams show her falling after slipping on a rug, the meaning is found in the context of where she falls. The dream starts out with her in a mad rush to get to her grandma's house. She arrives, rushes through the front door, slips on a rug, and thuds against the floor. The metaphorical meaning of falling is easy to identify when you know that she is constantly pressed for time and rushing from place to place, and in that state, she tends to overlook things. Sometimes, she even slips and falls and injures herself. But the dream expresses a deeper layer of meaning by using her grandma's house as a setting. Grandma's health is frail and the woman wants to spend more time with her, but it's hard when she's constantly busy, and her biggest fear is that one day, it'll be too late. She'll come rushing over to see her grandma and she'll be gone, pulling the proverbial rug out from under her.

When the rug is pulled out from under you or the ground disappears beneath your feet, you fall. The metaphor fits with situations like when relationships end and health downturns suddenly. What you thought was solid and dependable is suddenly gone, and you are off balance with nothing supporting you. When support of any kind ends and you have nothing to catch you, you fall.

Support also comes from the ground you stand on figuratively: your values, principles, ethics, morals, beliefs, and ideals. They are the foundation of your life and character. Take them away, and what's left? That was the situation behind one woman's dream about flying in an airplane that disintegrates in flight and she falls. It occurred after learning that crooks ran the idealistic charitable organization she supported with her time and money, shattering her belief in the charity.

But the dream is about more than the external situation; it also dramatizes her internal one. Supporting the charity "uplifted" her, a feeling that her dream shows as flying in an airplane. Then, suddenly, the airplane disappears, and she's falling through empty space, the dream's way of saying that she's unsupported. The idea in the imagery expands to include her internal support based on her belief that her internal compass always guides her true. When something you believe about yourself runs up against the hard truth of reality, it throws you for a loop. Falling perfectly sums up the situational and personal dynamics.

Falling dramatically expresses feelings such as being lost personally. A person who is lost has no ground to stand on. Stretch the idea, and it means that a person lacks authority, status, and power—they lack "standing."

> What you thought was solid and dependable is suddenly gone, and you are off balance with nothing supporting you. When support of any kind ends and you have nothing to catch you, you fall.

The symbolism of falling can be quite simple. When you are falling, you are between two places, meaning two places in life. You graduate from school but haven't yet found a job; you are between places. You leave a relationship but haven't yet found a new one. A decision faces you, but you haven't yet made it. We express uncertainty as being up in the air, and we know how dreams visualize the idea.

Another simple way of understanding falling is that it means a deadline. You look down and see the ground; you can't go any farther, you can't wait any longer. It's "the end," and hitting the ground means that something isn't going to end well.

Here's another simple idea for you. Falling means that you need help!

For a man with a pattern of waiting until the last minute to make decisions, his dream tells the story as somebody coming up behind him and pushing him off the roof of a building. It enacts the idea of being "pushed to make a decision." It's not a particular decision, it's any decision. He thinks and thinks and waits until the last minute. The dream imagery may also symbolize the idea of "getting out of your head"—he falls from the roof, and the roof symbolizes his head.

Simple questions may lead to figuring out what a dream means. You dream about falling—what do you think is going to happen when you reach the ground? It's going to hurt, right? The follow-up question is, are you expecting that something in ordinary waking life is going to hurt you? Asking good questions is the true art of dream interpretation.

Here's another question to ask: where are you expecting to land? The dream content may not show it—you fall through empty space and have no sense of where you are—but the right questions help you tap into subconscious knowledge of what a dream means even when not shown directly by the imagery. If you have nowhere to land, it leads to the question of whether that's how you feel: nothing is waiting for you.

The feelings and emotions a dream triggers leave a trail of clues. Dreams are known for creating scenarios to release and process emotions like a pressure valve. Falling creates a scenario that may help process stress, fear, dread, shock, horror, indecision, anxiety, hopelessness, and so forth. Reflect on your recent life and search for parallels with what you are feeling, have felt, or anticipate feeling. If your dreams recur without a resolution, it may indicate that the emotional processing isn't complete, so the dreaming mind responds with "rinse and repeat." The cycle stops when the emotions settle.

Falling can mean a change of circumstances or conditions—probably a sudden one—like when your life falls apart. It can mean a big letdown or feeling deflated. A hope, desire, or energy surge is the wind in your sails, and when it stops, you must come down. You come down from a high. You fall in love, and you fall into depression. You fall from grace. You take the fall. Those ideas are easy to express visually in dream language.

Falling up steps or stairs is a common dream theme, and it often means the idea of something that's tripping you up. You trip on a step and fall upward—the meaning of "tripped up" is right in the imagery. Steps in a dream can symbolize the steps you take to reach a goal. The goal is to reach the top, and something you encounter along the way trips you up. Look for variations of ideas expressed metaphorically, such as "falling on your face." A dream expresses the idea as dropping or falling ... on your face. Variations of this family of ideas are found in figures of speech like "drop the subject" and "fall into line," and the meaning of them is found in the dream imagery.

Falling dreams might symbolize the need to take a new path in life, perhaps one you almost literally fall into.

Falling in a dream may visually express the idea of falling asleep and the mind distancing from the body. You "fall" asleep by dissociating the mind from the body. One man's recurring dreams used the imagery of a vortex trying to suck him in, and it always occurred as he was falling asleep. He's dissociating his mind from his body, and it's natural, but for him, it's terrifying. On the other hand, trauma, abuse, and body dysmorphia are ripe situations for when the mind wants to escape the pain of its existence within the body.

Initiation is another ripe situation for falling dreams. Initiation means going into a dark and unknown psychological space for the purpose of learning a new way to live and be. One man's dream expressed the idea as crawling in a cave when suddenly, the ground gives way beneath him, and he falls into a deeper cave. He's terrified, but the feeling eases as he discerns that the deeper cave is full of subterranean life. He's finding out that much more is inside of him than he consciously knows, more "depth" and life. To fall means to descend, and his dream is a variation of the classic story of the "descent into the

> **Falling in a dream may visually express the idea of falling asleep and the mind distancing from the body.**

Underworld," told countless ways in myths and fairy tales as allegories for the descent into the depths of oneself. It may be like a death experience because that's what it is psychologically. The ego dies to make room for the deeper self to emerge.

Naturally, the ego reacts to a death experience with all its survival instincts supercharged—it says "screw that" and runs back the way it came. And it may be able to escape the initiation and go back to a "normal life," but it's at the expense of extinguishing the person's inner light.

See also: Crashes, Suicide, Teeth, Volcanoes/Earthquakes

FIRE

Start simple when interpreting a dream symbol. It helps you see the meaning despite the distractions. Start simple, generate ideas, and check if they fit into the bigger picture the dream paints. The dream author won't leave you hanging; it uses symbols in the context of a story, and the context defines what the symbols mean.

Take fire, for instance. Fire burns, and what burns also hurts. Fire as a symbol may simply mean that something hurts. Does a dream use fire in the context of a story that involves pain? If so, pain may be what it means by fire. You're dreaming and touch the fire on purpose, and the meaning is like the phrase "don't touch a hot stove." Why? Because it burns—it hurts!

Next, ask yourself if you're doing something that's causing pain to yourself or someone else or if you're headed in that direction—by falling in love with the wrong person, for example, and you know what the result will be but can't help yourself; you touch that fire anyway. In your dream, you can't help yourself because you're following the same pattern as your waking life. It's the script you follow subconsciously while dreaming. Dreams visualize ideas, and hurt is symbolized as fire, while being visualized physically and perhaps experienced as the sensation of pain while dreaming is probably the emotional, psychological, and existential variety.

Pain is something we want to keep our distance from, and so is fire. Fire as a symbol can mean "stay away."

Keep in mind, though, that the dream author cares most about the *idea* in the metaphor, not the metaphor itself. The idea behind touching a hot stove is that you should know better. The stove is hot, and you'll burn yourself by touching it—duh! The message is simple, and the dream author's options for expressing it are many. Instead of touching a hot stove, you pick up a hot object, and it burns you—what else did you expect to happen? It's the same idea.

The same point can be made by giving a dream character the role of enacting the idea, such as in the dream a teenager had where his brother sticks red-hot pins into his body and howls in pain but keeps doing it. The simple idea is that somebody—it's the brother who plays the role in the dream, but let's be more general and say "somebody"—deliberately causes themself pain. Now it's easy to find the parallel between the dream and the dreamer. He and his brother do *Jackass* stunts together that purposely cause themselves pain and injury. The dream projects the action onto the brother as a character because the dreamer blames him for instigating the stunts. But when he sees his brother in the dream, he's really seeing himself. The dream imagery "pokes holes" in his illusion.

Fire is dangerous. Uncontained, it spreads quickly and incinerates everything it touches. Dreams use those associations to create scenarios where fire is a symbol for danger. In this case, you and the other characters in the scene react to the fire as if it's dangerous. But it's also possible that the fire symbolizes a danger you flaunt, ignore, or don't recognize, and you are roasting marshmallows while everyone else runs for their lives—and vice versa when you see the danger that others don't. Subconsciously, you know what the fire means and react accordingly.

Fire can be merely a message that something is hurting you, or if you are seeing something burn, it could indicate the fear or sadness of losing something important to you, such as your home or a relationship.

A man dreams that he's in a packed nightclub and sees a fire start. He decides to get to the exit before warning about it. Superficially, his decision looks selfish, but subconsciously, his decision is driven by knowing that the fire means "putting out the fires that other people start." It's a pattern in his life to take care of the messes his friends make, allowing them to "party on." His decision in the dream to get to the exit before warning anybody about the fire reflects his determination to break the pattern.

Fire destroys, and while a lot of things destroy, a dream chooses fire over other options because it matches well with certain personal and situational dynamics. Jealousy and hot anger, for example, are destructive and like a fire in the heart. When somebody's life goes up in flames, it's a hot, destructive situation. For the dream author, it's like their home going up in flames or a city burning down—the imagery visualizes the idea. Cities are where people go to make a name for themselves, and a person's name is associated with their reputation. Put two and two together, and it's easy to see how a burning city is the picture of a person's reputation or self-image in ruins.

When buildings burn, it can mean that structures of thought and belief are changing. The imagery of a building burning to the ground is a dramatic way of saying "drastic changes," including physical and health changes.

Also, fire destroys completely. Ashes are all that's left, and they could be the ashes of your former life or self or all that remains of a big idea or hope.

The Phoenix rises from the ashes, a symbol of rebirth. In one man's dream, a dog that he loved—it was hit by a car and died—is trapped inside a building as it burns down, and he can't save it. In the next scene, he sees the dog's spirit leave the building and senses that it's returning to Mother Nature. He felt an internal shift soon afterward that allowed him to end his grieving.

> **Also, fire destroys completely. Ashes are all that's left, and they could be the ashes of your former life or self or all that remains of a big idea or hope.**

Fire spreads as it destroys, and that association comes in handy for situations and conditions that get out of hand and spread from person to person. Destructive rumors are like roaring flames. False beliefs and lies are, too. Take, for instance, a woman's dream that she picks up a piece of paper from her desk at work, lights it on fire, and throws it into a trash can. It ignites the paper already in the can, and the fire spreads rapidly, threatening her office. She wonders to herself, *Why did I do something so stupid?*, and the scene ends.

To interpret the meaning, she focuses on her work life—in the dream, she's at work, so that's the place to begin—and what came across her desk recently—in the dream, she's at her desk. It brings up the memory of reading something written by a coworker and discarding it. Why discard it? At first, she thinks that it's because the coworker's ideas are inferior. Then, she realizes that she never read what's written on the paper in the dream; instead, she lights it on fire and tosses it, and when she asks herself why she did that, the response from inside of her is, *It's not worth reading*. It makes her realize that she doesn't give her coworker's ideas a chance. And with further self-analysis, a revelation smacks her; her attitude is based on what she's heard about the coworker from other coworkers, not from honest evaluations. Their opinions are like a fire that spreads to her. She's a fair and rational person, but an assumption not based on merit is what? It's stupid, like lighting something on fire and tossing it into a trash can full of paper.

Subconsciously, she knows what that action means, and that's why her reaction while dreaming is to wonder why she did something so stupid. Sure, it's a stupid action on the surface, but the thought came to her *after* the fire spreads, meaning *after* she's influenced by the opinions of others. Dreams don't follow ordinary logic, and when they do, it's more by chance than design.

Fire consumes, and an all-consuming focus is like a fire burning within oneself. It's extreme passion, commitment, desire, and ambition, and it's not enough for a dream to say, "You're consumed by your work." Instead, it shows you on fire! A person "on fire" is on a mission and nothing will stop them, or they are on a roll, extraordinarily lucky, or zoned in. Or they are in a rage—fire is a great metaphor for hot anger. A dream may project the idea in the action onto a setting such as your home going up in flames to show you the consequences of work consuming your life or anger burning you up. That way, a dream shows the idea as a metaphor rather than as a boring memo, and you get the message.

For one woman, a nightmare about her home being on fire took her mind back to the time of life when she was a college student with a passionate love for art, who detoured onto another career path because the prospects seemed better. Two decades later, she witnesses the fire in her nightmare and remembers how the creative fire had once "lit her up." She's hit full force with the cold, dark flame of grief for what she lost. Her nightmare is not to torment her; it's a catharsis, a purge, and once the strong emotions pass, it becomes a catalyst for stoking her creativity and renewing her love for art.

For a man who dreamed about following Jesus through rough terrain and coming to a family home where they can rest and sit beside a comforting fire, the fire is a symbol for his spiritual zeal. In the dream, he wakes up in the morning, and the fire has died out. It's a great metaphor for his inner fire cooling off, allowing him a period of time to rest and recover.

Just as a phoenix rises from the ashes, fire in a dream may symbolize a kind of rebirth for the dreamer.

Fire burns. Yeah, that's obvious, but in dream-speak, it can mean anything from burning desire to something more literal. For example, a burning bed is a common metaphor for hot passion. That bed is getting a workout! But never assume without testing for other possible meanings. For one man who dreamed about his bed being on fire, it didn't mean sex or passion—none of that was going on in his life or occupying his mind. Plus, the dream seemed too literal by showing his bed in his bedroom and himself sleeping in it—alone—the same as he was while dreaming. So, after he woke up, he pulled his bed out from the wall and checked behind it. An electrical socket had gone bad, and the cord plugged into it was red-hot. While sleeping, he caught whiffs of frying electrical cord, and his dream translated it as imagery of his bed burning. His astute precaution may have saved him from his dream coming true!

Fire purifies, and now we get to an interesting and not so obvious association that dreams use as symbolism. The fire in your dreams may be making way for new life and growth, like how a forest fire burns away what's old and decayed. For one woman, her dream creates a scenario where she's a participant in a ritual at an ancient temple carved into a mountainside. She stands in a circle of robed priests around bluish-white flames rising high into the air from a huge mandala etched into the stone. Lightning streaks across the sky, and the sun is close to setting. She knows without being told what she must do.

She disrobes and walks naked into the flames, feeling the most intense tingling from head to toe as if the flames are inside every cell of her body. A voice coming from the flames says to her, "I am Agni, and I declare you worthy as a messenger of the gods!" The flames then form into the shape of a giant bird, and it carries her spirit into the heavens, where she meets great and ancient beings but remembers very little about her interactions with them.

She wakes up feeling like a new woman and, more importantly, like she's just returned from a trip to the stars. The darkness she'd felt within her is gone, burned away. She remembers the name Agni, researches it, and discovers that it's the Vedic god of fire and purification! Furthermore, the dream imagery of the lightning, the sun, and the bird are all part of Agni mythology. Before the dream, she was clueless about this Vedic god, so how did she dream about it in such detail?

The collective unconscious, that's how. The dream author works inside the world's grandest library, which offers detailed histories of all mythologies, religions, and more. Dreams that directly tap the collective unconscious like hers did—some dream theories say that all dreams in one way or another tap it—are highly important and sometimes life changing.

Fire is hot, and now the symbolism of it can branch off in many directions—the metaphorical possibilities are endless. Metaphors use heat to mean hot emotions and feelings, hot ideas and trends, and hot passions and desires. A hotheaded person is one whose temper easily flares. A fire in the belly means a hot pursuit.

The many meanings of "hot" are behind some of the possibilities for fire symbolism discussed already, but the one that's the most enigmatic is the use of heat as a counterpoint to cold, fire as the counterpoint to ice, and light as the counterpoint to dark. Those opposites are among the most basic in existence, and the "clash of opposites" generates the heat in the forge of Creation. From the opposite polarities of positive and negative in atoms to the opposite polarities of the archetypes in the roots of the psyche, it's the dynamic energy of all life. Fire is energy, and energy is a by-product of the interaction of opposites.

The burning ball of plasma in the sky that is our sun is the giver of life on this planet, the greatest source of energy in the solar system, and the association between the sun and the energy that fuels life itself is as old as humanity. The solar god is the original one, and heat and flames have long been associated with it. Fire is spirit, it is God, and regardless of one's beliefs about the subject, the most powerful dreams featuring fire can speak to one's spirit and existence.

It's one reason why dreams about a fire that can't be quenched or escaped are among the most haunting, regardless of the person's beliefs. Questions about mortality and death are behind those dreams—the flames of the funerary pyre. But the dreams are really about life and living it fully. In the heart of us all is a flame that energizes our personal transformations—the alchemical fire and light of one's consciousness. It's a sacred flame that you protect, knowing that the gales and gusts of earthly existence can blow it out.

When the fire in your dreams leaves nothing behind, when it forces you to adapt and respond to save yourself and those you love, when you know you must keep it burning at any cost, it may be a blessing in disguise. You, too, can rise from the ashes. You can be your own hero because you are the keeper of the sacred flame simply because you're alive and your fire still burns.

But the answer to what fire means may be simpler. The dream author within you translates physical sensations and conditions into images and stories, and fire is how it translates the sensation of excess heat, a feverish condition, a healing process of the body, and the burning sensations of neuralgia and acid reflux.

See also: Apocalypses, Armageddon, Dragons, Hell, Nuclear War, Volcanoes/Earthquakes

IMPRISONMENT/ENTRAPMENT

You are in a dream and can't escape. You are trapped, a prisoner, a captive. The scenery may be a prison, a torture chamber, or a grave, but the basic idea is the same, and you use the same approach to begin exploring what the dream means. Ask yourself, how am I trapped? It may be easy to figure out when a person is trapped in an abusive relationship, for example. Their answer to the question points dead at the person who treats them like a prisoner. But dreams show the ego what it does not know or understand, and even if the initial correlation between the dream content and your situation in life is apparent, dig deeper; you can find more.

Take, for instance, the young man's recurring dreams that place him inside a house with locked doors and windows. He runs from room to room desperately trying to escape and senses an older man inside the house watching him from the shadows and waiting for him to give up his struggle. He easily identifies the man inside the house as his boyfriend, someone he calls a "control freak." He identifies the house as the condo where they live together, which doesn't really look the same as the house in his dream, but it *feels* the same. And yes, in the condo, he feels trapped, too, because he can't afford to live on his own. His boyfriend knows it and uses financial dependency to play head games. Case closed.

But more is to it because his dependency and feelings of being trapped began long before he moved in with his boyfriend. While growing up, his parents dictated not only acceptable behavior but acceptability as a person, and for a young man, just realizing he is gay—completely unacceptable to his parents—no choice remained. He bailed at the first opportunity. Then, as a young man drifting from place to place, his vulnerability made him attractive to men who wanted to control him. He ended up with his current boyfriend, once again in the clutches of a control freak.

His recurring dreams tell the story of his life as being locked in a home with no way out. It's a recurring theme in his ordinary life reflected in his dream life. The home in the dream is an amalgamation of all the homes he's lived in and how it *feels* to live there—it's not only a symbol for where he lives, it's a symbol for his inner life. Everywhere he goes as an adult, he plays out the same drama that began in his family home. The trap is in his own mind, and the prison is the pattern of re-enacting the drama over and over.

Patterns of thought, feeling, and behavior trap a person within them. Dreams visualize the idea as a prison or trap. Beliefs are a prison when they are enforced with consequences. They are a trap when they restrict

Barred windows on a house can be just as powerful a metaphor of entrapment as an actual jail cell. You might feel trapped in a certain family situation, for example.

growth and freedom. In a dream where a man is a prisoner in Hell, his beliefs are the walls of his prison. They trap him inside a rigid conception of a "real man" and a belief about the consequences of being anything less.

When you think and feel that you have no other choice about something, a place of confinement is the dream setting that tells the story. A coffin with the crest of the elite school the dreamer attended symbolizes the trap of believing that the high-flying career he worked so hard to achieve must go with him to the grave—he'd be a fool to give it up. It's a common theme in the dream lives of people whose great achievements lock them on to a certain course in life.

> **When you think and feel that you have no other choice about something, a place of confinement is the dream setting that tells the story.**

Even a comfort zone can be a sort of prison if a person is strongly averse to leaving it. And technology ... whoa! It's a trap for people who are completely consumed by it through high-tech phones and entertainment systems. Increasingly, it's a source of nightmares, and no wonder—people are prisoners in a digital world.

Sadness, anger, depression, envy, and anything else that fixates or keeps a person stuck in life are all entrapping. It becomes the place where they live figuratively and hold a recurring place in their dreams. An example is given to us by one young man's dreams about his mom, who died a few years prior, being trapped somewhere in the afterlife, and he's unable to help her. He's trapped in grief, and it's he who needs help, not his mom.

For a young woman and her recurring dreams about being alone in a prison, it's a symbol of her feelings of isolation and her family's restrictions. Her parents rarely let her go out, and her family home feels like a prison. She's deprived of freedom and a social life, like a prisoner.

For another young woman, her father kidnapping her, holding her prisoner, and madly confessing his love for her are a dramatization of how she feels about him watching her every move because of his great love and concern for her welfare. *Dad, you're overdoing it!*

Horrible recurring nightmares about being held prisoner by a demented man haunted a woman until she figured out that the man wasn't a specific one in her life, he was a symbol for how she feels about *all* men. And it's not they who are demented, it's an exaggeration of her "men issues." It makes her sort of deranged, and realizing the personal truth reflected in her nightmares shocked her right out of the mental trap she'd created for herself. The nightmares then ended—which is usually the case when a person gets the message.

In another woman's nightmares, a sadist who keeps her bound and inflicts cruelties popped up in her dream life and hung around for decades after she was raped. Progressively, she was able to think through the situation as it occurred in her dreams and escape his traps. For her, the trap is a mental space created by blaming herself for getting raped. Her harsh self-criticism is sadistic.

Those dreams are pointing her to retrieve the lost and traumatized parts of herself trapped in the personal inner space and time where and when the crime happened. The dreams are a good sign, too—healing energy is welling up from her unconscious mind to help her. The situation is different, though, for another young woman who was savagely bullied as a teenager. Years later, the wounds are still bleeding, and in her nightmare, she is trapped inside a bathroom stall by her bullies and forced to perform oral sex on them. Defiantly, she bites off the penis of the lead bully, but he only laughs mockingly, as if expecting her to do it, and she vomits. The dream graphically shows her mental and emotional bondage to the bullying experience and her desire for revenge, which sicken her from within.

Anything that makes you feel like a prisoner or slave is fair game for symbolization as confinement, such as when a person is a slave to a sex or drug addiction. Prison is the right setting to tell that story because it adds associations with crime and punishment. Paralysis and possession are more ways for a dream to say you're trapped.

In a man's recurring dreams about serving a sentence in prison, the meaning relates to his guilty feelings over his many mistakes and the punishment he thinks he deserves. For another man, his prison dreams revolve around his association between serving time in prison and spending time alone to get himself together. It feels restrictive and confining, but in the dreams, he knows why he is there and resolves to make the most of it. Prison is a lonely place, too, and this dream theme expresses loneliness and isolation.

For a woman who dreamed about being trapped in a stuck elevator, the scenario dramatizes her feeling that her life is not progressing. Going up in an elevator symbolizes the idea of progress. No progress means no going up.

For a young transgendered woman, dreaming about being trapped inside a woman's locker room is a metaphor for feeling like she's trapped in her female body. The locker room is a place to get naked and change clothing, two associations that strongly correlate with her situation. One, she wants to change her appearance from female to male but is unable to because of her circumstances, and two, she doesn't feel safe around other females—especially while naked.

Imprisonment can take many forms, such as imprisonment in a drug or alcohol addiction, feeling like a slave in a marriage or to the wishes of one's parents, or being a cubicle drudge in a dead-end

See also: Charon, Hell, Medusa, Minotaurs, Paralysis, Possession, Suicide

PARALYSIS

The inability to respond is the simple idea that a dream can mean by paralysis, like in the phrases "paralyzed by fear" and "paralyzing anxiety." Before we take the plunge into the symbolism of paralysis, though, let's cover some physical causes.

When we talk about fight-or-flight response, "freeze" is the option often overlooked. Some people freeze when confronted by difficult, traumatizing, and emergency situations, and "paralyzed" is another word for frozen. The freeze response traps traumatic energy in the body if it's not shaken off once the danger or emergency passes. While sleeping, the nervous system relaxes enough to allow the trapped energy to release, and the dreaming mind creates imagery and scenarios associated with the discharge of that energy. Paralysis is a common feature of the experience.

For people with PTSD, the cause of their paralysis nightmares might be the manic energy of the trauma. It's trapped in their nervous systems and releases as they sleep. Their nightmares are horrendous and generally can't be interpreted conventionally because they arise as a response to their overloaded nervous systems. For good reason, we call the experiences "sleep terrors" and "night terrors." Embodied Dreamwork and physical activities that work with energy, such as qigong, yoga, martial arts, and vigorous exercise, are helpful. Milder variations of paralyzing trauma show up in conventional nightmares that can be treated with conventional therapeutic and dreamwork techniques. A go-to resource is psychotherapist Linda Schiller's book *PTSDreams: Transforming Your Nightmares from Trauma through Healing Dreamwork*.

Sleep paralysis is a normal condition while dreaming explained elsewhere in this book (see the entry for Shadow People). One way to tell the difference between sleep paralysis and symbolic paralysis is by whether paralysis produces a nightmare, or a nightmare produces paralysis. Sleep paralysis can carry over into the first moments of wakefulness and produce terrifying experiences because you're still dreaming even though your eyes are open, and the dreaming mind responds to your fear by creating fearful imagery. But you may also become aware of sleep paralysis *while* dreaming. It's especially common in people

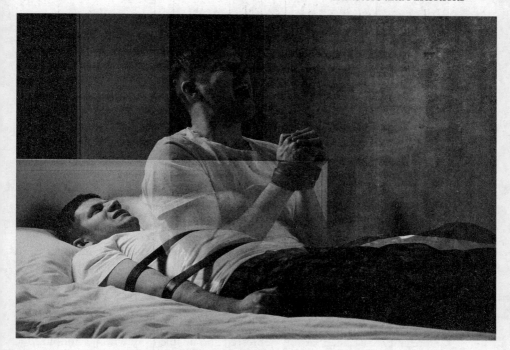

Sleep paralysis is a real medical condition that often affects people with sleep apnea or narcolepsy, but it can also be the result of "night terrors" from nightmares.

who sleep fitfully. They are closer to the surface of conscious awareness and more aware of what's happening physically than someone who's deeply asleep. They realize they can't move, and it can be terrifying. Their response to sleep paralysis produces their nightmares, but if the paralysis is a feature of a dream's story and it provides a reason in the narrative—for example, you're paralyzed because you're in a coma—the paralysis is more likely to be symbolic. The nightmare produces a simulated experience of paralysis.

One young man dreamed about being paralyzed and falling into a dark vortex every time he fell asleep. By resisting, he could force himself away from the roaring vortex painfully and slowly. The vortex symbolizes falling into unconscious sleep, and his feeling of paralysis is how his mind translates his muscles going slack as he falls asleep and his mind dissociating from his body. He has the rare ability to remain consciously aware while falling asleep, depicting in the dreams as moving away from the vortex, and it seems like a curse because the loss of bodily control is terrifying, but with training, he can enter the dream state fully conscious by controlling his fear and accepting that his mental awareness separates from his body.

Dissociation from the body is a condition that dreams translate as paralysis. In those dreams, the experience of being unable to feel with the physical senses is caused by the mind's disconnection from the body and may be rooted in traumatic stress response. Dissociation is a natural protective mechanism that turns harmful if a person can't find their way back to a healthy connection between mind and body. People who deliberately or recklessly cause harm to themselves create an antagonistic relationship with their body, and when they go to sleep, their body tells them how it feels about the situation. *Hello, nightmares!*

> **Paralysis as symbolism can mean the doubt that prevents or hinders you from making a move. You're frozen in place.**

Paralysis as symbolism can mean the doubt that prevents or hinders you from making a move. You're frozen in place. Paralysis can also mean lacking control—while paralyzed, you lack control of your body. You have a goal you want to reach or a place you want to be in your life, for instance, but lack the power or control to get there. Or you can't control certain emotions, feelings, situations, or circumstances. Or you just can't get your butt out of bed to face life. The dream author translates the ideas symbolically as paralysis.

A variation of the idea plays out in a dream a young woman experienced where her ex-boyfriend is comatose in a hospital bed. She holds his hand and tells him that it's all right to die. The scene dramatizes her situation after their breakup. She's been terribly depressed and unable to function, symbolized in the dream as her ex in a coma. Dying means letting go, and she's telling herself that it's all right to let go of him and emerge from her depression.

Paralysis can mean that something's holding you back. Depression, stress, panic, timidity, and character flaws are common causes of what can hold a person back, and so are heavy restrictions and a lack of options and opportunities. Dreams have many options for expressing this basic idea. For example, being wrapped up by a spider and paralyzed by its venom is a way of saying, "You are going nowhere." The dream uses that imagery to correlate with personal and situational dynamics. For example, an overpowering mother figure or devious lover has you wrapped in a web, paralyzed psychologically, or a thought process or feeling is paralyzing you.

Overthinking and overanalyzing create a condition we call "paralysis by analysis." For one woman, her dream author creatively spun a story about her tendency to overanalyze by showing her lying on a couch in a psychoanalyst's office unable to move. The setting is especially appropriate because her endless and fruitless analysis of herself paralyzes her ability to make decisions. Plus, the analyst in her dream talks in endless circles, tying her brain in a knot as she tries but fails to follow the reasoning. It's a graphic demonstration of her thought processes.

Circumstances that entrap you easily translate symbolically as paralysis. Abusive and controlling relationships can entrap a person, for instance, and paralysis is another way of saying "trapped." You are like a prisoner.

Social anxiety is a sort of paralysis. The idea plays out in a man's dream where he enters a building, sees a crowd of people in the lobby, and freezes in place. It's a dramatization of his typical response during social situations. Even the thought of interacting socially in a large crowd strikes him with paralyzing anxiety.

Paralysis is a worst-case scenario for some people, a worst fear come true. Their fear of helplessness and dependency is amplified into a scenario involving paralysis. It gives the dream author associations to work with that equate paralysis with terrible fears and worst-case scenarios. That's the idea behind a dream a man experienced where he wakes up paralyzed in a hospital and can't communicate to the staff. He's trapped in a body that doesn't function, and fear is the driving force behind the dream. His worst fear is to fail at life, and his dream boils down to a "note to self" to live every day to its fullest. He's not helpless but sometimes feels that way.

For one woman, her paralysis while dreaming begins with her laid out on a cold, metal table. She's a child. A man she can't see rubs lotion on her skin, then touches her sexually. She views the scene as if it's a cartoon, and as the sexual touching continues, it switches to stark reality. His hands move from her chest to inside her pants. She lies there helpless, just wanting the assault to be over.

> **Paralysis is a worst-case scenario for some people, a worst fear come true. Their fear of helplessness and dependency is amplified into a scenario involving paralysis.**

The dream is a replay of the sexual molestation she suffered as a child. The man symbolizes her original abuser and is also an amalgamation of other abusers she's been in relationships with as she repeats the pattern. Her childhood abuser rubbed lotion on her as an excuse to get his hands on her. When the abuse starts, she reacts by freezing—she can't fight, so instead, she sends her mind away while her body lies paralyzed and terrified. The switch from cartoon to stark reality symbolizes her shock as a child as she realized the true purpose of "the game" her abuser played, and it's a poignant expression of her forced loss of innocence.

See also: Molestation, Imprisonment/Entrapment, Shadow People, Spiders

POSSESSION

Something's not right—that's a simple idea behind the symbolism of possession. The dreaming mind observes that something's not right and creates a scenario to express the idea. It's vague, and in some cases, so is the source of possession. You don't know what's gotten into a person or into yourself, you just know that something's wrong, and that's the idea behind a "possession dream."

If you are possessed, you are not in control of your own actions, which can be a terrifying experience. The terror is compounded by not understanding what is controlling you!

Or, maybe, you do know what's wrong, and your dreaming mind decides to symbolize it as possession because it matches up well with the situational and personal dynamics. For example, an addiction changes a person's behavior and personality; the addiction *possesses* them. Possession is the symbol of choice for other extreme changes in behavior and personality: the relentless pursuit of love and sex; the obsession with attaining power and fame; the embrace of extremist ideologies and opinions. They take over a person from within.

A person possessed is not acting like their usual self. Something sinister enters the picture. A mood, desire, idea, feeling, emotion, or change of personality possesses them. And in cases where a whole mess of things possesses a person, the dream author responds with scenarios that involve legions. The darker it is, the darker the dream imagery. To be possessed by a ghost is one thing—it may symbolize the idea of being stuck in the past, for example—but possession by a demon or legion of demons is, on the face of it, a much darker idea. Dreams choose their details carefully. Use the list at the bottom of this entry to look up specific types of possession.

Possession is an exaggerated comparison with being stuck in a loop of thought, feeling, or desire. A person is in a loop when they aren't finding what they're looking for, or their way out of something, and possession comes into play when they're looking for something to satisfy an inner need or craving. People are said to crave attention, love, and recognition, for example, and nothing is wrong with that. The problem enters the picture when they go about it the wrong way, such as by getting attention through consumer items or trying to "buy love" through wealth, status, and excessive self-sacrifice. It's not an authentic experience, and deep down, the person is aware of it, but they don't know a better way or won't see beyond the desire for instant gratification. Secretly, they fear their inadequacy, and possession fills the void.

Possession means sacrifice in the sense of sacrificing your life, and wow, does that idea have legs. You may be sacrificing your life right now and not realize it for what it is, but your dreams know, and they tell the story in the starkest terms. You may not recognize that putting someone else's needs and priorities before your own is a type of sacrifice, even when done altruistically. *Here, have my life,* the sacrifice says, and at its heart, it's a type of masochism. It's martyrdom. It's possession through ego bondage.

Take, for instance, a woman's dream about standing at attention in a line of people as a plantation owner endlessly lectures the "servants" about proper conduct and attention to detail. They're roped together with their hands tied behind their backs, implying the idea of slavery. The woman proudly inspects their bonds to make sure they are secure. At the end of the line, she comes to a woman who is around her age and height. The dreamer notices that her bonds are loose and she's only pretending to be trapped, and the first opportunity she gets, she's going to bolt. The captive looks the dreamer in the eye as if to say "please don't say anything," and the dreamer reacts with righteous indignation. "Sir," she says to the plantation owner, "this one seems to think she can escape. What should we do with her?"

"I'll deal with her privately," he replies, and the dreamer secures the woman's bonds more tightly. "I'm sorry," she whispers, "but it's for your own good."

Passivity is a type of ego bondage, and that's the idea behind the dream. It creates a scenario for the dreamer's ego to act out its bondage to a male authority figure, represented as the plantation owner, by giving her the role of junior slave driver. She thinks she's only pretending that her excessive efforts to please male authorities by tending to their every wish and need are voluntary and that by secretly nurturing an image of herself as "better than that," she's somehow escaping the hold it has on her, symbolized in the dream as the rope tying together the servants.

> **Passivity is a type of ego bondage, and that's the idea behind the dream. It creates a scenario for the dreamer's ego to act out its bondage to a male authority figure....**

But in the scenario, she's in the same line as them, making her one of them. They represent the aspects of herself that are in service to the ego's attitude of self-sacrifice, and the woman with the loose bonds represents the part of herself that realizes the situation for what it really is. Internally, she treats that part of herself like a rebel slave, and through her internal dialogue, symbolized as the plantation owner "dealing with her privately," she keeps herself bound in service.

Beneath her martyrdom is a secret ego inflation. It's secret because she thinks of inflation in terms of superiority and arrogance like a plantation owner, but passivity is also a type of ego inflation, and a feeling of superiority hides in the personal blind spot created by its shadow. "It's for your own good" is a statement that pierces the heart of her inflation because she thinks it's better to go along passively and make everyone else happy rather than put her own needs and desires first. Her fighting spirit is then channeled into her perfectionism—she's exceptionally good at it, with close attention to detail and proper conduct, but it's driven by her fear of inadequacy, and every time a male authority figure says "great job" and recognizes her service, it covers over the fear and secretly feeds not only her inflation but also her internal rebellion. The response inside of her is, "Fuck you for not freeing me."

Her situation illustrates a common one behind possession dreams. In place of the plantation owner and what it represents, substitute "the company," "the church," "the family," or "the belief system," and you have a summary of the modern condition. Society is built atop structures that are sadomasochistic in nature, locking individuals into a duality of serving them by either borrowing authority and power from them or submitting oneself to them. Either way, you "buy in" by internalizing and personalizing the structures. Submission, a type of possession, simply means giving over the power to think for oneself and be responsible for your own life. Thinking for oneself is transcendence over the "either/or" duality, and it's no wonder that society's power structures and pressures of conformity target "free thinking" for especially cruel treatment.

Possession may be a dream's way of trying to explain the unexplainable. Take, for instance, the dream a woman had where her stepfather, possessed by an evil spirit, murders her mother and siblings. Naturally, the focus for understanding the dream is on the stepfather—what's changed or different about him that's unexplainable? But it was actually her mom who did something unexplainable by cheating—caught in the act by her stepfather and driving a knife through the heart of their marriage.

The drama of the dream plays on the idea that murders happen in response to extreme situations like catching your spouse in bed with another person. Possession in this case means "taken away" from her—the dreamer loves her stepfather and fears losing him as the family splits apart. It means that he's lost to her.

Possession can mean "out of control," and if you aren't in control, especially of yourself, what is? Jungian psychology uses the term *archetypal Possession* for a condition where the ego identifies itself with the powerful energy of an archetype. The energy inflates the ego and can take control of the personality. And the ego may perceive archetypes and other autonomous structures of the psyche like invisible entities with an evil agenda to possess them.

When things feel out of control, you can feel as if you are possessed, what Jungians call "archetypal Possession."

Archetypes are not dark or evil by nature but are inherently dangerous. Dr. Carl Jung says that the conscious side of the person—the ego—must have the strength to counterbalance them. You need a strong sense of yourself to harness the energy of an archetype rather than be possessed by it. The classic book *Ego and Archetype* by Edward Edinger is a great resource.

Possession happens when something nasty takes over a person from within. Typically, we think of scenarios such as addiction, psychosis, and spiritual darkness as parallels with possession, but the dream author's repertoire is broader, and its focus is on the ego. After all, a dream's plot is driven by the interaction of the dreamer's ego with the dream's environment. An archetype is a possibility for what possesses a person, but more commonly, the ego's creations possess it in the sense of taking it over, and nowhere is it more obvious than when the ego is possessed by ideas about itself. "I deserve to be famous," says the ego, and the idea possesses the person. The ego says that it must be the smartest, the most attractive, or the most popular—it's possessed by the idea it creates. Or the ego comes up with a concept or theory that grabs hold and won't let go. It becomes an obsession, and obsession rhymes with possession.

Finally, the potential for wordplay enters the picture when possession in a dream means that you feel like someone's possession. Possession can also mean material possessions, such as in a dream about a possessed Rolls Royce that, for obvious reasons, symbolizes the dreamer's obsession with wealth.

See also: Black-eyed People, Demons, Devils, Entities, Evil, The Girl from *The Ring*, Ghosts/Poltergeists/Spirits, Haunted Dolls, Imprisonment/Entrapment, Paralysis, Vampires, Zombies

STORMS/BLIZZARDS/HURRICANES/TORNADOES

Something big is building, and you sense trouble. You may not be able to put into words what's raising the hairs on your neck, but something's not right. Conditions are treacherous. Progress is impossible. Down in the deepest reaches of your heart and soul, a power swirls that's dark and wet. Those are the situations, conditions, and circumstances the dream author turns into stories about storms, blizzards, hurricanes, and tornadoes.

Those disasters provide the author with associations that differentiate them from other types of disasters—mainly their big buildup and longer running time. A crash or earthquake may strike suddenly, but the storm grows. The clock ticks. The intensity and drama climax. You may or may not have time to respond.

It's no wonder that stories of all types use storms for dramatic effect. Hear the perfectly timed thunder?

Storms are a big feature of the human experience. You may live for 100 years and never experience an earthquake, but we all experience the primal fear and thrill of storms. Memories of before, during, and after a storm provide the dream author with the raw material for telling stories—scary stories—and a smorgasbord of associations. But bear in mind that storms create atmosphere, and some details of a dream are more important for the atmosphere they create than for their symbolism. The intent may be simply to convey an ominous feeling. Plus, dreams can incorporate what we hear and sense while sleeping, and the boom-boom of a storm may be a dream's translation of what's happening inside of and around you while sleeping. For instance, you fall asleep while watching a war movie and dream about a thunderstorm, or something you ate is tearing through your digestive system like a hurricane.

As a symbol, a storm is great for comparing with something disruptive—storms disrupt plans and upend lives. The storm could be the family emergency that disrupts travel plans—after all, storms create emergencies, impede travel, and force plans to change. Or in the figurative sense, the plans are your vision for your future, and the storm is a symbol for the illness or misfortune that derails you. One young man dreamed about black clouds in the distance and a shaman next to him saying, "You should avoid that storm." The black clouds symbolized the symptoms of mental illness that he overcame, and the shaman's statement means "don't go there again."

> As a symbol, a storm is great for comparing with something disruptive—storms disrupt plans and upend lives.

A storm is also great for comparing with something you protect yourself from. For example, the "storm on the brow" that you see brewing. Uh-oh, stormy emotional weather ahead—better seek shelter!

A storm is a symbol for a dark mood, the person or event that storms into your life, or the stormy relationship that brings with it thunderous arguments and lightning flashes of anger. Or it could be the depression that comes between you and a loved one or between you and the sunny skies of feeling good about life. Meteorologically, a storm is a center of low pressure—aka a depression—and in that sense, it can symbolize something that causes or attracts unwanted feelings, misfortunes, and negativity. It's a picture of gloomy pessimism, and the worse the gloom and pessimism, the worse the storm.

Storms grow in intensity, comparable to situations and conditions in life. Take, for example, the dream a woman had that opens with a scene where her elderly father is missing from his home. She frantically searches the streets and sees him at a distance outside a retirement home. As she runs toward him, a storm begins raging. Then, a flash flood sweeps down the street between them and makes it impossible to cross. She cries out for her dad to get inside the building, but he's incognizant of the storm's growing intensity.

The context of the woman's situation with her father makes the dream's meaning rather obvious—one layer of it, at least. He's elderly, lives alone, and losing the ability to care for himself. She helps as much as she can, but it's not enough, and she fears a scenario like her dream coming true: she'll drop by his home, and he'll be gone without a trace. It's within the realm of possibility because he's forgetful and easily confused, but he stubbornly refuses to get help, and moving to a retirement home is out of the question.

Storms can represent being in a dark mood, being angry, being depressed, or being in a confrontational relationship.

The dream sums up the situation by showing him standing out in the open during a raging storm, while nearby is a shelter—a retirement home. The woman sees it, but he doesn't, meaning that she sees the solution, but he refuses. The dream uses the storm as a multifaceted symbol. First of all, it's the danger her father is in and her inability to "reach" him, symbolized by the pouring rain and the flash flood. Second, it's the danger she recognizes that her father doesn't. Third, it brings out her feelings and emotions, a mix of fear, sympathy, and sadness. Fourth, her father is like the implacable storm. And fifth, the situation is coming to a head, symbolized as the storm's intensity increasing as the dream progresses.

Dreams often begin with situations and conditions of daily life that then dramatize their impact on inner life, and the above example follows the pattern. The opening scene lays out the situation with her dad, then makes her worst fear come true. An observer may say that she's obviously worried about her dad and seeking resolution for the situation, and that's true—that's the surface layer. Beneath it is the personal layer the dream dramatizes. The storm is in her life with her father and her inner life, too. Resolution begins there.

A variation of the idea is dramatized by a dream where the dreamer and his sister visit their childhood home. The dreamer looks out the kitchen window and sees nasty, black clouds rolling in. The radio warns to take shelter; a tornado is coming. The dreamer dashes to the basement and finds his sister already down there. She cries out, "We should have seen it coming!"

You may think that she means that they should have seen the storm coming, but that's not the full idea. What does she—and the dream itself—really mean? Important statements by dream characters can summarize what a dream is about and, to follow the trail to the meaning of the sister's statement, turn it into a question. What should they have seen coming? "Should have" means the past, so the question becomes, what should they have seen coming when they lived in their childhood home?

Restating the details of the dream gives the dreamer the insight to answer the question. They should have seen their parents' divorce coming. It tore through their lives like a tornado, and on one level, that's what the dream means by saying a tornado is coming. The signs of trouble brewing in their parents' marriage were apparent. A huge storm rolling in is the perfect metaphor. But to the dreamer and his sister, it wasn't obvious at the time, and the divorce struck with suddenness. It's the situational dynamic behind the dream creating not only a nasty storm but also a tornado. Tornadoes strike suddenly, but you can see a storm coming.

When dreams refer to the past, they always relate it to the present. Something about the experience of the divorce is ongoing for the dreamer, and by analyzing the dream, he comes to realize that he ignored how the divorce tore him up inside. Turbulent emotions are buried within him, down in his subconscious mind and its storehouse of emotional memories, symbolized as the basement of his childhood home. The dream announces that he's about to revisit them and enter a time of healing. Stormy weather is ahead in his emotional life, and it's an opportunity to heal the past. The resolution begins inside of himself.

> **Tornadoes as dream symbols can be like storms but with specific features that differentiate them. They drop from the sky and destroy everything in their path....**

Tornadoes as dream symbols can be like storms but with specific features that differentiate them. They drop from the sky and destroy everything in their path, a great symbol for a sudden onset of anxiety and other sorts of chaotic and confusing thoughts and emotions and how they twist up a person's insides. The worse the anxiety and chaos, the worse the tornado. The landscape of the dream symbolizes the dreamer's internal psychological landscape, and the tornado is the thing that tears through it. It may also symbolize the person's life, and the tornado is the thing that rips a path through it. The swirling turbulence of a tornado makes it a great choice as a symbol when a dream speaks about turbulent emotions or something that goes around and around, such as a bad argument. It makes you feel all twisted up and tight inside.

Fear, though, is the emotion of choice for the symbolism of a tornado. Picture in your mind the black funnel cloud bearing down—do you feel a fear response in your body? Now, multiply that feeling by 1,000 when you not just imagine it, you dream it. Sure, other disasters can elicit the same response, but for many people, a tornado is a picture of their worst fear. Once it's upon you, you're powerless to do anything but hope and pray that you survive. It gives the dream author a combination of associations to work with.

A man dealt with chronic tornado nightmares throughout his life. It felt like an affliction and a curse. He'd be dreaming something ordinary when suddenly, here comes the funnel cloud and he's running for his life. Like a black panther, the tornado tracks him with no way to escape, and inevitably, it finds him cowering in mortal fear.

He decided one day that he'd had enough, and the next time he dreamed about a tornado, his response was, "Come and get me if you want." And it did. He was riding in a train, and the funnel ripped off the roof and sucked him out. Up, up, and away he went, but he refused to be scared. He stared into the eyes of the beast, and when it didn't get what it wanted from him, it let him go. He never dreamed about a tornado again, and in his waking life, his courage grew to face the things he feared.

For another man, his chronic tornado nightmares brought out the same extreme level of fear and struck with the same suddenness. His path to facing the fear took him on a deep inner journey. He came to realize that the tornadoes were like portals that took him to an inner dimension, the same use of symbolism as the tornado in *The Wizard of Oz*. When Dorothy wakes up at the end, it was "all just a dream," but she insists that it was real, and that's how the inner journey is, too. The dreams forced him to reckon with himself in the deepest and most personal ways, to break patterns of self-destruction and confusion, and to transform. It took him to a place of mystery where the rules of the daylight world don't apply. In other words, it took him into the unconscious.

> A counterclockwise spiral shape that leads the traveler inward is classic symbolism for that process of inner development by consciously facing the unconscious.

A counterclockwise spiral shape that leads the traveler inward is classic symbolism for that process of inner development by consciously facing the unconscious. But whereas walking a spiral staircase implies a voluntary journey, a tornado implies an involuntary wrenching away from ordinary reality and its patterns, habits, and comforts.

Anger is another emotion that the image of a tornado captures perfectly. Anger makes your head spin and takes you around and around. It's destructive and can strike suddenly. Elevate anger to the level of fury, and the equivalent is an F5 tornado, the most ferocious of all.

Like a tornado, a hurricane spirals and produces tremendous power and destruction. Metaphors compare hurricanes with the strongest and most destructive forces—"rocks you like a hurricane." In that sense, a hurricane is a next-level storm, and all the possibilities for a storm's meaning discussed above apply to hurricanes, too.

A hurricane has an eye around which massive forces gather, and it's an association the dream author can use as a symbol for something that's powerfully attractive and has its own center of gravity. For example, one's life revolves around a job or person, and a dream has good reasons for choosing a hurricane or tornado as a symbol—perhaps to mean that it's all-consuming and destructive. Another sort of center of gravity is a belief or idea about yourself—everything about the ego and personality organizes around it. The immature ego typically sees itself as the center of life and the world, and it's the "eyes" from which people view and understand their life. In that sense, a hurricane may be a symbol for a raging ego and, on the milder side, a childish temper or a sense of entitlement.

If an island is a symbol for the conscious mind and the ocean a symbol for the unconscious, a hurricane inundating an island is a symbol for the powerful forces of the unconscious overwhelming the conscious mind. The same idea applies to dreams about a coastline battered by a huge storm. The coastline is the boundary area where the conscious mind and the unconscious meet, and when something big sweeps in from the unconscious, it overwhelms the conscious mind.

A blizzard matches well symbolically with certain hazardous and treacherous conditions in life and in oneself. Swirling snow hindering vision can symbolize difficulty seeing your way forward to a goal. Deep and driving snow slows you down, making progress difficult or impossible. It gives the dream author a versatile symbol and story motif.

Depression is among the most common conditions behind "blizzard dreams." Living with depression is like a perpetual blizzard: the heaviness, the slowness, the hazards, the cold feelings. All those associations show in a dream a woman had where she struggles in a blizzard. Each step forward requires great effort, and on top of that, she doesn't know where she's going—the en-

The white-out conditions of a blizzard can represent your inability to see your way toward a goal in life.

tire landscape is whited out. But up ahead, she spots a white horse, the very image of strength and power, and knows it's there for her. She hurries forward to take it by the reins, but a man dressed in black gets there first, grabs the reins, and pulls the horse away from her.

After waking up and thinking about the dream, she senses that her life is at an important juncture. She's aware of her depression and recognizes the metaphor of struggling in a blizzard. But what does her dream mean with the horse and the man pulling it away from her? She thinks of the horse as representing her inner strength, and more importantly, it is help that arrives right when she needs it. Dreams and other sorts of stories commonly use white animals in that capacity, showing that something deep inside of us is responsive to our needs. The man who grabs the reins symbolizes the part of herself that keeps her in depression and saps her strength. Its dark appearance and malicious behavior identify it as the shadow side of the ego. In psychological language, it's a complex—a cluster of thought processes, emotional processes, and aspects of the personality that have "gone rogue" against the ego and work behind the scenes to usurp its decision-making power.

Realizing this, the woman feels wronged. The white horse is hers, and she wants it back!

She then dreams that she's back in the blizzard and sees the horse. The man is near and about to repeat the same action of pulling the reins, meaning taking control of her inner strength and preventing her from leaving her depression, so she rushes forward and jumps onto the horse before he can get to it. He's furious! She snaps the reins, and the horse moves swiftly, but soon, they come to a cliff. The bad man closes in. The only way out is forward, so she jumps the horse off the cliff. They splash into the icy water far below. The dream ends.

Knowing that the blizzard symbolizes her depression is the master key for decoding the rest of the dream. The final scene where she jumps off the cliff is the proverbial leap of faith and a reflection of her decision to push forward despite being unsure about where she's going—it's better than the alternative! The bad man isn't done with her, though. He continues to appear in her dreams, and through inner work, she traces him to his source of power

> **Knowing that the blizzard symbolizes her depression is the master key for decoding the rest of the dream.**

within her in her pattern of trying to please the men in her life and consequently sacrificing her desires. It's also a source of her depression.

Nothing says "stuck" like a blizzard. The above example uses it to mean "stuck in depression," and other possibilities for meaning include the ideas of being stuck in a situation, in work, and in an obligation. The imagery can also mean "blanketed," as in "covered up"—the true, authentic you is buried somewhere under there. It can mean "bad prospects"—a blizzard is the wrong time to start something new.

Your personal experience with storms may create associations that your dreams use. For example, a blizzard may remind you of a specific incident when an important person in your life got stuck in a blizzard and you worried yourself to death. A blizzard in your dream may therefore symbolize worry, concern for a loved one, or fear of being alone or helpless. Use your associations to uncover the unusual and unconventional ideas behind a blizzard as a symbol.

Also, explore the feelings brought out by the dream and the scenario it creates and analyze the content for the ideas it expresses. A dream doesn't say "stuck" by showing you easily skiing over a snowy landscape or say "depression" by showing you happily playing in the deep snow. Usually, it expresses the same idea multiple ways, including through your feelings. It may be a simple idea like that the storm is big and it's a problem, so to find the personal parallel with the dream imagery, you search your life and yourself for a big problem. It may be a feeling, such as dread, so you follow that feeling to find the personal parallel. What do you dread coming up like a storm?

See also: Apocalypses, Crashes, Falling, God, Tidal Waves/Tsunamis/Floods, Volcanoes/Earthquakes

TEETH
Just about everyone's been there: suddenly, your teeth crack into jagged, porcelain pieces; a loose tooth falls out; or your mouth gushes blood and chunky bits of gums. You've been there one way or another because nightmares and bad dreams about teeth are so common, it's safe to say that they are universal.

"Teeth dreams" are universal because we all have teeth and use them for chewing, talking, smiling, and so on, and these uses are a starting point for the dream author to tell stories about diet, articulation, appearance, and much more. The symbolism builds atop the uses and functions of the teeth and mouth and their many associations and metaphors.

Begin with the use of teeth for chewing and the associations with diet and eating. Dreams give us feedback on how the body responds to what we eat, and when the body likes what we feed it, dreams create pleasant experiences involving food and dining. A rule of thumb from the tradition of dream interpretation is to eat more of whatever you enjoy eating in your dreams and less of whatever your dreams present in a negative context. Take, for instance, a young man's dream that puts him in the cafeteria at his high school; he goes through the line and picks out boxes of processed foods to eat. He and his peers go to a dining table and chow down … on cardboard. He chews up the tasteless cardboard and notices that the cafeteria workers are giving him dirty looks.

The interpretation begins with a review of his eating habits—it's the obvious starting point because the dream creates references to food choices. He jokes that everything he eats comes from a box or bag, and all kidding aside, he might as well be eating cardboard because processed foods lack nutrition. The dirty looks of the cafeteria workers reinforce the idea. They symbolize the organs and systems of his body involved with digestion. Then, he remembers that the day before the dream, he and his friends joked about how everything they eat comes from a box. His dream began with the memory of joking with his friends and spun a deeper story around it, amplifying the message to eat better.

A common meaning behind dreams featuring the teeth and mouth involves ideas related to speaking and articulation. It's a storytelling bonanza of associations, references, and memories. The act of speaking begins with movements of the mouth that involve the teeth, tongue, and throat. We speak to articulate, to communicate. Communication is the basis of our personal and social lives, and because of the high importance and the potential for problems and issues with communication in our personal and social lives, "teeth dreams" are among the most distressing types.

Take, for instance, the young man who dreams about sitting across from his father in a restaurant. He tries to say something, opens his mouth, and a tooth falls out—then another tooth and another, and soon, he's lost an entire row of teeth, followed by a torrent of blood. Distressed and confused, he wants to ask his dad for help but is unable to speak, and his dad just stares at him.

For anyone fluent in the symbolic language of dreams, it's easy to see that this dream spotlights an issue with communication, first with the setting. The dinner table is traditionally a place for family members to talk. Then, to be more obvious, the dream has him opening his mouth to speak and his teeth falling out. The dream puts the icing on the cake

Dreams of teeth can have something to do with one's diet. Unpleasant dreams involving teeth may indicate your body is telling you that you are eating the wrong foods.

when he is unable to ask his dad for help, and Dad is playing the role of the "wall of silence." Put the clues together, and it raises a question. What is he having trouble communicating to his father?

It appears to be the dream's subject, but we need to know the context of their relationship before we can say more. Dreams cleverly use the people you know as characters to help you understand yourself better. They bring to life inner aspects of yourself, and it's easy to mistake the actual person with a character that plays them in your dream. Usually, the appearance of the character is like a mask, but some dreams replay recent memories, and when those memories involve the people you know, they may appear as characters. A deeper idea hidden may still be behind the mask, but the process of winnowing down the possibilities begins by reviewing your memories and the current situations, conditions, and circumstances involving those people.

That context clinches the interpretation of the young man's dream. He'd recently told his father that he thinks he's transgendered. Dad didn't take it well. He didn't yell or scream. Instead, he threw up a wall of silence, and now, the son doesn't know what to say to break through. He desperately wants his father's support but isn't getting it, and the dream dramatically tells the story. Plus, it brings forward his feelings of distress and confusion about the situation. One dream scene summarizes the personal and situational dynamics.

In a dream where a young woman feels a loose tooth in her mouth and pushes it with her tongue, that action begins a domino effect. The loose tooth falls out, then another one, then all her teeth fall out, plus fleshy chunks of her gums and a bucketful of blood. She calls her boyfriend. He answers and says he'll take her to the hospital. Working backward raises an obvious question. Why call her boyfriend when an ambulance is a better choice? Dreams have their own logic, so it's not to say that she made a bad choice; it's to highlight a subconscious thinking process. Co-creative dream theory teaches that dreams unfold based on the dreamer's choices. Her choice to call her boyfriend suggests that the underlying subject of the dream somehow involves him.

> **Co-creative dream theory teaches that dreams unfold based on the dreamer's choices.**

With that observation in mind, next we analyze the symbolism of a loose tooth. She pushes it with her tongue, and the domino effect kicks in. Speech and articulation are where to begin the interpretation process because of the dramatic action set in motion by the interaction of her tongue with her teeth. Is she having communication issues with her boyfriend? Her initial answer is no, they communicate openly. Now, add to the picture the loose tooth and the old saying about being loose with the truth. She says that she doesn't lie to boyfriend … *unless you mean the little white lies that everyone tells.* Hmm, teeth are little and white, right? Looked at that way, the symbolic meaning is clear, but it requires a bit more explaining.

The psychology behind telling white lies is that they cast the dreamer in a better light. She does it with her boyfriend as a protective measure. She's self-conscious about her personal appearance—most young women are—especially with him. Teeth are a big part of one's appearance. She tells white lies to present herself better. It's a type of posturing, but telling even white lies pings her conscience and raises the potential for embarrassment if caught, and the mixture of knowing that she lies and why she does it is a potent psychological brew. Her dream dramatizes it as a torrent of blood, teeth, and gums gushing from her mouth that begins innocently as playing with a loose tooth, which means playing loose with the truth!

Loose teeth are weak, and now, we get into ideas such as "weak arguments" and saying things you don't mean—weak speech. Solid teeth correlate with solid arguments and feeling sure about what you say and how you say it. On the other hand, if you don't explain yourself well, the dream author reaches into its bag of tricks and pulls out imagery involving loose, weak, broken, and missing teeth.

Pulling on a loose tooth can mean that you need to say or relieve yourself of something. Perhaps you must force yourself to say it no matter how painful, like the meaning of the term "pulling teeth." Children are told not to pull out loose teeth, but how many of us avoid the temptation? It gives the dream author a clever association that comes in handy for telling stories about acting against advice, doing something you aren't supposed to, or wanting to do something because you are told not to.

Losing baby teeth is a rite of passage that a dream can use to symbolize ideas that relate to transformation, maturity, and adulthood. New teeth growing in may signal a time of growth, a new addition to your personality, and improved communication ability. But growth can be painful, and when we try to hold on to something past its expiration date, we may dream about trying to put back in teeth that have fallen out naturally.

Losing a tooth can mean "losing face"—you lose part of your face when a tooth falls out. Losing face means loss of status, prestige, and reputation. It can mean a blow to one's self-image. Those are big reasons why the ideas and associations related to losing face are found in many distressing dreams about losing teeth.

Losing teeth causes anxiety and stress. We use language such as "cracking up" and "falling apart" to describe the bad effects of anxiety and stress. The dream author visualizes the meaning as teeth cracking and falling apart, a common type of anxiety dream.

A tooth falling out on its own can mean that you allow something to come out of your mouth that you wish you could take back. That meaning is

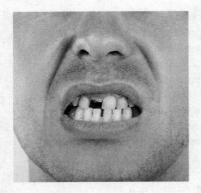

Anxiety and stress in one's life can instigate dreams about losing teeth, which is a sign of a loss of control over the course of one's life.

especially likely in dreams where you try to put back in teeth that have fallen out, and it applies to other regretful communications, like written ones. The simple idea is that something has gotten out that shouldn't have—it may cause regret, embarrassment, or trouble. On the other hand, pulling out your own teeth carries the idea of the difficulty in getting yourself to do something. It's the same meaning as the term "pulling teeth," and dreams visualize it.

An insidious urban myth makes people believe that dreaming about the loss of teeth means that someone important to them will soon die. It's insidious because it creates fear around a dream theme that's common, and it's untrue. However, dreaming about losing a molar can symbolize the loss of something that's deeply embedded in yourself and your life. Important people are embedded in your life, and the loss of them is major and painful, whether through death, separation, or circumstance. One woman dreamed about losing a molar after she had a miscarriage. The baby was deeply embedded in her womb, and like her mouth, the womb is a warm, dark, moist place.

Now you see how we begin with what the mouth and teeth do and then add in symbolic actions to convey more complex ideas. It enables us to interpret the symbolism of swallowing teeth. It can mean swallowing your words—holding back from speaking your truth or saying what you really think. When the dream teeth are broken and sharp, it adds the idea of holding back sharp words. Swallowing broken glass conveys the same idea.

A mouth full of broken or fallen-out teeth symbolically expresses the idea of the difficulty in saying something. The meaning is right there in the imagery—it's hard to talk when your mouth is full. Chewing on your thoughts translates in dream-speak as chewing on something, and when the situation involves difficulty in communicating, a dream may show it as chewing on a gummy substance. The situation is "sticky," and you're not sure how to say what needs to be said. Picking something out of your teeth can symbolize clearing up a situation, being self-conscious about something you said, or a pattern in your communication such as a pattern of lying or choking when the pressure is on. It may express self-consciousness about your appearance or being "picky" about something.

The symbolic combinations of the mouth, teeth, and other details go on and on. Take, for instance, a high-anxiety dream where the person finds a big gap between his teeth. He gets a checkup, and the dentist says that everything will be fine. The dream expresses his concern about a "gap" in his ability to pay for college, and the message is that he shouldn't worry about it. He's only a junior in high school and has time to figure it out. A gap in your teeth can symbolize a difference in opinion because it's a sort of gap between people. It can symbolize a gap in reasoning because teeth are part of the head, and the head is used for reasoning.

A trip to the dentist in a dream can mean that you're working on what you say and how you say it, correcting or improving your communication, or thinking through the right

> **When the dream teeth are broken and sharp, it adds the idea of holding back sharp words. Swallowing broken glass conveys the same idea.**

way to say something. Perhaps something needs to be "straightened out," or you would like to present yourself better. The dream's intensity corresponds with the intensity of the underlying situation, and it incorporates related thoughts and feelings. If you are very afraid, anxious, or stressed, it'll show.

Consider the difference between appearance and reality that a woman's dream dramatizes in a story about taking her new boyfriend to meet her girl-friends over dinner at a nice restaurant. Everything is great until her gorgeous boyfriend opens his mouth to speak and reveals a train wreck in there—it's not even true; the woman who had the dream wouldn't be caught dead dating a man with bad teeth! Instead, the dream highlights her concerns about how her girlfriends will perceive him because she knows he tends to put his foot in his mouth and say things that may embarrass her. The dream is helping her realize the potential for embarrassment if her girlfriends see deeper into her new boyfriend than what she's comfortable with. Teeth are great symbols to use in dreams about personal presentation and appearance and the difference between appearance and reality.

Bad teeth can mean bad prospects, outlooks, or attitudes.

False teeth in dreams can symbolize uttering falsehoods. That meaning is behind a dream where a young woman gets false teeth. She pulls them out of her mouth, and an awful smell punches her in the nose. A plethora of distressing emotions course through her. The dream imagery concisely sums up a memory from the previous day where she deliberately lied—said something false—to her mom, and she feels awful about it. The dream tells the story by using false teeth as a symbol and correlating the awful smell with her guilty feelings.

The first rule of dream interpretation is to consider the obvious meaning before launching off into an analysis of the symbolism and story. Dreams about teeth may have a physical source. Bruxism can cause recurring dreams about grinding and clenching teeth—it's what the person is doing in their sleep. Analysis of the symbolism may be helpful because while bruxism is a source of the dream imagery, the reasons behind it are likely to be emotional and psychological. Anger, stress, and anxiety are common culprits for grinding and clenching, but also think in terms of holding tightly to something or holding back from saying something. It's a common psychological response when the

> **Bruxism can cause recurring dreams about grinding and clenching teeth—it's what the person is doing in their sleep.**

ego is challenged and made uncomfortable, and it's the meaning behind the phrase "grit your teeth." You may be holding back from speaking your truth.

One man's dream about a visit to the dentist may have saved him from bad trouble with a tooth decaying beneath a filling. In his dream, he randomly sees a dentist's office and decides it would be a good idea to get a checkup. The dentist takes an X-ray of a specific molar and vaguely indicates a problem. The man wakes up with a strong feeling that he should visit his dentist. During the checkup, he points to the molar and asks for an X-ray, and that's how the dentist discovers the decay beneath the filling. By catching the problem early, he saved himself from a root canal or worse!

See also: Cancer/Disease, Falling, Vampires

TIDAL WAVES/TSUNAMIS/FLOODS

You are in a dream looking out at the ocean; you see a humongous wall of water barreling toward the shore with no way of escaping it—unless you have superpowers such as flight. But for most people, the only choice is to wait for the inevitable.

The inevitable.... Do you see that simple idea in the symbol of a tidal wave, tsunami, or flood? It may not be obvious when you're the tiny human about to be crushed by a wall of water, and it may not be what the dream really means, but you begin there. Start simply when interpreting a dream and test the possibilities that come to mind. You know subconsciously what the wave symbolizes. You sense and *feel* it, and your brain goes "ding!" when you think of the right meaning. If something big and inevitable is facing you, you may quickly find a parallel between it and the wave, like if it's the night before you're about to get married and something inside of you is screaming "help me!"— oh, yeah, it's obvious what the wave represents. But is it obvious why you feel that way? Probably not, judging by the powerful imagery the dream creates to get your attention. Dreams amplify when we aren't listening or getting the message. They maximize when we minimize. A tidal wave or tsunami is a maximized wave. Your work is just beginning after you see the obvious.

But the inevitable may not be obvious, and your work to find the meaning isn't easy when you're trying to see into your blind spots. You don't know or understand something, that much is clear. That's why you dream about it—to make clear to the conscious mind what the unconscious already knows and understands. And when you don't know or understand something, your job is to find out.

The ego is a small part of a big system, and it's the most important part for navigating the world of daily life. The ego is the decision maker. Now, imagine the person in a powerful position, the leader of a company, government, or military, and they think the entire organization owes its success and prosperity—even its existence—to them. Call it a God complex—it's common to one degree or another. The unconscious mind really doesn't care as long as the ego doesn't threaten the system—the psyche. But when the ego threatens the system, when it won't allow needed changes, when it stifles personal growth, the unconscious responds.

Hello, tidal wave!

The wave is the force of change, or it is forced change. Nothing less will do the trick—the unconscious has already tried milder dream imagery to get across its message. Now, the big guns come out. Forcing a needed change is a common reason for chronic nightmares about tidal waves, tsunamis, and floods. The ego's boundaries prevent the changes needed as a person develops and matures, and the psyche, as a self-regulating system, compensates to balance the system by overwhelming the boundaries if necessary.

Ironically, the opposite situation may be just as common. The ego's boundaries are weak and can't hold back the powerful forces of the unconscious. A shoreline is a common dream symbol for that boundary, and a huge body of water such as the ocean is a common symbol for the unconscious. Now you see why tidal waves, tsunamis, and floods are common symbols for pushing past the ego's boundaries. It's the perfect metaphor.

Tidal waves are an obvious symbol of abrupt, irresistible, and dramatic change, disasters that irrevocably alter an entire landscape.

Whether the boundary is too weak or too strong, the idea is the same, and it may not be an ego boundary that the dream means. It may be a personal boundary, and the wave or flood is the force that crosses it. Other symbols are at a dream's disposal for symbolizing a boundary: a door, a wall, a defensive position. Why choose a tidal wave instead as a symbol for crossing it? It may be to express the extreme force behind it or the feeling of threat. If it's a person who crosses your boundary, it may be fair to describe them as a "force of nature." If it's a fear, the fear is *really* big.

The big buildup—that's the symbolic idea behind a tidal wave, tsunami, or flood. You see the wave growing or a landscape overrun, and in your life, a confrontation is building. Emotions are coming to a head. They hit hard like a tidal wave or keep coming like a tsunami. A relationship that ends quickly and dramatically is like a tidal wave, but if the drama goes on and on, it's like a tsunami or flood. New phases of life are "sweeping changes" across the landscape of our lives. Symbolically, the wave is something that sweeps in and impacts in a big way, and it parallels situations and conditions such as job loss, bad illness, or unplanned pregnancy.

> **The associations between emotions and water are many, and they intersect with the associations for a flood, tidal wave, or tsunami.**

For one woman, "big decision" is the idea behind the wave in her dream. She looks out at the ocean from her apartment balcony and sees a humongous wave, but it stands still, looming in the distance. It's a symbol for a decision that's "on hold." She hasn't been in a new relationship since her divorce, and recently, her neighbor made an offer to start a "friends with benefits" arrangement. It's intriguing but also complicated. She can't decide, and her dream sums up the situation as an unmoving wave. A new relationship would mean a big change for her, and her dream reflects it in the size of the wave. After analyzing the dream, she decided to go for it.

The associations between emotions and water are many, and they intersect with the associations for a flood, tidal wave, or tsunami. When you are at a "breaking point," a dream may show it as a wave breaking or breaking apart whatever stands in its way. When you say "wave after wave of emotions," it's a tsunami or flood of emotions. When emotions overwhelm, the water overwhelms, and its darkness may symbolize their dark and murky nature. We say that emotions pour out of us, and the dream author makes the connection with water that pours out. A trickle of water may symbolize the shedding of a few tears, but a wall of water is an outpouring of tears and related emotions such as sorrow and shame.

Take, for instance, a woman's recurring dreams that a tidal wave is about to hit her home, and she reacts the same way every time by retreating upstairs and barricading herself in her bedroom. The wave hits, and water floods under the bedroom door. She stands on top of her bed to escape it. The water keeps rising, inundating the bedroom. She's terrified of it touching her, and at the last moment, she always wakes up, still hearing her screams echoing in her mind.

The recurring dreams dramatize her emotional life, and fear is the word that summarizes the situation. Everyday sorts of emotions are manageable for her, but long ago, she experienced severe emotional turmoil and never dealt with it. The dreams express the dynamics as a wall of water that reaches her home from a distance. Her home is the point in time where she lives presently, and the water comes from a distance because the emotions originate distantly in time. The water is murky because so are the emotions. She's terrified of reexperiencing the emotions, so in the dream, the water terrifies her. She doesn't want to "touch it," meaning touch the emotions it represents.

In another woman's recurring dreams about tidal waves and floods, the one word that summarizes the situation is "devastation." The waves and floods devastate her dreams' landscape, and it symbolizes her psychological landscape. Plus, she has experienced losses and misfortunes that left her life in ruins.

Symbolically, an outpouring of water applies to emotions and to contents of the unconscious that pour into the mental space occupied by the conscious mind. But we also use the word "outpouring" to describe surges of creativity and productivity, and the subsequent dream imagery and scenarios that use it are generally milder in comparison to the above imagery and scenarios. The difference is found in the subjective experience. When an outpouring is manageable, the flood in a dream is more manageable. But when a creative or productive outpouring overwhelms a person, the flood is overwhelming. The same idea applies to the other uses of the symbolism discussed above.

The body reports to the mind while asleep, and dreams translate the reports into imagery. Dreams about floods of nasty, brown water may precede a diarrhea attack. Yellow water is associated with the need to urinate.

If the flood in your dream contains brown water, it might be your body warning your subconscious of an impending attack of diarrhea.

Sounds from your sleeping environment can seep into your dreams and translate into your dreams as imagery related to water, such as the sounds of a toilet flushing or rain falling. News about flooding may seep into dreams, too. When dreams about a disaster follow news about a disaster that doesn't personally affect you, it may not have symbolism specific to the disaster. Instead, it refers to what you were thinking and feeling when you heard the news.

For example, a teenage female dreamed about a flood the night after watching a news report about heavy flooding. The flooding had no personal impact on her, but hearing about it gave her anxiety, and that's what she feels while dreaming. But the anxiety has nothing to do with the flooding; it stems from what she was feeling as she watched the news report. She felt anxious about her appearance in comparison with the beautiful newswoman. Her dream is about the trigger for her anxiety when she sees a beautiful woman.

Dreams about flooding and related disasters may correlate with actual experiences. For one man, his flooding dreams occurred during times of financial stress, correlating with an experience long ago when his home flooded and cost him heavily not only in terms of money but the time and energy to rebuild.

For another man, dreaming about finding signs of flood damage in a home he was considering buying correlated with his thoughts about what would be required to rebuild his marriage. The new home in the dream symbolizes the new space where he'd like to move the relationship, and the flood damage symbolizes the damage to it, which goes with them wherever they go in the relationship with no escaping it.

See also: Apocalypses, Crashes, Falling, God, Storms/Blizzards/Hurricanes/Tornadoes, Volcanoes/Earthquakes

VOLCANOES/EARTHQUAKES

What do volcanoes and earthquakes have in common? Rumbling and shaking. And what do rumbling and shaking have in common? They are signs of trouble coming. A shake-up. An explosion, calamity, or disaster. In dreams, it's shown visually and even felt physically but meant figuratively.

The author of your dreams can run with those associations to create symbolism and stories about something that rocks your world or threatens to.

It's great metaphorical imagery, and volcanoes and earthquakes as metaphors are similar in many ways and different in ways that are handy for matching with personal and situational dynamics.

Take the metaphor of the volcano that blows its top. A huge explosion releases the buildup of pressure. We all know of situations in life where we use the metaphor—maybe you have experienced it firsthand. The dream author also knows when to use it, and in true dream style, the imagery is spectacular. Boom goes the volcano!

The boom happens when tempers flare, emotions explode, arguments blow up, and feelings sizzle. The top of a volcano is its head, and the meaning is rather obvious when the top blows. Somebody lost their head! We use that language for major meltdowns and manic episodes, and dreams do, too, by showing the meaning rather than saying it.

The closeness to the action says a lot about the underlying dynamics and its personal impact. Are you in the thick of it or outside of the blast zone? Are you feeling the reverberations and seeing the repercussions? Is lava raining down? You could say that the lava is the fallout, and the fallout is the aftereffect of a blowup.

In one woman's dream, lava explodes from the mouth of a volcano as she's driving nearby. Chunks of hot rock fall from the sky and hit her car. She starts to panic, but suddenly, her female cousin is in the passenger's seat and points to the mouth of a cave where they can shelter. She drives into it and looks over to thank her cousin, but now, a little boy is sitting there in her place.

Her dream dramatizes a situation that occurred the day prior to the dream when she witnessed a violent argument. That's what the explosion from the "mouth" of the volcano means. The dream reflects her proximity to the argument by showing her driving close to the volcano when it explodes. The fallout that hits her car symbolizes the argument's "impact" on her—the "sizzling" words that the people "hurled." The outside of the car symbolizes her protective emotional skin, which took a beating, so while dreaming, she's searching for a way of protecting herself. A basic function of dreaming is to help us search within ourselves for answers and solutions to things that are unresolved from the previous day.

The next scene is the resolution. Driving into the cave symbolizes turning within oneself, a tried-and-true response to emotional and fearful situations by focusing mental attention inward. She associates her cousin with the qual-

Violent, heated, and explosive, a volcanic eruption in a dream can be associated with extreme anger, pain, and panic.

ity of being coolheaded, and that's why she appears seemingly randomly in the car and points to safety. Her cousin is an example of someone adept at handling emotionally charged situations. The little boy symbolizes the woman's sensitive nature and serves as a reminder of what she's really protecting. The transformation from cousin to little boy visualizes a process of inner transformation.

With a volcano, much of the action is below the surface—it's unseen and unnoticed until erupting at the surface. For example, one's true feelings finally surface, and boy, are they hot! An earthquake is a better metaphor when emotions are hidden, internalized, and misdirected—they remain below the surface but are felt up top. An earthquake is a release of pressure that causes spectacular effects, like a volcano. It rumbles and shakes and then erupts suddenly after a long buildup, sometimes without advance warning. No wonder we compare volcanic eruptions to sudden emotional eruptions.

Another reason why the dream author chooses an earthquake as a symbol is that two big objects or forces are clashing, such as when the head wants one thing and the heart wants another or when neighbors are in dispute and the border between their properties is the fault line. The fault line is where tension builds, and it's the weak spot that suddenly gives way.

The ground moves beneath you during an earthquake. Think of it in terms of your stability; an earthquake symbolizes instability. The idea applies broadly to situations and conditions: mental and emotional stability, financial and job stability, relationship and family stability, home and health stability. A dream may reference what's unstable in your life by putting you in a related setting, such as a workplace or family home. If the ground beneath it shakes, it's unstable.

Groundedness is another related idea. When you are grounded, you are stable because of deep connection and depth. Take, for instance, the dream a man experiences where he's walking along the busy city streets near where he lives when an earthquake strikes. Before he can think of a safe place to go, the asphalt around him crumbles, and he's left standing on a pillar of rock above a lake of lava. He stays perfectly still, afraid that any movement will tip the pillar and plunge him into the lava, and he doubts that he can remain that way until help arrives.

> **The ground moves beneath you during an earthquake. Think of it in terms of your stability; an earthquake symbolizes instability.**

His dream dramatizes a condition of his inner life. He'll be going about life as usual, shown in the dream as the city setting that's familiar from his daily routine, when suddenly, he feels like he's on a distant planet—it feels unreal. He wonders, *What am I really doing here?* It's an existential question that can be phrased as, *What's the point of life?* The point, as far as he can tell, is to be busy, but in the back of his mind, he knows that being busy is a circular track that always returns to where it starts. Life has no meaning—it's the proverbial hamster wheel. One day, the wheel will stop turning, and all the busyness will mean nothing after he's dead.

The ground crumbling away beneath him is a visual metaphor for becoming ungrounded by questioning his fundamental assumptions about life and finding that they're insubstantial.

The dream's final scene where he stands perfectly still atop the pillar shows him the situation and the path to its resolution. The basic idea of the imagery is that he feels utterly alone when he stops his busy mind and really considers his situation in life. He feels no real connection to his environment or to his inner being, and now, a resolution enters the picture. When a person feels centered, it doesn't matter where they are or what they're doing—the point of their existence is found in that centered place within them. *To be or not to be?* is no longer a question.

Now, picture the man standing atop the pillar. First of all, it says "centered"—he's literally at its center. Second of all, it says "alone"—he's literally alone, which in the end, we all are in the sense that we must answer the questions about our existence. And third of all, it says "stillness"—that's the state of mind he needs. The lava surrounding him symbolizes the idea of annihilation. He could easily lose himself completely if he doesn't find stable, centered ground within himself, and the dream paints a scenario where he has no choice if he wants to survive. It's a classic example of a nightmare's bitter medicine.

For another man who dreamed about a major earthquake, it happens while he's at work and symbolizes the rumors that layoffs are coming. The rumors really shook him up. In his dream, aftershocks follow the earthquake, reflecting his internal condition as shocking thoughts struck him one after another: how will he manage things with his family; are his savings enough to get them by; what else could he do for employment?

You could say that the layoff rumors set off a seismic shift inside of him. Also, forces are moving like tectonic plates beyond his control. The idea stretches further to correspond with situations like a major shift in attitude or opinion. An earthquake is a good symbol for it because it's a seismic shift. An earthquake can mean that something about your world is changing or threatens to change in a big way. A volcano, on the other hand, can symbolize the same idea but corresponds with hotter and more explosive situations and conditions.

When earthquakes and volcanoes flatten and destroy structures in dreams, think first in terms of belief and thought structures. When a new building replaces an old one, the old one must come down, and the same goes for new structures of the mind and personality. In terms of personal development, we may go through times of reevaluating everything we think we know and consequently feel like we're falling apart—and you know by now how a dream visualizes that feeling. Dramatize it! Flattened structures may also convey the simple ideas of devastation and loss.

The man who had the above dream feels shaky inside. That's the simple idea of the earthquake and its aftershocks, and it's a common meaning of the symbolism. He's also in a state of emergency, and his dream tells the story by creating an emergency that corresponds symbolically with the situation. Dreams spotlight our internal conditions, especially our emotions, and dramatically express them.

Grumbling is a situation that a dream may translate as a minor earthquake. Volcanoes, too, grumble when barely active. It's a dream's way of saying that something barely affects you or has a minor impact. However, it may also be a warning sign of something bigger brewing. Deep down within you, it's coming to life.

Dreams anticipate what's ahead in life, and many of our cognitive processes do, too. Those processes are mostly subconscious, and dreams bring important subconscious processes to your attention. Anticipation theory asserts that anticipation determines outcomes. In other words, what you anticipate is a big factor in determining your future. The rumble of an earthquake or volcano may be an anticipation of trouble ahead, and the anticipation may contribute to trouble materializing. Therefore, it's wise to respond by heading off the trou-

Earthquakes necessitate a rebuilding in the aftermath, and so they might be a symbol that you need to get rid of the old "buildings" in your life in order to start anew.

ble and searching within yourself to see if you are the source of it. People who always expect trouble have an uncanny way of making it materialize.

Anticipation builds, and in that sense, a volcano or earthquake is a good metaphor for a buildup of anticipation. For example, the anticipation of sex. It's a pressure that builds internally, then (hopefully) releases with a bang! Dreams that anticipate something good and beneficial tend to be very different from ones that anticipate something bad and destructive.

Earthquakes and volcanoes are features of some apocalypse dreams, and this book includes a fascinating discussion in the entry on Apocalypses. A dream's major features are probably meaningful but may be part of a bigger picture or larger idea such as apocalypse, separation, loss, collapse, anxiety, fear, dread, entrapment, and being "under fire."

Take, for instance, the dream where a woman is going up in an elevator when an earthquake strikes and the elevator stops between floors, trapping her inside. The earthquake is part of a bigger picture about wanting to "move up" in life. Being trapped in an elevator, a means for moving up, symbolizes the idea of feeling stuck and not making progress. The earthquake sets the scene for the main action of getting stuck and its personal meaning for her.

Many of our most powerful dreams dramatize the ego's relationship with other parts of the psyche—the deeper parts. Earthquakes and volcanoes result from deep forces coming to the surface, and in psychological terms, the surface is ego territory and the planet is the psyche. The ego senses something going on "down there"—in the unconscious—and its reaction determines how a dream unfolds. A bad reaction or negative stance is nightmare fuel because the psyche uses dreams to compensate for imbalance. Reacting by saying "I don't care" is akin to ignoring trouble in an important relationship—how does that usually work out? At that point, you can only go one way: go down within oneself to confront what's being avoided or hidden and is unknown.

Such eruptions from the unconscious may occur at the worst possible time—when stress is high, problems are mounting, and the ego has other priorities and shit to deal with. But from the psyche's point of view, the timing couldn't be better. Perhaps the solutions to the ego's problems are down inside of oneself. In that sense, the eruption is a slap in the face to bring you back to reality.

The internal pressure may result from stuffing too much down inside of you, and the eruption is the psyche vomiting it up. That circumstance is quite commonly the reason for chronic nightmares that feature eruptions and powerful shaking. The person can't take it anymore. One man's dream told the story as a volcano of shit erupting from his toilet. He'd stuffed so much (shit) down within himself and held down so much pressure, its release was like a bomb going off!

Finally, an earthquake or volcano in a dream may be a response to something that's heard, felt, or experienced while sleeping; for example, a low-flying helicopter rattles your house, sparking a dream about an earthquake, or a fever ignites a dream about a volcano. A volcano is also a great metaphor for hot and turbulent conditions inside of the body—maybe you shouldn't have eaten those hot peppers. Hot lava going up a volcano's conduit (think esophagus) and entering its throat is a picture of the burning feeling of acid reflux, a condition commonly experienced while sleeping.

See also: Apocalypses, Fire, Hell, Storms/Blizzards/Hurricanes/Tornadoes

Spiritual Nightmares and Dreams

Body, mind, spirit—the first two are acknowledged as areas of life and need. We need to nourish and support the body and mind—this is clear. But spirit? For the most part, spirit as a part of oneself that survives physical death is not acknowledged or accepted rationally, yet spirituality has been part of the human experience for as long as humans have been around.

Dr. Carl Jung's psychology acknowledges that humans need what spiritual experience offers: a life of meaning and purpose, an experience of oneself as more than a body and mind, and a connection to something greater. The very structure of the psyche demands it because at the core of everyone is an archetype that originates beyond body and mind. He calls it the Self, the central and most important archetype of all, which psychologist Robert Moore says is a superstructure composed of four primary archetypes. The relationship between the ego and the Self is best described in spiritual terms, and dreams are the primary way of experiencing it.

While dreaming, the ego enters a space with different rules than ordinary waking life. There, the Self can speak to the gestalt or wholeness of a person, which includes spirit along with body and mind. The Self views each as equally important despite the bias against nourishing and supporting a person's spiritual life. And because the psyche is a self-regulating system that uses dreams to compensate for what's lacking or imbalanced in it and spiritual life is the most likely to be lacking or imbalanced, the stage is set for the most powerful and impactful dreams revolving around spiritual themes and ideas.

But just because a dream features something spiritual doesn't mean that spiritual life is the source or subject. Dreams can just as easily use the symbols as part of a story that has little or nothing to do with the spirit. Dreams use associations to create the meaning in symbols, whether it's associations with cars and people or with God and Satan. The story may go deeper in some cases, but we always begin exploring the meaning of a dream from that baseline.

> **Dreams use associations to create the meaning in symbols, whether it's associations with cars and people or with God and Satan.**

Some traditions in dream interpretation view all dreams through a religious or spiritual lens, and because dreams layer meaning and consciousness experiences itself as an intangible thing having a physical experience, they could just as well know a truth that's hidden from rational inquiry. Unfortunately, that "we know better" stance is also used as an excuse to impose interpretations with a religious or spiritual slant. Remember always that you are the only one who knows what your dreams mean.

Spiritual dreams can be slippery. Interpret them for yourself. You're about to learn how.

DEMONS

Like other evil characters in dreams, demons are misunderstood as the presence of spiritual evil. It must be bad if a dream features demons, but they are characters in a story and must be understood as actors playing roles who just happen to be cast almost exclusively in horror flicks and nightmares.

The dream author uses associations to create the symbolism of demons and inserts the character into a story. To see the symbolism and understand the story, you step back and observe objectively—difficult to do with a type of dream character that carries many bad implications, but otherwise, you are likely to get lost in your subjective thoughts and feelings and fail to see the hidden meaning.

The demon is a symbol. Start there. Make associations with the character—the first thoughts that come to mind as you think about it. Oftentimes, your initial thoughts provide the path to the meaning, provided that your approach is objective. Your next step is to compare your associations with the context of how a dream presents a demon as part of a story, the role it plays, and the patterns in your dream life that feature similar imagery and themes.

Like nearly all things in dreams, a demon is a symbol, one that is often misunderstood.

Take, for instance, the dream a man had where he is trapped in Hell. Unseen demons in high guard towers prevent his escape. He finds a tunnel that leads under the walls and follows it to an exit on the side of a mountain face. Below him is a steep drop with nothing to grab on to. The implication is that he must jump if he wants to escape.

Notice the role the demons play as his prison guards. They are not interacted with or even seen. Their physical remoteness expresses an idea that's important for understanding what they symbolize. Compare that scenario with what they're not; they're not slave drivers lashing him with whips. That imagery would imply something closer personally to him, like a slave-driving inner voice or an overbearing boss. No; the demons are distant, and they symbolize the man's beliefs that imprison him within a mental structure, symbolized as the prison. He grew up in a family with rigid beliefs about what makes a "real man" and what he is supposed to think and feel. It's a mental prison, one that's so old and ingrained that it's distant in time, thus the dream shows it as distant walls.

He has learned to see his beliefs for what they are and found a route within his own mind to escape them, the tunnel out of Hell, but now he is at an impasse, symbolized as the long drop down the side of the mountain. He escaped the old belief structure without a new one to replace it. Metaphorically, he stands at a precipice and faces a leap of faith.

Demons and beliefs walk hand in hand because people either believe or don't believe in them or don't know either way. It's probably a negative belief if a demon is cast as a symbol for it. On the other hand, an angel is more likely to symbolize a positive belief, but it really depends on the person and the dynamics involved. For example, a belief that you are cunning, clever, and powerful is inherently positive, and a dream could symbolize it in the form of a demon instead of an angel because of associations between those qualities and demons. But another reason why a dream could choose a demon to symbolize a belief about oneself is because it inflates your ego or brings out your dark side. Now the clever casting of the role is obvious.

Contrast the dream about demonic prison guards with a recurring one that a person had featuring vicious demons as overlords that torment and torture him: scenes of flesh ripped and torn; people burning eternally in liquid fire; his loved ones targeted for especially brutal treatment. The dreamer is helpless, and his demonic overlords delight in terrorizing him. His punishment, seemingly, will never end.

On the nightmare scale, this one ranks a 10/10. Analyze its story and notice that the demons are main characters—they are shown in detail and drive the action as opposed to being unseen and not part of the action. Based on how the dream presents the imagery, it's safe to say that something severe is happening in this person. The dream author deliberately created scenes that symbolically express an idea that we can summarize simply as "a tormented soul."

Life inside of the man is a living hell, driven by endless guilt over what his torment is doing to himself and the people closest to him—it's like an eternal punishment, and demons are your characters to play the role. The nightmares occur in a setting that's enclosed, in Earth's center or Hell, a way of saying "inside of you" or "inescapable." It's a symbolic representation of his inner life and a metaphorical expression of its conditions. The recurrence of the dreams suggests an ongoing situation in his life and the need to focus there for resolution.

But why torment him with such a nightmare if it's not going to help him? The nightmares offer no resolution or relief in their content, and that seems cruel, like pouring acid on one thirsting for water. But let's assume that Dr. Carl Jung is correct when he says that all dreams—*even the worst nightmares*—are for our benefit. Now we can see how the nightmare may help him by starkly framing his situation. His nightmare is self-created through the interaction of his ego with his unconscious mind. The unconscious is objective when it says, *This is how it is; this is you reflected in the mirror.* When a situation is as bad as it gets, you only have two ways to go from there. Either dig your grave and crawl into it or fight for your life with everything you've got.

> It's not the nightmare's fault when a person's life is such a mess. You can't blame a mirror for what it reflects.

It is cold, Saturnian wisdom and the paradox of Dionysus, the bringer of both despair and ecstasy. Lucifer and Dionysus are bringers of light. Embrace life and all that it is—that's what nightmares do by backing us into a corner in the hopes that the bitter medicine will break the hold of whatever drives us to ruin. Pain and angst give way to joy and unlimited freedom. It's not the nightmare's fault when a person's life is such a mess. You can't blame a mirror for what it reflects.

Picture the demon (or demons) from your dream and ask, what do I see about myself? Observe it objectively, separated from the powerful emotions and connotations. It's going to be difficult—by nature, dreams show us what we don't know or understand; it's unconscious and trying to become conscious. When a dream pictures it as a powerful demon and presents it in a powerful story, something big and important is at hand in your life.

Amplify—that's one reason why the imagery is so dramatic. Dreams amplify to get your attention, to express urgency, to straighten out priorities, and especially to counter imbalance in the psyche. In the image of a demon, you may see a dark personality trait, a bad attitude, an intractable problem or situation, an emotional disturbance, disregard for your own welfare or the welfare of others, or something that looms over you like a black wave. Dreams amplify for good reason, and you can bet that something is out of whack if the imagery powerfully affects you because dreams amplify for good reason. It may be what's needed to shock you out of a stupor or make you realize just how bad or destructive something really is.

The exaggeration of dream imagery is a fitting comparison for whatever it symbolizes, a metaphor that matches up cleverly with it. The mistake when interpreting dreams featuring demons is to think they're a statement about you. It may fit symbolically with something about you or your life, but it's figurative and not literal, except in rare cases that we will discuss later.

A demon is a fitting symbol for fear, so figure out why the author of the dream thinks it's the right symbol to match with the fear it symbolizes. You can get a look inside of the author's mind if it uses demons, plural. They are "legion," and when a person faces a plague of fears, their dreams can reflect it as a plague of demons. Fear is like Pandora's Box; open it, and out pops all sorts of nasties. A singular fear, on the other hand, is not a plague of demons. But the *symptoms* of a fear may be legion: anxiety, paralysis, self-criticism. It's not to say that demons automatically symbolize many fears, but perhaps they symbolize many symptoms, consequences, or causes.

In the example where the man dreams that demons guard his prison, they are many and unseen, symbolizing the complex nature of the belief structure that imprisons him. We may say that something is a belief, singular, but it has many aspects, plural, and that's why the dream says many demons in the plural.

For a woman with an eating disorder, the legion of demons in her nightmares are the various voices in her head that drive the disorder: "You're fat," says one. "You're ugly," says another. "You're lazy, and that's why you're fat and ugly," says a third, and on and on. A variation of the idea is shown in the dream a woman experienced where demons torment her with insults and criticism, and she sees a hideously ugly reflection of herself in a mirror. Each time a demon lashes her with an insult, a new wound appears on her body, symbolizing the wounds to her emotional body that she inflicts on herself through harsh self-criticism. She picks at every perceived flaw and thinks her flaws are legion. With that insight, it's obvious why many demons populate her dream instead of just one or two.

Life can be hell, and when external situations and conditions are hellish, queue the demons in your dreams. It may not be hellish by objective standards,

Being teased or tormented in real life by mean people can translate into a vision of demons in a person's dreams.

but that doesn't matter to the dream author that creates dream imagery subjectively. So, for instance, the person you can't stand or the problem that won't go away is hellish, and the dream author uses demons to tell the story. Abusive and traumatic situations, especially, are prime material for demonic dreams. They make life a living hell.

But the intensity of dreams depends on the person and how they handle their life, especially their emotions. Studies of dream content and how it corresponds with mental health show conclusively that the better a person manages their emotions, the less intense and more pleasant their dreams are. Imagine Napoleon returning after a long day on the battlefield experiencing intense emotions and sleeping like a baby. Other soldiers in the same battle may return so traumatized that they never sleep well again. Their "inner demons" forever haunt them.

Inner demons—it is perhaps the most common source of nightmares about demons. Anything inside of a person that haunts, taunts, torments, hurts, or wounds is ripe for symbolizing as a demon—or *demons* if the torments and wounds are many. The job of the dream author is to give form and expression to what is intangible. Throughout known history, people have described inner torment and distress in demonic terms because it captures what they feel and perceive. The author of dreams merely follows our lead. But another reason why the author chooses demons to play the role is that they can be invisible, and emotions and feelings are invisible, too. You experience them, but you can't point and say "here's my emotion" except to where you feel it in your body. In the same way, a demon can be invisible but you know it's there, and if it possesses you, it's inside of your body.

Take anxiety, for example. It's invisible, and the dream author needs to visualize it or at least refer to it. Bad anxiety is a constant torment, and in the person's mind, it's like an invisible presence that's nothing but bad. Dread is another feeling that can have mysterious origins within a person and that dreams cast in dark tones. And let's not forget the feeling of being lied to! It's something you sense, and demons are master liars.

When something is wrong or feels that way and it eludes explanation, dark dreams express the dynamic, and demons are apt representations of something that is wrong or, at least, isn't right. We may not know the source or be able to explain what we sense and why, so the dream author creates a demonic presence to symbolize it. In those dreams, we may sense it but not see it, reflecting our ambiguity about and lack of awareness of the dynamics involved.

A demon is a superb symbol for temptation—temptation is how evil beings bring about the ruin of souls. Plus, a person's temptation may be "all in their head," and a demon is a symbol for anything that gets into your head like that. The temptation to steal, for example, begins as covetous thoughts.

Personal boundaries also exist in your head. You say that *this* is the line that won't be crossed, but it's a mental construct, and the author's job is to give it a physical form or express the idea through a scenario. Take, for example, a dream that represents a personal boundary as the front door of a woman's

> **A demon is a superb symbol for temptation— temptation is how evil beings bring about the ruin of souls.**

home. It's a great symbol for a boundary because a door is a boundary line where you can choose what to allow in and what to keep out. In her dream, demons stand outside her door and taunt her, but she feels confident that her door will keep them out. But then, she turns around, and they are already inside her home, symbolizing the crossing of her boundary. When something or someone crosses her boundaries, it feels like a personal violation, which is why the dream chooses demons for the role. They are serial violators.

The line between right and wrong is another boundary and mental construct, and demons are on the wrong side of the line.

The shadow of the ego is another source of demonic dream imagery, and the reasons are obvious when you understand the shadow as the ego's dark side. First of all, you could describe demons and their behavior as the ego running amuck—they are strongly egotistical. Second of all, demons work in the shadows. And third of all, the extreme manifestations of the shadow are the driving force behind the evils that human beings inflict on other people, the world, and themselves. The parallels are so obvious, it's no wonder why dreams symbolize the shadow of the ego as demonic.

But evil exists in the world and in people in the forms of psychopathy, aberration, extreme egomania, and narcissism. It's evil! When we brush up against it, whether through direct contact or something such as a true crime story, our dreams respond, and evil is the forte of demons. We often attribute evil deeds and thoughts to demons and, indeed, investigate the history of serial killers and their statements about what drives them to kill, and you find demons. And not personal demons—they say it's real demons, though their psychiatrists may disagree. Either way, the association between evil and demons is particularly strong.

American serial killer Dennis Rader is a well-known case. He said he was possessed by demons and told his psychiatrist that he had torture chambers in his dreams. He claimed it was the source of his idea to include binding and torturing his victims before sexually assaulting and killing them. But it's unclear whether he meant his sleep dreams, his fantasies, or both.

> **American serial killer Dennis Rader ... said he was possessed by demons and told his psychiatrist that he had torture chambers in his dreams.**

Understanding the true nature of demons in dreams requires discernment. You may read the above example, compare it with the demons in your dreams, and jump to a conclusion that something truly evil is haunting or possessing you. Your demons haunt you with violent sexual fantasies, for example, but is it truly demonic, or is it a repressed aspect of your sexuality? Is it an addiction to sex, pornography, or a drug that metaphorically is like your demonic lover? Is it raging pain, a raging ego, or a raging sense of injustice? Is it an exaggerated depiction of how you feel? Is it sleep paralysis or another type of dream-related hallucination? Demonic possession in dreams is widely misunderstood as literal when it's meant figuratively, such as when a person is possessed by a dark idea, mood, feeling, or compulsion.

A guilty conscience; a repressed aspect of oneself; an emotional disturbance; a dark side of life or oneself—those examples and others are the true demons in your dreams.

A case that could be confused for true evil played out in the recurring dreams a man had about a humanoid demon he interacted with directly and extensively. Over the span of a couple of years, the frequency of the dreams grew until becoming a nightly occurrence. In a dream that occurred late in the series and is typical of their content, he's a spectator watching a pale, humanoid demon construct a world for itself. Crimson swirls of grass; rocks with bright-red veins protruding from the ground; giant blocks with carved symbols and unholy abominations surrounding a massive, white throne on which the demon sits and controls every corner of its domain. The dreamer, a passive observer, hears agonized human moans and sees people impaled on stakes, some lifeless, some crying. It scares him.

Around the room, he notices human dolls. Some are on shelves, some limp around. They are well-fed, spotlessly clean, and fully clothed. Then, he sees a man pinned to a table and the pale demon standing over him. The demon tells the man that it wants his skin—all of it. It grabs a scalpel, makes an incision, and peels off the skin from top to bottom, laughing maniacally as the man screeches. Left on the table is a bloody mass of exposed muscle, fat, and organs. The demon gleefully parades around its "skinsuit." But it's not finished.

Now the man, still alive, is tied to a pole, fully exposed without his protective skin and feeling every breath of wind like spikes jammed into his body. The demon cuts up the skinsuit and sews it back together so it can fit inside. The feet are its shoes, the legs and waist are its pants, the torso and arms are its shirt, and the face is its mask. The demon laughs loudly and joyfully, mocking the man's pleas for help. "No one can save you! You are in my playground, where I have absolute control!"

The scene shifts to show the man inside a glass tube shaped around him like a body. "I built this machine just for you," the demon says, hinting darkly at what's to come. "It will purify you by removing all the filth from your heart." The machine then fills with water, turning red with the man's blood. The man shrieks, and the demon continues its monologue. "It is fun to watch you cry— I make it into music—the beauty of it is inspiring. Your kind disgusts me. You are filthy and corrupted. My world is sheer hatred for you. Every square inch of this dimension is nothing but my hatred, and here I will make your kind kill, rape, cut, slice, and devour each other! Then, I will drag all of you into my world."

The monstrous demon turns the machine up to full power and watches the man's chest. A blue light shines from the heart. Satisfied, the monster turns off the machine and gently removes the man, then takes him to a room where it transforms him into a life-sized doll with buttons for eyes and patches of skin sewn together from other humans—he's a doll like the others in the opening scene. He wears beige slacks and a vest over a light-blue Marcus Regency shirt. Not a spot of blood mars the outfit.

Holy smokes, what a nightmare! The long and graphic description gives you a taste of the experience. Now, imagine having such night-

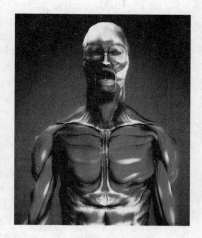

One poor man dreamed of a demon that cuts off his skin and then wears it as a skinsuit.

mares night after night and being lucid during most of them. Or maybe you don't have to imagine it because your nightmares are similar.

It's a tall order to be objective when analyzing a nightmare with horrifying content, but the man does it readily, and after careful consideration, he says that the demon is a manifestation of his dark side. The belief that gives it life is that humans are terrible, but he wants to be close with them despite it. The paradox is epic. The skinsuit the demon makes symbolically expresses the idea—a theme also found in *The Silence of the Lambs*. People are objects, and for this man, they are objects of his deepest love and utter hatred. As the vile, filthy beings they are, he can't ever be close with them unless they are purified first. The desire to be so close to another person that you are inside their skin is the deepest yearning for love, and it's infantile because it refers to life in the womb as part of the mother's body.

> **A glimmer of hope is that he is aware that the demon is his dark side and the roots of it are in his childishness. An analyst may be able to lead him out of the darkness.**

The psychology behind the nightmares really shows itself in the content. The demon expresses through its deeds and words what's happening internally in the man. The dolls, especially, fit a pattern found in neuroses and nasty complexes where a person is twisted by their mother's withholding of love and learns that they must be perfect to receive it—depicted in the dream as the dolls in the opening scene and making the victim into a perfect doll in the final scene. The mother or a mother figure may change diapers with utter disgust and react to every spot and blemish as if the Devil itself just appeared. People who have not lived through or been close to such circumstances can scarcely imagine what it's like.

Inside of the person's psyche, it creates a world under the control of their dark side. In the dream, the demon says that its world is a domain it has created where it's in full control. In psychoanalytic terms, it's a split-off aspect of the person's psyche, and it doesn't take a psychologist to recognize the potential for psychosis. The man is a walking time bomb and is perhaps one triggering event—like, say, falling in love, then being dumped—away from acting out the fantasies of his "inner demon."

A glimmer of hope is that he is aware that the demon is his dark side and the roots of it are in his childishness. An analyst may be able to lead him out of the darkness. By integrating the demon consciously, it may become his daimon, a Greek word that means the energy or entity that gives us our fate or destiny. It's the "inner genius." Dr. Carl Jung refers to it as something alien in the unconscious, archetypal and numinous and driven by an imperative and a higher authority far greater than the human intellect. Because it is autonomous, it behaves within us like a god—do you see it reflected in the dream above? Famous people in history who have claimed to be possessed by their daimon are Greek philosopher Socrates, German poet Goethe, French ruler Napoleon, and Dr. Jung.

The path to harnessing this tremendous energy is to recognize it as something of your own. Its origins may be in the heart of a star or a supernova, but when it enters the psyche, it's in your domain. With superhuman willpower or just the tenderness of a loving heart, it may be tamed and integrated consciously, turning the consciousness of the person into a force of nature with access to powers that are inconceivable to the uninitiated. The stakes are all or nothing, and the prize is to become godlike in the sense of rising far above the ordinary human condition. But first, the person must crawl through its darkest, ugliest depths.

Use the list below to continue exploring this subject.

See also: Armageddon, Dark Magicians, Devils, Evil, Hell, Lucifer, Possession

DEVILS

While dreams can use devils and demons interchangeably, they usually have reasons for choosing one or the other as a character in a story. First of all, a devil is more personal, and second of all, it's singular—"the Devil"— whereas demons are less personal and tend to come in groups or legions. The mythology and theology of demons and devils distinguishes them as separate types of beings, but the dream author takes its first cues from their interchangeable use in our language and the stories we tell.

This book has already covered a lot of the same ground in the entry for demons as what can be said about a devil as a symbol and as a character playing a role in a story. For this discussion, the emphasis begins with a devil's personal nature—it implies something close and personal to the dreamer, like the dream about being raped by Satan, which dramatizes the personal and severe nature of a conflict with a classmate. Satan is right for the role because the situation is as personal as it gets. Plus, the Devil is God's adversary, and the classmate is the dreamer's adversary.

Devils are at the top of Hell's hierarchy. Demons are right under them. Here, we get into the potential for confusion because only one Devil—Lucifer or Satan—exists along with many demons, but popular culture offers diverse devil imagery and may not differentiate "a devil" from "the Devil." When the dream author needs to express the idea of a greater power, it has a devil to use as a symbol and

In the ranks of hell, devils are above demons, and the Devil, with a capital "D," is the lord of Hell.

character, and for the greatest power, it has the Devil. And when we say power, we mean dark power.

The dream author follows our lead with how it translates the idea of dark power and uses it to compare with the darkness that has power over and in oneself. Take addiction, for instance, and the level, nature, and power of it. In the early days of an addiction, when it doesn't have as much power over a person, the dream author may choose a demon to symbolize it. But after an addiction has fully taken hold, the author may change the symbol to a devil, or the Devil, to express the idea of a greater power. A good role for a devil in a dream is to symbolize the most powerful among many temptations or addictions. Heroin, for example, is a top dog among recreational drugs because its effects are so powerful and the addiction is so insidious. The person may have other addictions, but heroin is their one true love, their devil.

The same can be said of anything with power or control over a person. For example, during the late stages of brain cancer, a woman dreamed about her disease as a talking serpent, just like the Serpent in the Garden of Eden. The character dramatically and pointedly promises that it's going to kill her. At that stage of brain cancer, it had taken full control of her life, and while many similar stories do not end like hers, she beat it with the help of a powerful dream ally, a black panther, which symbolized her powerful spirit. Like most of us, she knew the story of the evil Serpent well, giving her dreaming mind the perfect character for the role of a personal adversary bent on killing her. And perhaps the point was to arouse her fighting spirit. After all, a fight against the Devil is a fight to the death.

The possibilities for what a devil can symbolize gets especially interesting when we think of it as a symbol for "the devil inside," the thing that drives a person to darkness, despair, and destruction. Following that logic, the devil inside of the person must be really nasty, but dreams exaggerate and dramatize and have more reasons for creating such a powerful character. For example, it may be a warning that a situation or condition could grow to "devil level" if something isn't done about it now. In this case, a dream may—but not automatically—show a devil as small in stature or not particularly powerful. The imagery implies the potential for things to get much worse.

On the more playful side of devil imagery is the "little devil" that might be the impish behavior of, say, a rather naughty and disobedient child.

A playful side to the imagery also exists, such as the dream a woman had where her young son has devil horns—he's a "little devil," and she even calls him that affectionately. The kid is a real handful. The dream author's job is to get your attention—you dream a lot during the average night and might remember only a fraction of it—so it uses every trick in the storyteller's playbook to maximize the dream's impact and memorability. Its tricks include puns, wordplays, humor, satire, irony, and even dark sarcasm. It also likes to poke holes in the inflated ego and, conversely, pump energy and life into the deflated ego, and it can use a devil in a story for either purpose and other unexpected ones.

Take, for instance, the recurring dreams a woman experienced that all play out the same way. She's in public, in a busy setting just doing her thing, when suddenly, she realizes that she's ventured too far into the territory of some devils. They snatch and carry her into a subway tunnel. She's helpless to escape as the devils fly past hundreds of witnesses and don't try to help her; they just gawk with blank stares and empty eyes. At the end of the final dream in the series, they drop her off at the other end of the tunnel. She sees sunlight.

The woman can't identify any issues that would be the driving force behind her recurring dreams but does say that a feeling of loneliness began creeping in around the time they started, and its intensity increased along with the dreams. She searches the dream content for the idea of loneliness and finds it in the opening scene where she's alone and in public—a public setting populated with people could symbolize the idea of public and social life. Then, the devils snatch and carry her into a subway tunnel, another public setting. The witnesses stare at her blankly with empty eyes, suggesting the idea of lacking connection and the spark of life, and they are distant from her as the devils carry her through the tunnel, another way that a dream can say "separate." The tunnel is enclosed and underground, and that imagery implies the ideas of constriction and going within.

The analysis helps her realize that her loneliness is worse than she consciously knows. In a sense, she's ventured too far into that personal territory, an idea the dream symbolizes as venturing too far into the territory of the devils. She's waiting for a shift to fix the situation, such as meeting new friends or renewing old relationships. It highlights her passivity—she's not taking action to address the situation despite being aware of her unmet need for social contact and interaction. Instead, she's going about her daily routine waiting for something to happen, which is a simple summary of the dream's opening scene.

Enter the devils. In one sense, they are like the daily routine that carries her along passively—they physically carry her, and she's passive when in their clutches—but in another

Devils in dreams are carriers of discord, chaos, and upset into a person's life. They are creatures of a dark and mysterious world that is foreign to us.

sense, they are the break in the routine—they snatch her off the street. The final scene, at the end of the tunnel, is forward-looking. Inside of herself, she's building toward creating resolution, and with the help of the dream analysis, she consciously decides that the time has come. She senses "the light at the end of the tunnel," the end to her isolation and loneliness.

The devils in her dream play a role like dwarves and elves in folklore and aliens in modern mythology. They come out of nowhere and shake things up, even by kidnapping the unsuspecting humans who lack magic in their lives. As aspects of the psyche, they represent autonomous parts of a person that work subconsciously on their behalf. But they are creatures of the dark and the deep and the mysteries of life, too, and their ways are foreign to most of us. Her devils, contrary to the typical image of evil, serve a good cause, but they go about it in their own way.

In a dream another woman experienced, she's inside her brother's home office, seated on a couch next to a coworker she has a crush on. They are flirting and having a great time, then suddenly, the lights go out, and she decides to get to work. She gets up to turn on the lights and hears a voice, childlike yet gravelly, say, "Hey, you turned out my light!"

"I don't remember doing it," she replies as she searches for the source of the voice. She reaches a staircase leading up to the second floor of the house, and at the top of it, she sees her young niece. But something is wrong about her. The niece character starts walking down the stairs, and the woman sees that her skin is scaly and that her eyes are yellow like a reptile's. The Devil is inside of her, the woman thinks, and terror suddenly flares hot inside of her. "You turned out my light," the Devil says again, sternly. "Don't you have better things to do?" The woman chokes the Devil, and it just stares coldly at her. Right as she's about to scream for help, she wakes up.

This dream screams "conflict of work versus family." It features a combination of a work–family setting plus work and family characters. The home office is a work setting. The coworker is a work character. The brother's house is a family setting. The niece is a family character. The dreamer's head says that work is very important, and her heart says that family is very important. But her work is taking priority over family—that's the conflict.

It's not a willing decision; it just happens because of her job's excessive demands, brought forward in the dream with the detail about the lights going out but her not remembering doing it—it's not her fault that she must sacrifice family for work; it's just the nature of the beast. The dream chooses a coworker that she has a crush on to symbolize the idea of loving her work, and it chooses her niece because she loves her, too, and wants to be part of her life as she grows up. But when it comes down to it, her job comes first.

The dream then highlights her inner conflict in the image of her niece turning into the Devil. The drama begins when the lights go out and the woman decides it's time to get to work—that's an odd reaction under the circumstances, and it highlights the conflict between work and family. She's in a family setting but decides she must get to work. In other words, work is taking priority over family. When the niece says, "You turned out my light," it means, "You are taking time away from me and the family I represent." In other words, when she sacrifices family for work, the light in her life goes out. Notice also that the girl says *my* light and not *the* light and that the woman describes the thing that possesses her as *the* Devil and not *a* devil.

The Devil is a symbol of the conflict between the woman's head and heart, but it goes deeper than that. "Don't you have better things to do," it says not as a question but as a loaded statement hinting at iron authority. Hell is a hierarchy, with the minions doing as they are told without question, and when it comes to work, the woman knows that if she wants the great career in the corporate hierarchy, she does what she must and makes sacrifices without comment. She hates it, an idea she acts out when she strangles the Devil, but she can't help it; it's an idea brought into the story when she's about to cry out for help, but no one is around.

The dream has a hint of hope in the details about the woman wanting to turn the lights on and in encountering her niece on the staircase leading up. Turning on the lights means bringing light back into her life. The second floor of the home is above the place where the dream begins, and up in that context means advancement. The dream is forward-looking by suggesting that she will soon "take steps" to advance toward resolving her conflict.

Dr. Carl Jung said that all of the details of a dream must be accounted for to be reasonably sure that the interpretation is correct. In the above example, all of the many details connect as part of a big picture. The dream also falls into a category that Dr. Jung calls "Big Dreams." They highlight the most important parts of life and can stick with us for a lifetime.

See also: Armageddon, Demons, Evil, Fire, Hell, Lucifer, Possession

ENTITIES

Like a creature in a dream, an entity is undefined relative to other types of dream characters. The dream simply says it's an entity. It may not have a body or distinct form, but the dreamer feels a strong presence. Oh, it's there, all right, no mistaking it! It's like a word on the tip of the tongue, in your mind but just beyond your grasp. The dream author hunts for a comparison that captures the idea, and an entity is something that's there but can't be seen or defined. The picture isn't clear. The source isn't known.

That comparison is how the dream author looks ahead in life and sees what's coming, or you have a conscious sense of a probability materializing. You don't know what it is yet, and the lack of definition or comprehension combined with a feeling of foreboding is why the author chooses an entity to symbolize it. And since an entity is an intelligent awareness, it's the right symbol for the aspects of oneself that are soon to emerge from the unconscious and are still unknown to the conscious mind, which simply senses that something is coming.

Who and what you are—those are the most important things to the unconscious mind. From its perspective, the good part comes when it can speak to what's happening in the core of you as a person, as a being, as an "entity." Then, it crafts dreams with deep stories and lasting personal impact. It wants to engage you with the most important story of all—the story of your life— and give you the perspective to make informed choices about the chapters that are soon to be written and the entity that you are becoming.

Take, for instance, the recurring dreams a young woman experienced that feature a character known simply as "the Entity." Night after night, she struggles with an invisible force that seems bent on destroying her. In one set of dreams, it stands in the background as her family is murdered and she's helpless to stop it. In another set of dreams, the Entity tells her that it can help her if she'll swear her allegiance to it. And in the next set of dreams, it takes form as a mist that envelopes her. She can't escape and ends up falling flat on the ground, sobbing and crying out, "Just leave me alone!"

An entity is a kind of undefined character in a dream, a thing without a distinct body but whose presence is sharply felt.

She feels cursed, and the Entity feels real, a spiritual force bent on destroying her. Her reaction is natural, but she's missing the critical fact that her dreams are self-created experiences. They are not acting from outside of her or imposing anything on her; they are acting from inside of her and are self-imposed. It's her unconscious mind forcing her to engage with the deeper aspects of herself, and since she doesn't know consciously what they are, her dreams simply call them the Entity.

Murdering her family is the first step. She knows who she is through her experience as a member of a family unit, but her unconscious mind knows that she's much more and unable to realize that it is her conception of herself as a family member. Murdering her family means, in a sense, removing them from the picture. Initiation into the deeper aspects of life often begins this way; otherwise, people are almost sure to remain within the bubble of what's familiar and comfortable. Her family life is good, but it blinds her from seeing the bigger picture of the person she can become. Initiation in some cultures begins with removing the initiates from their families and social groups. She's alone after her family is murdered, and that's the point.

Once that point is reached, the next set of dreams present the next challenge of making her find within herself the resources she needs. People who are cleaved from the comfort of what's familiar tend to then look for something they can swear their allegiance to that substitutes for their family and social groups. It's a dangerous phase. The lure of ideologies, hierarchies, and belief systems are particularly strong, and extreme shifts in personality are a clear and present danger. The Entity promises that it will take care of her problems in return for her allegiance, but it doesn't really want her to accept the offer; it wants her to tell it to screw off! It's a test of her resolve. She is unable to do that, though, because she's clinging to the false hope of returning to her normal life where all is well and her challenges are manageable within the framework of what she already knows.

Her reaction triggers the next set of dreams where the entity becomes an enveloping mist. It's a symbolic message that she has no escape. She's creating the experience for herself and unconsciously knows why. The personality she has developed is her prison because it prevents her from developing her full potential, or what Dr. Carl Jung calls "personality #2." Many spiritual traditions describe this process as being born again, and people tend to overlook or skip over the part that comes before it: dying.

Dying to your old self. Wiping away everything you were and starting over. Figuratively, it's like Armageddon or nuclear war, a complete and total change.

But why does the dream author choose the entity over other ways of telling the story? The answer goes back to the self-created experience and the reasons for it. The young woman needs a nemesis character to drive her out of her comfort zone. It's more than an enemy or opponent, more than a monster or shadow figure. It's more personal. She's trying to actualize her full potential by answering an inner call to rebirth and greatness. The entity is merely doing its job.

She must know her ordeal as life and death because that's what it really is—if she doesn't go through the ordeal and at least start on the path to realizing her personality #2, her greatest potential as a human being is lost. An angel's other face is a demon, and both are terrible to behold. For some people, the ordeal experience is a life-threatening physical or mental illness, an addiction, or a run-in with evil. It's a shattering experience, and if the ego gives up its illusion of control, it may find out what comes next when it aligns with the power of life that's greater than itself.

The entity in her case defines itself through implication. We can say about it without being told that it's powerful and in control. It's able to influence events and fulfill desires. It's archetypal, too, a type of character that appears in the dreams of people around the world and throughout history. Hidden behind the entity as a symbol in dreams could be the idea of power, a hidden problem, or an unfulfilled desire. Because of her dreams' recurrence and theme, though, they are understood by their pattern. The ideas are present in the entity as a symbol, but the symbol is part of a sequential story that plays out over many nights of dreaming, and the meaning emerges from that big picture. Her experience points toward more happening than the usual dream symbolism.

Her experience is also notable for the lack of an apparent source of the entity in herself or her life, for example neurosis, personality disorder, illness, trauma, or abuse. Dig into the life of a person who is stricken by terrible nightmares, and usually, you find a source. But in this case, her life is great, and she's well-adjusted and smart. Her nightmares have no apparent source, and in such cases, traditional psychology is useless, even counterproductive, and traditional religion may even make the situation worse by convincing her that the entity is a malevolent spirit and that exorcism or a similar extreme measure is the only way to free her of it. What she really needs is a teacher to guide her through her initiatory ordeal. What modern medicine is likely to give her is a prescription for powerful drugs to suppress it at the expense of extinguishing her spirit.

"The Entity" is also a description commonly given to experiences of being attacked while asleep. People wake up bruised, scratched, and sore. Their dream content may contain references to an entity, but on the other hand, it may simply be the best label for an experience with no rational explanation.

They may think their house or an object such as a doll is haunted. People fall back on paranormal explanations when rational ones don't seem to fit, but in some cases, they can't find a rational explanation because they don't have the information they need.

For example, they may have a parasomnia—a group of sleep disorders involving undesirable physical events while sleeping, such as sleepwalking and injuries. A person who is sleepwalking doesn't usually feel pain—they get hurt but don't wake up. In a severe case reported in the medical literature, a sleepwalking patient jumped from a third-floor window and sustained multiple bone fractures but didn't wake

Nightmares of being attacked in bed often involve a hard-to-identify entity of some kind; such dreams can be tied to actual sleep disorders.

up! Other parasomnias include punching, kicking, thrashing, and scratching. Injuries experienced while asleep have rational explanations.

But some cases of so-called entities attacking a person in their dreams include waking up paralyzed and/or with an evil presence in the room. Again, a rational explanation for such experiences includes sleep paralysis and hallucinations that occur while going into and out of sleep. Well-documented cases also exist of injuries appearing in areas of the body where a person dreams about sustaining an injury, showing the power in the complete believability of dream experiences—so believable, the body responds as if the injury is real.

A few cases exhaust the possibilities for rational explanations, and paranormal ones are all that remain. Is the person really being attacked by an entity while asleep? Can invisible beings enter our dreams to do good or ill? The parapsychological literature suggests that yes, something abnormal is definitely happening—or it *can* happen. The people who experience being attacked in their dreams say it's an entity or a similar spiritual or alien being. If it happens and you can't find a rational explanation, it may be time to look into Spirit Releasement Therapy as taught by William Baldwin. It takes a dual approach of treating psychological sources along with spiritual and energetic ones.

That's what you might call the "nuclear option." A less drastic approach uses the narrative framework of an "entity dream" as a guide to resolution. Like a somatic metaphor—the expression of the body's illness or disease through physical symptoms and conditions—spiritual metaphors express the soul's illness and pain. An entity may be a lost part of oneself that's trying to make itself known or a result of trauma that fractures the personality. The entity may be a lost or fractured part of someone else that attaches to you because something resonates in common between you. Dream content can tell the story and provide a map to healing and reconciliation. Active Imagination techniques and Gestalt offer tools for working with dream content, and shamanic techniques may also be helpful.

See also: Aliens, Black-eyed People, Creatures, Evil, Ghosts/Poltergeists/Spirits, Haunted Dolls

EVIL

The word "evil" comes up a lot in relation to the darkest dreams and nightmares, and it may or may not be obvious why the dream or the dreamer characterizes something that way. Murder is evil. Demons are evil. But what about an evil house or an evil presence—what makes it evil? A dream may not offer anything obvious for the characterization. It may be vague in comparison to things that are obviously evil. But it still offers a way of discovering the meaning by following its logic on a path into the mind, heart, and life of the dreamer.

Simply put, the dream author may choose to characterize something as evil for a few different reasons. Follow the logic and you may find abuse, for example. Severe abuse produces terrible nightmares, and in cases of molestation and violence where abuse is obvious for what it is, the corresponding dreams tend to be more specific with identifying what is evil and why. It's not to say that they always directly identify or depict the abuser or the abuse, but in general, the better something is known consciously, the more detail it is given in dreams.

But when a dream is vague about what is evil and why, the reason may be that the dreamer is less aware of where the abuse or other sort of evil is coming from. If it's from a personal narrative, the voice saying "I'm a bad person" may be so ingrained in the person's mind that they don't recognize it as self-abuse. Internal conditions such as anxiety and neurosis and external ones such as poverty and stress may be subjectively perceived as just a normal part of life. The unconscious mind, though, views the situations objectively and calls them like they are. Evil is evil, whether it fits figuratively or literally with the personal and situational dynamics.

The insidious sorts of conditions mentioned above may not be something that a person can throw a punch at. The evil in their lives is harder to put their finger on and stand up against, and it shows in their dreams as evil that's difficult to define. The dream is a mirror that reflects only as clearly as a person's awareness or understanding, though the objective psyche knows evil when it sees it and uses dreams to help you see more clearly.

Evil can be a catchall word to describe anything bad: bad influence, bad feeling, bad person. While following the path into your life to search for what the dream characterizes as evil, look for the subjective characterization rather than the objective or literal characterization. The snag for most people who are

It's can be difficult to define the nature of the "evil" in a dream when a dreamer might not understand the source of their torment.

new to dream interpretation is that they say that something is bad but not evil, failing to see the subjective and metaphorical truth of evil as a characterization.

How often, though, do we encounter literal evil? And even when something is considered evil, it's still a definition given to it. Yes, we all agree that serial killers are evil, but is it the person that's evil or what they do? We may say that a serial killer who is mentally ill or driven to kill because of a brain tumor is not evil, but to other people, evil is evil with no differentiation. The dreaming mind models its characterizations on our subjective criteria. It also dramatizes and exaggerates and is anything but objective, usually. We must follow its logic rather than our own to understand what it really means by evil.

Dreams create symbolism through comparison, so when a dream says that something is evil or you perceive it that way while dreaming or afterward while reflecting on it, you ask, this is evil in comparison to what? Take, for instance, the recurring dreams a woman had where an evil shadow chases her through public settings, and she tries to protect her young children from it. To her, the world is full of evil, and she wants to protect her children from it. She could name specific things that she considers evil—drug abuse, crime, war—but her dreams are not specific about what's evil, and it's because they reflect her sense that the world in general is a bad place. Evil is a comparison her dreams use to characterize her subjective perceptions and feelings.

In another example, a man experiences recurring dreams about an evil shadow chasing him. It's huge and vaguely demonic, but other than chasing him, it does nothing else. He reacts to it with a high level of fear, and since normally he does not scare easily, he traces the dream imagery to its source with a simple question: What's my greatest fear? The answer comes readily; it's failing to provide for his family. When the dreams began, he'd left a salaried job to start his own business. Times of financial instability ensued, and he feared that he was only one misfortune away from financial disaster. The nightmares made him fully realize his unwillingness to risk his family's well-being, so he took another salaried position, solidified his financial position, and the nightmares stopped.

A few years later, they started again. The same evil shadow pursued him, but its symbolic meaning changed to reflect his new greatest fear: physical decline. He pushed himself to his physical limits, and as he got older, his body didn't respond like it used to. He could see the downward trajectory and the inevitable loss of strength and endurance. He responded by entering contests such as marathons and martial arts tournaments that forced him to train harder than ever. And he did it knowing that his physical decline was inevitable, but he'd go down swinging!

Fear is the sort of emotion that's ripe for comparison with evil because the two words often go hand in hand, such as in the phrase "fear no evil." But if the dreamer does not fear the evil in their dream, they are either learning one of life's most important lessons—fear nothing—or they subconsciously know that they have nothing to fear.

Take, for example, the dream a college student had about a demonic young boy following him around campus and saying the vilest things imaginable. The boy floats above the ground, speaking blaspheme and obscenities, but the dreamer just tolerates the boy instead of fearing him, and that's a huge clue that he knows subconsciously that he has nothing to fear. And it's true. The day prior to the dream, in his abnormal psychology class, he'd been shocked by case studies of severely disturbed children. His dream drives the lessons home by bringing to life a severely disturbed child.

The same logic holds when the dreamer overreacts to or senses evil in something seemingly innocuous and nonthreatening. Subconsciously, the person knows what the evil symbolizes. One example is sensing evil in a room such as a basement. It's not like the room is a portal to Hell, but if a basement represents buried memories and those memories are bad, it explains why the dreamer senses evil about the place. The dream visually represents bad memories as a bad place.

An evil place can visually represent something about the dreamer's interior psychological landscape. It's the dark spot in the mind where evil thoughts spawn or the dark corner of the heart where evil feelings dwell. It's the grudge that's nursed or the criminal plan that's hatched.

A woman dreams that she plants black stones like seeds in the soil around the roses growing in front of her mom's house, intending to kill them. The

A place, such as a creepy basement, can evoke a sense of evil simply by being in its location. Evil in a dream can just be a feeling rather than taking a definite form.

dream visualizes the evil schemes she comes up with to make her mom feel bad by attacking her favorite things and cherished notions. The roses, her mom's favorite flower, represent her mom's spirit, and the black stones represent the hardened, spiteful places within the dreamer that hate how her mom treated her while growing up. Seeds take time to hatch and grow, which is true of both the dreamer's black feelings and her evil schemes to destroy her mom's spirit. The dream doesn't explicitly identify her actions as evil, but it's a fitting description. Dreams may leave it up to you to label your actions. They don't judge (usually); instead, they teach by reflecting you back to yourself, and the label for

> **A shadow is, by nature, what the ego doesn't know about itself—bad, good, and in between.**

what you do in a dream is easier to see when you describe it as simply as possible. What's another term for killing your mom's favorite flowers? Evil scheme.

The dreamer is aware of her scheming and dark feelings. That's why the dream gives the actions to her as a role to play and she's consciously aware of what she's doing and why. Also, the flowers are in front of her mom's house, in full public view, the dream's way of saying "out in the open." For a person who is unaware of her spite and how it drives her actions, their dream might change the scenario to being accused of killing Mom's flowers instead of doing it herself. Or maybe she doesn't know why she kills her mom's flowers, revealing that she doesn't know why she acts, thinks, and feels the way she does.

This is the territory of the psychological shadow, a subject in dreams that's most likely to be labeled as evil. A shadow is, by nature, what the ego doesn't know about itself—bad, good, and in between. It's maligned as evil and has earned its reputation. Dr. Carl Jung said it's the driving psychological force behind most of the personal and collective evil in the world. But he also defined the shadow as everything that should or could be conscious about a person but isn't. It's unconscious and therefore under the control of the unconscious ego, the shadow. When we do something bad or wrong and don't know why, whether awake or dreaming, it's a sign of the shadow. Evil things we encounter in dreams are almost certainly projections from within ourselves because everything we encounter in a conventional dream is a projection from our inner world.

But an objective psyche speaks literally in dreams—not nearly as often as the subjective psyche, but when it says evil is afoot, it's not being figurative. It may speak metaphorically, but the message is literal. A dramatic demonstration is given to us by a woman's dream that the charming man she was dating was evil. She listened to the uneasy feeling and broke things off with him, and later, she found out that he had a long history of swindling the women he dated. She may have subconsciously sensed his dark side and her dream amplified her uneasiness, or the objective psyche made her aware of what it knew about him.

Also consider the dream that warned a man against going with his friends to a drug buy. In the dream, he and the friends drive to a house in a rural area, and he knows that something evil is there. He refuses to go any closer despite his friends cajoling and harassing him. In his waking life, he backed out of the buy. They cajoled and harassed him the same as in his dream, but he couldn't shake the bad feeling it left in him, and he tried to talk them out of their plans. They went anyway and were never seen again.

> **Nightmares are like high voltage for the nervous system and tend to leave a person feeling edgy and trepidatious, so feeling that way is not a sure indicator of a literal warning.**

The body's nervous system is a receiver for vibes, and it pulls no punches about what it senses. The felt sense of something in a dream is your best means of differentiating the figurative from the literal. It's subtle. Nightmares are like high voltage for the nervous system and tend to leave a person feeling edgy and trepidatious, so feeling that way is not a sure indicator of a literal warning. After calming down and sending a request within yourself for clarity, sit with the feeling and let it speak to you. The body is the seat of the unconscious mind, the generator of dreams, and feelings are the body's way of speaking. Clarity comes by searching within oneself, sorting through the feelings, and holding focus for as long as necessary. Some dreams require days, weeks, or longer until revealing their secrets.

A struggle with evil in nightmares is essentially a struggle for clarity. Prolonged struggles with evil in nightmares are usually caused by prolonged struggles with something in your life. Willful ignorance is another cause, and clarity is the antidote for ignorance. Evil is what you don't want to know; it's suppressed. The longer it remains in the shadows, the more power it gains. When evil grows in power in a succession of dreams, it either reflects worsening conditions internally and/or externally or it's like an alarm getting louder—or both and all of the above. Changing the condition and heeding the warning are the only ways to stop the nightmares.

See also: Armageddon, Black-eyed People, Dark Magicians, Demons, Devils, Entities, Hell, Lucifer, Murder, Pennywise the Clown, Possession, Serial Killers, Shadow People, Slenderman, Witches/Warlocks

GHOSTS/POLTERGEISTS/SPIRITS

The author of dreams *loves* to use ghosts, poltergeists, and spirits in situations where they work well as symbols and metaphors. In some cases, this is the best way of making a comparison that captures an idea or set of ideas. Take, for example, the feeling of being invisible. Ghosts may be invisible, and now you have the perfect way of expressing the idea. For one young man, he can't be seen or heard by anyone in his dreams. They ignore him despite his attempts to be noticed. He comes to realize that he's a ghost but doesn't remember dying. In his waking life, he feels invisible—unseen and unnoticed—and in his dreams, he's a ghost, an invisible being.

In a later dream, he decides to use his ghostly powers to be a trickster and move objects and make sounds that scare the people who can't see him, corresponding with a change in his feelings and behavior—he's sick of being ignored and is starting to act out.

A variation of the idea plays out in another dream where the dreamer knows she's a ghost and only her pet dog sees her and cares that she's there. It's a poignant way of saying that she thinks that only her dog loves her.

And another variation comes from the dream a woman had about her sister's ghost haunting her family home. Her sister left home and hadn't been heard from in many months when the dream happened, and the family didn't know if she was alive or dead. The dream tells the story by using her sister's ghost as a symbol for the idea that she's physically absent, but her memory remains, and the family is haunted by not knowing what happened to her.

In some cases, a ghost or spirit in a dream is a symbol for sensing the presence of someone or something that's absent physically, such as when you still hear the voice of a parent and feel their influence long after they are gone from your life. It's a common theme in dreams following the death of a loved one, especially when you live in the same home as they did.

Talk about a situation tailor-made for ghost dreams! The logic of comparing the person to a ghost under the circumstances is easy to understand. That's not always the case, of course, but usually, an association with ghosts is noticeable in a dream's content. One such association is that ghosts and spirits are "relics of the past," and in the following example, a dream tells a story of the dreamer experiencing himself as a boy again and he's in bed very sick. The ghost of a woman crawls into the bed and under the blankets with him, and he tells her to leave. She complains, "Can't you see that I just came from the river and I'm very cold?" It's a scene within a long dream that symbolically recounts his experience of catching ty-

The classic spooky nightmare image is, of course, the ghost and its variations such as poltergeists. Ghosts might represent a longing for someone who has passed or they could be trickster spirits.

phoid as a child and almost dying. He caught it while swimming in a river, and subsequently, during the worst phase of the illness while his life hung in the balance, he felt colder inside of his body than he'd ever felt. The ghost symbolizes typhoid—it "came from the river" and is a relic from his past, and its statement about being very cold hits the nail on the head.

An encounter with someone who had typhoid sparked the dream—he smelled it on the person's breath before they knew they were sick, subconsciously triggering his memory and his dream. The memory is a relic of his past, something he hadn't thought about in many years. In other cases, the relic that takes form as a ghost or spirit is something that actively and presently haunts the person. Ghosts and spirits are the leftovers of people who died, and the memories, thoughts, and feelings that haunt people are leftovers of their past. When the author uses a "ghost dream" to mean haunted by the past, it usually offers other details in addition to ghosts and spirits that express the idea of haunting. It gives you not just a ghost but a haunting, and it may include other details such as people and places that refer to one's past.

> **A haunted house is a fantastic symbol for those sorts of long-lingering feelings and situations because figuratively, they dwell within you.**

Memories and feelings, like ghosts, can linger. Ghosts are people who held on or wouldn't let go when the time came, making them the perfect symbols for the people and times of life we can't let go of. In a related sense, ghosts and spirits can symbolize a condition that's holding you back or keeping you down, such as depression, grief, or fear, and circumstances such as poverty or illness.

A haunted house is a fantastic symbol for those sorts of long-lingering feelings and situations because figuratively, they dwell within you. Your life is, in a sense, where you live and dwell. Your body and mind are where you live. And when something haunts you, it's inside your house because it's inside of you. Real hauntings and haunted houses are another story, a subject addressed later.

Ghosts and spirits are a frequent motif in the dreams people experience who are on the downside of a bad breakup or involuntary parting or ending. Something inside of them dies. Feelings of regret, grief, and resentment linger, and so does a feeling of the beloved's presence. It's one reason why people can dream about the ghost or spirit of their ex long after the relationship is over. They are still haunted. It's true of widows, too. For bad situations that involve anger, vengeance, and violence, a poltergeist may be the best symbol for the personal and situational dynamics.

Furthermore, situations like breakups and bad endings can leave behind things we can't or won't face, and oh, boy, does it stir up a strong response in the unconscious mind! The unconscious is *made* for reconciling us with ourselves and each other and is clever about putting in our path what we avoid so that it *must* be reckoned with. When the past haunts a person and needs to be reconciled, the dream character of choice for telling the story is a ghost or spirit. Add darkness or evil to the mix, and a poltergeist is a strong option.

The dream content usually reflects the degree of severity of whatever is haunting the person and its nature. The stronger the emotions and other dynamics, the stronger the dream's imagery and intensity. A poltergeist or evil spirit in a nightmare is strong stuff and carries the potential for adding hatred, violence, and other extreme associations to the dream author's repertoire. A poltergeist is basically a bad-news ghost or spirit with a penchant for destruction. It's a stronger use of the symbolism, perfect for roles that relate to corresponding situations in life such as extreme guilt or fear, emotional disturbance, or black thoughts or feelings.

Since fear goes hand in hand with ghosts and poltergeists, they correspond well with fears associated with them such as the fear of death, the dark, the unknown, or the past—especially a past that could catch up with you. Ghosts are said to linger because they carry a grievance or secret that must be dealt with before they're willing to move on. If a ghost in your dream won't leave, ask yourself if something is preventing *you* from moving on. A poltergeist or evil spirit in such a scenario suggests a greater severity to the underlying situation.

Fear is a test in dreams. They create scenarios involving ghosts, poltergeists, spirits, and monsters not just to scare you. It's a test of your response to fear and an opportunity to make lasting changes in yourself.

Imagine the dream space as a simulator and the deeper aspects of yourself as the observers. The test is to see what you're ready for and determine what's able to emerge from the unconscious mind and become a conscious part of you. The unconscious delivers the downloads for everything in the human repertoire, including everything you can be as a person. The potential exists for basically anything—what's right for you? What can you handle and use wisely? You find out in the dream space, and handling fear is among the first tests.

In that sense, you might say that poltergeists and powerful spirits are final exams used for the big tests because they carry with them a more powerful charge of fear and energy, but it depends on the person. People who don't fear spirits are likely to face different types of characters to test their fear response.

People fear what they don't know, and while they tend to look outside of themselves for what they don't know, dreams look inward. The dreaming mind sees everything about you,

Poltergeists are mischievous, trickster spirits that are noted for causing damage to objects around the house.

including what you don't know about yourself, and acts as a sort of relationship counselor. It introduces you to the vast and amazing things within yourself, and introductions can be messy. You may not comprehend it or like what you see and may even run like hell from it, but like a spirit, it follows you wherever you go because it *is* you.

Nightmares and dark dreams involving spirit characters are well-suited for illustrating your relationship with unconventional aspects of life, the mind, and the human experience. Conformity pressure tries to squeeze out everything about the human being that doesn't fit preconceptions to limit the range of acceptability to the narrow parameters of what can be quantified and explained conventionally. It creates a paradox for people who can't or don't want to ignore and suppress what they discover about themselves that's unconventional.

Precognition, for example, is a natural human ability, and research science has *proven* its existence, yet it isn't widely known and accepted. It's even rejected despite the evidence—vehemently, in some cases. Go online to a dream-sharing site such as dreams.reddit.com and peruse what people say about their first experiences of precognitive dreams. All too often, they encounter incomprehension and superstition, and in cases where what they dream about is dark, they may think that dreaming about it will make it come true!

Now imagine the author of dreams observing a person reacting with fear and incomprehension to an experience of precognition. How does it tell a story about interacting with an inner power that seems supernatural? How does it illustrate the ego's relationship with aspects of oneself that are unknown and mysterious? One way, and perhaps the best way, is by using supernatural symbols and themes and the many associations with ghosts and spirits because they are all of the above—unknown, mysterious, feared—and more. And precognition is just one of countless things about a person that falls outside the conventional boundaries—things that all too commonly we'd rather ignore and reject than know and accept.

That response is also common when we bump up against things we don't understand about people and life. It can seem as if something invisible is behind the scenes, and a strong human tendency is to hate and fear what we don't know and understand. The dream author observes those reactions and creates something evil and dark to symbolize it, leading to nightmares about ghosts and spirits. They are perfect for the role, and that is how you understand them—as characters chosen for roles based on how well they match up with the dynamics behind a dream.

Ghosts, spirits, and poltergeists exist autonomously and are hidden from view, and those two aspects together spell "shadow side." It and other autonomous parts of the psyche are mostly hidden from the ego's view. A person may have no awareness of anything more than what they know of themselves as an ego, and that's an invitation for ghost dreams, with poltergeists and evil spirits readily available for use as characters in dreams about a nasty shadow side, psychological complex, or neurosis. A trickster ghost in a dream, for example, can symbolize the trickster within a person that trips up their ego and creates their misfortunes, and they blame it on external factors when the trouble comes from within. The discussion in the entry on Dark Magicians illuminates that subject in greater detail.

Dreams that illuminate hidden areas of the psyche and the factors that cause a person to act compulsively and for unknown reasons are notable for their storylines that involve things happening outside the dreamer's reach and control. It may show that something in the psyche is pulling the person's strings from behind the scenes. Expand the idea, and it includes unseen influences, hidden emotions, inexplicable shifts of mood, and subconscious memories. A dream may convey the ideas through imagery such as doors and windows opening and closing on their own, objects moving, or lights flickering.

On the milder side, ghost imagery and references may be a dream's way of visualizing emotions, feelings, and thoughts that have a life of their own in the psyche and linger in the mind and heart.

In one woman's dream, she's a spirit in a classroom hovering over a guy she'd sort of dated. A woman next to her says, "You should tell him you're dead, so he doesn't think you're ignoring him." She writes him a letter and throws it at him, then cries as he reads it and cries more as he gets on his knees and screams. She wakes up soaked with her tears.

> A trickster ghost in a dream … can symbolize the trickster within a person that trips up their ego and creates their misfortunes.…

The dream dramatizes her lingering regret about the demise of their relationship. She was unable to engage emotionally with him because she felt dead inside. She's a spirit in the dream; thus, she's dead. Plus, she "ghosted" him by suddenly cutting off contact and disappearing from his life. The woman next to her is a projection of the side of herself that wants to explain to him why things didn't work out. The guy's reaction of falling to his knees and screaming dramatizes her feelings about the situation. The classroom is the perfect setting to tell the story because of its association with finding out things. Her tears are tears of anguish.

Instincts are mostly unconscious and beyond a person's conscious control, and animals are instinctive creatures. Combine these ideas together, and it spells "ghost animal"—the ghost means "unconscious," and the animal means "instinct." Like ghosts, our instincts work behind the scenes and mostly out of sight. It's desirable to increase our awareness of the instincts that drive us, and that's a big reason behind dreams where you interact with ghost animals. The interaction may enable you to "level up" by gaining conscious access to unconscious aspects of yourself and aspects of the personality that are coming online.

Animal spirits can come in many forms, but a popular species is the wolf spirit, which many favor as a power animal that can come to their aid.

Take, for example, the dream a man experienced where the image of a ghost wolf is tattooed on his shoulder. The vividness of the experience even made him feel the tattoo on his skin for days afterward. The ghost wolf symbolizes a new maturity emerging in his personality, especially in how he handles himself—wolves are shrewd and patient and show ferocity when needed. The dream wolf is a ghost because what it represents is not yet fully formed in his personality, and it's a tattoo because it's built atop the sense of himself gained from his history. In other words, it's personally meaningful, and people get tattoos that are personally meaningful. The wolf characteristics are becoming a permanent part of him, like a tattoo, and it's a landmark in his spiritual journey. People get tattoos to commemorate landmark events in life.

Ghosts are said to be spirits, and that association opens the door for the dream author to use ghost animals to represent spirit animals. They are like daimons—powerful spirits that attach to a person at birth—in the sense that they are inborn, and they are the source of great personal powers associated with the animal, like in the ghost wolf example. Dreams about spirit animals and ghost animals show the relationship between the person and the deeper aspects of themselves represented as the animal. Dreams about being hunted or pursued by a ghost animal may tell a story about a person's avoidant, fearful, or antagonistic relationship with these deeply instinctual structures of the psyche known as spirit animals.

People dream about a great variety of ghost animals—way too many to have that discussion here. Thorough and insightful discussions of the meaning and purpose of animals in dreams are available in *The Dream Interpretation Dictionary: Symbols, Signs, and Meanings* by J. M. DeBord; look up the entry for Animals there.

"Spirit." In one sense, it means zest, enthusiasm, and love for life. The dream shows a spirit or ghost, but it means spirit in the alt sense. Expand the idea, and it includes a person's goodness, better nature, and desire for truth and meaning. In another sense, spirit means a deep and important inner aspect of a person, giving the dream author a handy character to use whenever it speaks about that subject. And when it needs to speak to troublesome aspects of oneself and events in life, it also has available the word "spirit" and all it means. Imagine how a dream can convey the idea of a crushed spirit. We use the term to express how we feel, and a dream gives it shape and form. A dream could very well show the idea as a spirit or ghost crushing, squeezing, or pinning you to the ground. If you feel like you are a "ghost of your former self," a dream could visualize the idea as the ghost of you. A "lost soul" becomes a lost ghost in a dream. Alcohol spirits become actual spirits. It's up to you to translate the symbolic language and find the idea in its story; a dream may not directly state it.

Ghosts and spirits in dreams may represent the lost and fractured parts of oneself. Severe abuse and trauma are known to fracture the essence or spirit of a person, and the dream author tells the story by creating scenes where they interact with the split-off aspects of themselves in the forms of ghosts and spirits—and, in particularly bad situations, as poltergeists and malevolent entities. But less traumatizing experiences can cause fractures, too, such as rejection, failure, isolation, and disappointment. The fractured parts of oneself continue to *exist separately* from the ego and *live a life of their own*, and those are two definitions of a ghost or spirit. Even taking a fork in the road in life is a fracturing experience, and in dreams, we may travel the other roads to satisfy a need to know where they could have led. It's like a ghost of yourself is living that other life.

> **Ghosts and spirits in dreams may represent the lost and fractured parts of oneself. Severe abuse and trauma are known to fracture the essence or spirit of a person....**

A live spirit is a "spiritual life," and a dream can use it in a story to speak to spiritual life. If it's a dark story, it may mean that a person is "in the dark" spiritually or that they have dark associations with spirituality and its stepsibling, religion. At its heart, some of the most powerful nightmares and darkest dreams about spirits and ghosts are about spiritual life, either conflicts over it or the lack of it. Strip away the baggage, though, and the term simply means feeling "in good spirits" and living in close connection with the "true you." Your dreams want that for you. If it's not where you're at in life, your dreams will attempt a course correction. Their intensity depend on how much correcting you need. Nightmares are a major correction!

Many people think the spirits in their dreams are real, but the dream author also likes to use spirits to deliver messages because *we're more likely to listen*. The objective is to get a message across, and the author uses the best means to do it, including by delivering it from the mouths of deceased loved ones and other spiritual figures who come in dreams. They are characters playing a role, and it's very convincing. If the dreams are dark, it may simply reflect the subject matter.

Take, for instance, the dream where the spirit of a woman's deceased father comes to her in a dream and he looks worn out and tired, like he did before his passing. He begs her to save him, saying that he's afraid to die again. The woman says of course she'll help, but already, his condition is deteriorating. He fades away before her eyes, and she's helpless to stop it. The terrible nightmare made the woman wonder if her father's spirit really needed help, but its meaning is about the passage of time and fading memories. Her father died after a long illness when she was a teenager, and now, a decade later, she's a wife and mom. The memory of her father and the feeling of him are fading. She doesn't really want to dig it all up because it will only fade away again, which is what the dream means when her father says he's afraid to die again. But simultaneously, something inside of her is begging to hold on, an idea the father also expresses in the dream by begging her to help him.

> **Real spirits almost always come bearing gifts, insights, helpful advice, and love.**

The dream isn't about her father's spirit visiting her; it's about her memory of him. The fact that he looks tired is the first clue to what the dream is not because real spirits of loved ones always look like they're in their prime. And they never, ever drop burdens on the living or cause pain and distress.

Real spirits almost always come bearing gifts, insights, helpful advice, and love. A prime example is offered by the dream that radio host and psychic intuitive Wendy Garrett had about a visitation from famous and now deceased psychic Alex Tanous, who demonstrated his abilities numerous times under controlled, experimental conditions as documented by the Society of Psychical Research. In her dream, Alex emerges from a limousine and hands her the gift of a young plant, symbolizing the personal growth she is experiencing as a psychic and foreshadowing her future development. She knew of Tanous and his amazing body of work and sensed that his work continued in the afterlife as a guide for people walking the same path he did. His visitation elevated her game. Psychics, shamans, and other gifted people report that visitation dreams are common for them. Mathematician Srinivasa Ramanujan experienced hundreds of dreams where a goddess revealed to him deep secrets about mathematics that astounded scholars.

But sometimes, visitation dreams are dark, and the things that visit are nasty. Evil is the word, and evil things feed on fear or worse. Many poltergeist cases, documented by witnesses and researchers, provide compelling evidence of the existence of something way outside normal human experience, and the first inkling for the experiencers often comes via their dreams. It's a world that most people don't know exists, but it's absolutely real for the people who live it. The number-one piece of advice from parapsychologists who study the cases is to first think of the entity as a parasite that feeds on attention and the fear and havoc it causes. Then, starve it by ignoring it.

The discussions in the entries on Entities and Evil provide more guidance.

See also: Dark Magicians, Demons, Entities, Evil, God, Haunted Dolls, Witches/Warlocks

GOD

God is the mother (and father) of the most powerful and misunderstood dreams. God was in a dream, so it must be … God! The opposite reaction is also common: God was in a dream, so it must be meaningless nonsense. Why? Because God. Doesn't. Exist.

But take belief out of the equation, and God certainly does exist as an archetype. It's one of Dr. Carl Jung's great contributions to the world. By understanding God as an archetype, we remove it from a belief framework and put it in a psychological one. Now we can discuss God in terms of what it means as an idea or set of ideas and means personally to you. In dreams, God is a symbol or representation. That's where you begin.

As a symbol, two common associations behind the meaning of God in dreams are God the creator and God the ultimate authority figure. We see them at use in a dream where the dreamer is floating in a galaxy full of beautiful colors and stars. He reaches the center and sees a figure seated in a lotus posture, shrouded in shadows, and he assumes it's God, the Creator. God then speaks many voices in one: "You need to…." The dreamer waits for what comes next, but the voices only repeat, "You need to…." He asks, "I need to what—what do I need to do?" But again, the reply is, "You need to…."

Messages from God in dreams clearly have something to do with authority figures in one's life demanding you carry out certain tasks in your life or change a behavior.

Fill in the blank—what does the dreamer need to do? His initial reaction to the dream is to assume that he's forgetting to do something cosmically important, and you can imagine how a person would feel under the circumstances. Forgetting to take out the trash is one thing, but forgetting what God wants you to do is quite another! However, insert the idea that God in this dream means authority and observe the repetition of the statement, "You need to…." Then, picture the person who is always being told by authority figures, "You need to…." You need to study harder. You need to spend less time on your phone. You need to play sports. You need to go out more. And on and on.

God isn't telling him what to do; authority figures are. To him, it seems like everyone is telling him what he needs to do, and that's why God's voice is many in one in his dream. Perhaps the takeaway is that he needs to fill in the blank for himself.

A young man experienced a dream where God teaches him how music creates the universe. He hears otherworldly melodies and sounds and wakes up inspired to re-create them. He doesn't know music theory or even how to play an instrument—instead, he uses a software program to approximate what he heard in his dream. God is a symbol of creativity, and the dream bridges a gap between his desire to create musically and his ability to do it. The dream inspired him to overcome that gap.

One "God dream" put the dreamer in the role of an omnipotent creator. With a mere thought, he creates a planet and populates it with life, including a

Since ancient times, God has frequently played the dual role of creator and destroyer. God dreams likewise can be about both loving creation and wrathful destruction.

tribe of primitive people. Then, with intense fascination, he observes their evolution. They have families and build homes; they multiply and expand their territory. They worship him, their creator, as a God and sing praises. He is pleased.

Then, they start fighting among each other. Battles turn into wars. They abuse each other and their planet and indulge in perversions. Greedy people hog resources, causing deprivation, sickness, and death for others. They curse his name and turn their backs, refusing to believe he is real, decrying that a loving God would never subject them to lives of misery. He wants to intervene, but it would violate the condition he set at the beginning that the people will have free will and he will stay out of their affairs, only taking a hand in small ways to bless the ones who love him and help the ones who can't help themselves. Finally, conditions on his planet are so bad that he, as an act of mercy and with the most intense anguish, wipes it out with a global flood.

His dream is an answer to his questions about why God would allow misery and deprivation. Instead of telling him the story, it shows him by putting him in the role of God to know what it's like to love your creation but be unable to intervene when it goes awry.

In another example of the relationship between God and creative power, we have the nightmare a child experienced where she's outside in her yard playing on a sunny day. God speaks to her from the sky and says she can have any power she wants. She thinks about it and asks for the power to send a swarm of bees to sting the people who hurt her—only them, no one else. She sees a swarm of bees fly away into the distance, presumably to carry out her wish, and it pleases her. But then, the sky turns black and the voice of God thunders down saying that because she abused her gift, she is cursed to live like a mongrel dog in the dirt and muck. She screams that she's sorry, but God's presence has already left.

That's a very unusual nightmare for a young child. It reads like a parable but was experienced as an actual event—it felt like a true encounter with God. Twenty years later, as the woman recounted her childhood dream, she didn't remember anything that would spark it but did offer that it fit a pattern of having dreams that taught her the ethics and morality of using her power. She was quite gifted psychically, and by concentrating on her desire, she could make things happen in material reality. In her childhood dream, God is an archetype; more than a standard symbol, it's a living presence in her psyche, and like the God of the world's religions, it plays the role of teacher (and punisher!) and possesses unlimited power. Her dream taught her the most important lesson about using her power to manifest—do no harm. And she learned that if punishment is to be dished out or corrections made to people and their behavior, that's up to God, not her. Judge not lest ye be judged!

Dreams are a common way for people to become aware that they possess such gifts and abilities and how and when to use them.

Her dream demonstrates a "God association" that dreams can use: omnipotence and its opposite, powerlessness. The dream author can run with those ideas whenever it wants to tell a story about subjects such as grandiosity and ego inflation, feeling small in comparison to something, and lacking control or ability to affect change. Nightmares about being powerless use God as a symbol for the idea.

In the dream a teenager had, everywhere she turns leads to a dead end, and every person she meets has it out for her. The landscape is bleak and dark, and she has a sense that it's always that way and never changes. She decides that suicide is the only way out, and it's the same decision for the same reasons that she's made for real; she really is contemplating suicide. In her dream, she finds a bottle of pills and thinks to herself that she will swallow them and leave this world, and God better speak up now. Her thought gets no response, so she opens the bottle. She sees a ring inside and recognizes it as one her grandma used to wear. Her grandma was the light in her life, but she passed away, and ever since then, the dreamer has felt alone. The ring is the sign she needs, and she thanks God as she puts it on her finger.

The opening scene of her dream creates a scenario that can be summed up in one word: powerless. It also expresses her feelings of loneliness and hopelessness. She has ideas for the life she wants to live and the person she wants to be, but they seem impossible to make happen. All her efforts lead to dead ends and people in general feel menacing, two ideas clearly present in the dream. Its content also reflects her thoughts about suicide and how she's planning to do it and hints at her feeling that no one will miss her when she's gone. The one person who would miss her—her grandma—is already gone.

But her grandma's love is a memory she'll never forget, and to carry on with her life and fight the good fight, she really needs to remember it vividly and viscerally. Her dream provides it in the form of her grandma's ring. To find it inside the bottle of pills is especially poignant.

People who are suicidal or contemplating suicide are known to have powerful dreams about God and related subjects such as the afterlife and beliefs about what happens to people who kill themselves. The dreams are often taken as divine messages or divinely inspired, but they actually mirror the dreamer's beliefs.

> **People who are suicidal or contemplating suicide are known to have powerful dreams about God and related subjects such as the afterlife....**

For example, the dream a person had about a friend who committed suicide involved her being tormented in Hell. She thought that the dream was a message from God and that she was being told to pray for her friend's soul but came to realize that it merely mirrored her worst fears. Dreams that bring up such subjects are easily confused for being something they're not, so it's especially important to see the subjectivity of them. Dreams mirror our thoughts, feelings, beliefs, and perceptions.

A young man dreams that he can't escape the scrutiny of an all-seeing eye. It follows him everywhere, and he can't masturbate while being watched. Talk about annoying! Though he is agnostic, he wonders if God is sending him a message, but the dream's simple idea is that something's always watching him; turning it into a question reveals the true nature of the all-seeing eye as a symbol. What's always watching you and can intrude into your thoughts while masturbating? Answer: his conscience. Many dreams that cast God in such a role are really about the person's conscience—especially a guilty or conflicted one.

God is said to save people from damnation. Christianity gives that job to Jesus—"Jesus saves." A fascinating variation of that idea was made into a story by a man's dream where he flees a cemetery and runs to his house ahead of a mob of zombies. There he finds Jesus looking worn out and deeply asleep in his bed. Since Jesus is in no condition to fight, he takes on the zombies by himself.

The cemetery symbolizes the "old, dead" religious beliefs of his past, and the zombies—also old and dead—are symbols of those beliefs pursuing him. His home in the dream symbolizes his inner personal space, his being. Inside the home means "inside of himself." He finds Jesus there, looking worn out because the dreamer is tired of fighting the same old internal battles. Be-

In one dream, zombies invade a man's home. Jesus is in his home, but he is asleep in a bed and the man must try to save himself.

liefs are tenacious things that refuse to die, and religious beliefs are especially hard to shake—like zombies!

The dream puts Jesus in the dreamer's bed to show a close personal connection formed from the many times that the man thought about and prayed to Jesus while in bed. Another layer of meaning emerges from the fact that the dreamer protects Jesus. The man is gestating a new belief system that includes a new idea of and role for what Jesus represents in his life—"elevated consciousness"—but it's still under attack from his old beliefs, the zombies. In the meantime, he must fend for himself against the mental attacks and doubts. Finally, a moral of the story is that sometimes we must save ourselves and can't expect someone else to fight our battles for us.

In another dream, a man is drowning and calls on God for help. A bright light appears over him and saves him. One way of viewing the scenario is that it shows the man relying on his faith to save him from drowning in his problems, but the idea doesn't resonate with him. Instead, what resonates is knowing that a God above responds when called on. He thinks deeply about the dream and senses that the moral of the story is this: Don't wait until you're in trouble before calling on God; make praying a regular practice.

Some of the worst nightmares feature God as an antagonist character: a God that smites, pursues, and even terrorizes. A commonality among people who have such nightmares is that they are wayward or "back-slidden" in their religious faith and deeply conflicted about it. Religious beliefs are among the most entrenched and powerful of beliefs, and some religions insist on terrible retribution for abandoning or going against them. The angry God in dreams is a symbol of conflict and must be understood as a character given a role and nothing more. It's not "God."

But it's not to say that something bigger and beyond oneself can't take form as God in dreams. In some cases, this is the best way to describe an experience of contact with an archetype or for seeing through the illusion of material reality. Physical matter is, according to Albert Einstein and theories from physics, condensed energy, and the entire universe is energy of various densities. Most of what exists in material reality is literally beyond the human ability to perceive, and the best and sometimes only framework we have for labeling and understanding it is God. And since the dreaming mind uses what we know to compare with and describe what we don't know, naturally, God is a versatile symbol for anything that's unknown.

Another common reason for God to play an antagonist role in dreams is because the person resists a calling. In the story of Jonah and the whale, God tells Jonah that he will be a prophet and speak truth to the powers of his time, but Jonah says no way and tries to escape by sea. The whale swallows him, coughs him up near Nineveh, and the rest is history. The metaphor fits perfectly in cases where a person tries to escape from doing what they know they must, should, or could do, and the response from deep within them is to force a reckoning. Similar allegories feature caves as the setting and something inside waiting for the person to grow the balls to face it.

The calling may be to live fully, not to be a prophet or zealot. The agenda of the unconscious mind that creates dreams is to do everything in its power to help a person live one heck of a life and actualize their potential.

A force appears to be built into consciousness itself that creates dynamic energy through opposition, what Dr. Jung calls "the conflict of opposites." Human nature is dualistic, and on one end of the spectrum, you have inertia and complacency, and on the other end, you have vitality and initiative. Without a contradictory opposite to inertia, humans follow Newton's Law that a body at rest tends to stay at rest.

In this sense, the antagonistic God of dreams and nightmares is the fire that gets your butt moving. Highly creative and mission-driven people are known to have a godlike presence in their dreams that tells them, either directly or through signs and messages, when it's time to get to work.

Another message that's common to dreams that feature an antagonistic God is summed up simply as "do the right thing." It's not to say automatically that the person who dreams this way is doing the wrong thing, though as we've seen in examples given already, doing the wrong thing and going against one's conscience are like putting gasoline on a

> **A force appears to be built into consciousness itself that creates dynamic energy through opposition, what Dr. Jung calls "the conflict of opposites."**

fire. But maybe a person doesn't know what the right thing is or they don't think much about it. Life can be full of decision points that come down to simple choices between right and wrong—yet knowing what's right or wrong isn't easy in cases where, for example, you want to spend more time with family, but your job is all-consuming, or you want to live morally and ethically, but the people around you take advantage of your goodness.

The God of those dreams isn't always clear about what it wants of you, and the ambiguity may be deliberate because children know right and wrong based mostly on what they are taught, but adults must decide for themselves or else they project that power onto a person, object, or authority, creating a different mess of issues. If God is truly within a person, it must be sought after, and it's not always butterflies and unicorns when dealing with the most powerful and enigmatic force in the human psyche. Sometimes, the better word for encountering the God within is "confrontation."

Atheists are known to have wild and powerful dreams about God, much to their bewilderment—why dream about something they insist isn't real? Then again, why dream about ghosts, aliens, or demons—they also aren't real, right?

The dream author isn't limited by beliefs about what's real or not. Its criteria are what works as a symbol, as part of a story, or as a self-created experience. The atheist who questions their dreams about God should question why they create the experiences and what they show and teach because the images they see and the experiences they have are their projections.

> **God in the dream of an atheist or unbeliever is a symbol of something they reject, but fear could be true and real and could come back to haunt them....**

An example is given to us by a dream where a young man dreamed that God would become real in three minutes. Three minutes later, he was awake and recording the dream. Nothing supernatural happened, no voice of God, no light from above. He breathed a sigh of relief because he feared the prospect of God being real. Earlier in his life, he'd embraced Satanic beliefs, and it planted a seed of fear in him because his rejection of God was based on the belief—you might say the hope—that God isn't real. Becoming real would be a nightmare come true.

In that sense, God in the dream of an atheist or unbeliever is a symbol of something they reject, but fear could be true and real and could come back to haunt them, a personal association with God that haunts the dreams of the back-slidden and formerly religious, too.

Conversely, for someone who wants to believe that God is real but isn't sure (the word "belief" implies "not sure"), God in their dreams can symbolize their hope. Expand on the basic idea, and God becomes a symbol for what a person hopes is real, puts their hope or belief in, or secretly questions or doubts.

See also: Dragons, Entities, Jesus, Hell, Lucifer, Suicide

HELL

Take a survey of the most common settings for nightmares, and Hell tops the list or is close to it. As a metaphor and symbol, it matches well with many and various aspects of life. And since "life is hell" is as bad as something gets and goes hand in hand with pain, anguish, and misfortune—and nightmares go hand in hand with those situations and conditions—its popularity in nightmares is no wonder.

"Life is hell" can be true in both exaggerated and all too real ways. The dream author takes its example from that use of the phrase and ones like "You're going to burn in Hell," and it hits you with a "Hell dream" when the time is right, the symbolism fits, the metaphor comes in handy, and the setting is ideal for a dream's tone and atmosphere. The dream communicates an idea by using Hell as a symbol and a story setting, so when interpreting those dreams, you look for the idea or set of ideas it communicates.

The severity of the dream imagery tells you a lot about the underlying situation it correlates with. The worse that one is, the worse the other is, generally. A dream has reasons for creating scenes of burning in Hell and similar imagery that say, "Oh, it's bad—as bad as it gets." And knowing those reasons helps you work backward to find the meaning.

Hell is a versatile symbol and story piece, so it's hard to say what's the most popular way dreams use it, but if we had to pick one, it would be its use as a metaphor and symbol relating to a person's "psychological landscape." The dream space is a space within the psyche, and a dream setting in this case is a representation of it. Imagine the dream author wanting to create a visual representation for the phrase "I'm in a bad place in my life" and match it with the personal and situational dynamics behind the thought or statement. When you are in a really bad place, Hell is the metaphor that easily fits. Hell fits well when

Nightmarish visions of Hell have been displayed in religious art for centuries, such as in this fresco by Giorgio Vasari. In dreams, the Hellscape is a setting established by the dreamer's psychological landscape. The archetype imagery is a clear message of "I am in a bad place."

the bad place involves factors such as punishment and guilt—it's a place of punishment for guilty sinners. Emotional and physical pain are dynamics that Hell symbolizes because it's a place of torment. Keep in mind that the truth must only fit loosely with the imagery to be fair game. It's subjective, mostly.

On the intense side of how dreams can use Hell as a representation of one's psychological landscape is the nightmare a man experienced where he finds himself in a fiery and sulfurous landscape—Hell, he thinks—and sees a man burning and being crucified on a gnarly, dead tree. One sharp branch impales him through the length of his body, and he burns in eternal flames that don't kill him. Instead, he writhes in the most intense agony, seemingly forever. Semiconscious while dreaming, the dreamer feels pity for the man and wants to help. He calls down a deluge of water to quench the flames.

The image of a man in agony dramatizes what the dreamer is experiencing. He is in intense psychological pain, and he describes that time of his life as "passing through the fire and flames." Hell is the metaphor that matches his condition. His reaction of wanting to relieve the agony by calling down water demonstrates the creative power of dreams. Even though it is him who's experiencing the pain in his life, the dream projects it onto the crucified character, creating space for him to observe and react. Soon afterward, in ordinary waking life, the man's personal agony lessened, and he emerged from that time with the ability to heal his wounds and move forward with passion and vigor.

That example shows beautifully how the dream space not only reflects current and recent conditions of a person's life, but it's also a workshop for creating the future, with a big contribution from our decisions and reactions while dreaming. Now, imagine if the dreamer looked at the burning, crucified dream character in Hell and thought, *Sorry, buddy, can't help ya.* Do you think his subsequent healing would have happened? It's unlikely, it's safe to say. For sure, he knew subconsciously what he was doing and why and decided that he was tired of suffering and wanted relief; his creative response by calling down the water to put out the fire quickened the process.

The prisons in which we find ourselves, and which take on a literal imagery in dreams, can definitely be a form of Hell.

Now you see the enormous potential for healing and growth. Add nightmares to the picture, and it becomes clear why *nightmares are for healing.* First of all, they discharge bad energy, and second of all, they give us a stage for playing out our dramas. And how they play out is the biggest determiner of one's future because of the power of belief.

Hell is a setting and a *place* you go to in your dreams, a projection of your inner world in *every detail.* The details give definition to what Hell means as a symbol and as part of a story.

In the "Hell as a prison" dream discussed in the entry for Demons, demons are the guards around a prison in Hell. The details define Hell as a prison. To interpret the dream, we figure out what's imprisoning the dreamer and discover that it's a belief system about "real men." The belief system is the psychological landscape represented as a prison in Hell, a subjective depiction based on the man's feelings and perceptions, and it's a milder use of the symbolism because the situation in his life is milder than "burning in Hell." The dream imagery corresponds.

In another dream discussed in the entry for Demons, Hell is the backdrop for eternal torture by demonic overlords, a dramatization of the dreamer's "inner demons" and personal torments. The setting is right out of a horror movie, and the dream imagery corresponds with his condition. He's a tormented soul, and his life is hell.

While interpreting a dream, cycle through the metaphors and figures of speech you can think of and see if they match its content and your feelings. Do parallels exist with what's happening in your life? It's a quick way of getting to the meaning or at least starting down that road. Metaphors like "guilty as hell" and "hot as Hell" can be rather obvious and easy to find in dream content once you know what to look for. But a metaphor like "the road to Hell is paved with good intentions" is not on most people's radar, and the corresponding dream imagery may not outright show the idea of the metaphor. Instead, the path to the meaning is found in the dreamer's thoughts and reactions while dreaming, in associations that come out of the blue, and in a simple summary you give to the dream or a scene within it.

Take the example of a woman's dream where she's at her aunt's house and many family members are there. They are waiting for her sister to arrive, and someone says she needs to be picked up at the airport. The dreamer says she'd do it, but her old car is having mechanical issues. It's a flimsy excuse and she knows it, but it's one that her family can't argue against. Plus, she thinks, *It's not like Sis can't afford a cab ride!* The scene then shifts. She's outside the home, and her car is parked on the road and is on fire. Her sister appears next to her and says, "I'd help you buy a new one, but money is tight right now." The dreamer knows it isn't true and gets angry.

The dream brings together a complex set of personal and situational dynamics and concisely expresses them metaphorically. The opening scene at her aunt's home with the presence of other family members points toward family life as central to the story. The correlation isn't automatic but is a place to begin. The dream then creates a scenario where the dreamer needs to decide whether to pick up her sister at the airport. When dreams create decision points, they provide opportunities for the dreamer to react and, in doing so, reveal their true thoughts and feelings because their reaction is based on subconsciously knowing what's really being asked of them. Those decisions also determine the direction the story takes from there.

> **When dreams create decision points, they provide opportunities for the dreamer to react and, in doing so, reveal their true thoughts and feelings....**

Picking up her sister really means "make a sacrifice for a family member," and her reaction sums up how she feels about it. She doesn't want to, so she makes up an excuse, and that reaction summarizes her family life. When presented with a situation that requires something personally of her, she tries to think of a way out of it if her analysis concludes that the cost isn't worth the benefit. The dream creates a scenario involving the use of her car because her cost–benefit analysis, a habitual pattern that colors all of her decisions, is particularly noticeable when it comes to doing anything with her car. She thinks about the costs of the gas and the wear and tear and compares it with the benefit it may bring in return. And when those decisions involve family, the benefit is mostly in terms of the potential for reward. She wants to be seen in a good light, but what will it cost her?

The dream chooses her sister because of the competitive dynamic that colors their relationship. Recently, their competitiveness has centered around wealth, and in that regard, the dreamer is losing. Her sister has more wealth, drives a nicer car, can afford to travel in style, and certainly can afford a cab ride. Picking her up at the airport is exactly the sort of scenario that would earn the dreamer points with her family but also gall her to no end, and thus, she makes up an excuse and thinks to herself that her sister can afford a cab ride.

Now we get to the scene where her car is on fire and search for how it could express an idea metaphorically. Keep in mind that the imagery a dream creates after the opening scene is normally in response to what happened in the previous scene, and the meaning is the connector. We can assume that her car is on fire because it connects with her decision to make up an excuse for why she can't pick up her sister. It may not be obvious at first glance, but the idea is a variation of the metaphor, "The road to Hell is paved with good intentions." It's commonly thought of as a proverb or aphorism meaning that it's not enough to merely *mean* to do well; one must take action to *do* well. For our purpose, we think of it as a metaphor because the dream enacts the meaning, and the scenario is modeled on the idea it expresses. The dream author creates poignant irony by making the woman's car the center of the action, and it puts the car on a road and sets it on fire. *The road to Hell is what?*

The icing on the cake is the sister's statement about helping to replace the car if she could afford it. It's not enough to mean to do well!

See also: Armageddon, Demons, Devils, Evil, Fire, Lucifer

JESUS

As a dream character, Jesus is common in the big and important dreams of Christians and non-Christians alike. People who study and interpret dreams professionally may just say "Jesus dreams" to summarize the huge impact they make. When Jesus shows up as a main character in a dream, fireworks are likely to go off.

What are you projecting into the dream space? It's a fundamental question to ask about all your dreams. You see Jesus in the dream, and naturally, you think, *Hey, it's Jesus!* But Jesus is a symbol. It's a projection. As a symbol, an idea or set of ideas are behind the image, and as a projection, you can see yourself in it.

As an archetype, Jesus represents a set of ideas associated with higher consciousness and morality, and for people following in those footsteps, he's a perfect character to play the role of guide, teacher, and helper. But it's a different story for people following a darker path in life. Jesus is the fuel for their nightmares, the enemy of the self-serving ego, and the voice of the unconscious that disagrees with their choices. The psyche is a system made of opposite polarities. When a person is full of dark energy that imbalances the system, their dreams compensate with symbols that add weight to the other end of the scale. The psyche doesn't say that one is better than the other; each has a place and a role. The psyche says that they must be in balance. Achieving balance can involve wild swings to the extremes, and it's a recipe for hot and spicy dreams.

When Jesus appears in a dream, He is a positive symbol for such characters as a teacher, guide, comforter, and helper.

As an antagonistic character, Jesus can appear in dreams that highlight personal conflicts—for instance, when a person is being selfish or doing the wrong thing. Think of Jesus as the image of their conscience or as the embodiment of authority figures and belief structures and their messages, strictures, and rules for living. Conversely, when a person is going too far with their personal sacrifices or is self-righteous or "holier than thou," the psyche uses Jesus as a compensatory force to help the person come back into balance.

For one recently baptized young man who then started having nightmares featuring Jesus, his baptism triggered a new awareness of the idea of sin. In one nightmare, Jesus strikes him with paralysis, symbolizing the doubts and fears that paralyze him figuratively. Christian doctrine's subtleties and contradictions about what is and is not sin confuse him, and his doubt and fear paralyze him. In his mind, anything he does or even thinks could potentially be sin, and sin carries the worst consequences imaginable.

In another nightmare, Jesus curses him with leprosy. His fingers turn gangrenous and rot away. He wakes up wondering what he's done wrong, but the nightmare is simply the response of a young mind encountering new and terrible ideas. He read that leprosy is a curse from God—what could a person do so terribly wrong for God to curse them like that? Could *he* do something wrong and not even know it? His fingers rotting off is great symbolism for fear of punishment for something he does because fingers are closely associated with a person's actions and intentions.

Fear is at the heart of his nightmares, which is true of most nightmares. Tracing feelings brought forward by a nightmare is a first step to interpreting it, so you ask, what fear is the dreaming mind translating into nightmare imagery? With Jesus, the obvious place to begin is with fear that relates to religious concepts such as sin. Also, fear is an umbrella emotion that may have deeper roots in emotions such as guilt and remorse. Through dreamwork, the person releases the fear, creating mental room for the emotions and memories behind it to come forward into conscious awareness.

An intense fear is behind a dream a young woman had about Jesus impregnating her, then denying that he is the father. One way of looking at the meaning is that she's denying the "fatherhood" of Jesus, a concept from Christianity about Jesus being one with God the Father. Being pregnant with his baby could be a way of saying that Christian teachings are trying to take root in her, but she is denying them. However, the dream plays off the idea of immaculate conception to express her fear of getting pregnant. If it happened, she wouldn't know who the father was because she's promiscuous.

The fear dramatized by a "Jesus dream" isn't always so intense. Take, for instance, the dream a woman had where Jesus says repeatedly, "You must wake up!" Then, she wakes up and checks her phone, and it's 4:44. The timing seems propitious because 444 is a sequence of numbers associated with God, like how 666 is "the Devil's number." But she looks closer at her phone and realizes that the battery is almost depleted. In her dream, Jesus tells her to wake up, and she really does need to wake up and plug in her phone or else her alarm won't go off! The dream chose Jesus as the messenger because she had a good deed planned for that morning and that's why she wanted to wake up early. She feared that something could spoil her plans, and her hypervigilance prevented it from coming true … with a little help from Jesus.

The dark dreams of committed Christians commonly feature Jesus as a character or just a presence, and they report being able to banish dark dreams by calling on him or saying his name with authority. All too often, people confuse the dreams as spiritual attacks, but they are reflections of internal struggles. Either way, for some people, the name of Jesus carries the power to banish darkness in dreams when evoked with conviction.

A more complex psychology enters the picture when the person is trying to improve themself spiritually, morally, and personally. Their dreams become a battleground between the new person they are becoming and the old person they are leaving behind—and what a perfect combination because one of the main reasons why we dream is to create a simulated environment for personal growth and encountering what's emerging in us psychologically. For some people, Jesus is a figure of inspiration and a model for higher consciousness. He's also a "personal savior" and an unseen presence that feels very close, and it is close because it's part of the psyche. It's inside of us. Nothing is more personal!

Dream figures of this type tend to take a form that is familiar to the dreamer. For the Muslim, they may dream about the Prophet Mohammed instead of Jesus, and the Buddhist may dream of Gautama Buddha. Saints and other holy figures can play the role, too. For example, Hindu Saint Ishu is remarkably like the Jesus of Christianity and Islam. Think of them as symbols for personal potential and a bridge over a gap between where you are now and where you want to be. In this way, among the thousands of figures that reside in the psyche, Jesus and others of this type are the highest in terms of personal impact when encountered in dreams. The dreams are unforgettable and sometimes life-changing.

And they are often difficult. Transformation is messy. It can feel like dying, and in the psychological sense, it's the best word to describe the experience. Naturally, dreams that relate to transformation are among the most powerful dreams a person is likely to experience. Death and rebirth and confrontations with evil beings are par for the course.

Similarly, the dream author can use Jesus as the face of the Hero archetype. The Hero brings with it an electrifying energy to face the unknown and conquer challenges, and "Hero dreams" top the scale in intensity and drama. But more is asked of the Hero, for it's a structure of the psyche that must eventually die— or "transform"—for wisdom to emerge. It's designed to be a temporary bridge to get through the first stage of adult maturity. Then, the person realizes their limits and how to do battle by means other than force and conquest, which the Hero is not designed for.

Obviously, people of religious persuasions other than Christianity will more likely dream of figures appropriate to their beliefs such as Gautama Buddha appearing in the dream of a Buddhist.

Jesus is perfect for the role because through resurrection, he transcends his mortal limits and emerges with greater power. He taught his followers how to conquer Rome without lifting a sword, but the Hero would leap into battle anyway ... and die. "Hero dreams" featuring Jesus as a character can address issues such as tempering impulses, realizing one's limits, and attaining wisdom. The stories are like parables and allegories.

Jesus is associated with resurrection, and as an idea, it can symbolize feeling reinvigorated and "rising from the grave" after a time of depression or calamity. He's associated with sacrifice, selflessness, and doing the right thing.

> **Dreams can reflect such struggles in scenes of fighting Jesus, running or hiding from him, or him being a mountainous presence who won't let up.**

Jesus was a mystic—it's another association with him mainly from Gnostic, Essene, and esoteric traditions. People who feel called in that direction may dream about Jesus in the role of messenger or instigator of their initiation. The call comes from a source that's deeper than ego or personality, and a common response is to resist or reject it. The ego has other ideas! And who can blame it—the mystic path is a lonely one. Often, it chooses them rather than them choosing it, leading to inner struggles that can be epic.

Dreams can reflect such struggles in scenes of fighting Jesus, running or hiding from him, or him being a mountainous presence who won't let up. The meaning can be milder than an indicator of a personal calling—for example, fighting Jesus can symbolize resisting one's conscience, and hiding from him can mean refusal of a truth or other such revelation. After all, he told the bald truth and pulled no punches when it came to calling out what he perceived as wrong or bad. And he paid for it.

But if a person searches with wide-open eyes for a meaning of disturbing Jesus dreams and doesn't find it in the usual sources, they are wise to explore the possibility of being called to greatness. It's an unusual reason for nightmares and something to consider when no other interpretation rings your bell. The dreams are essentially an initiation to higher consciousness. The discussion in the entry on Entities features an analysis of a series of initiatory dreams.

If dark dreams featuring Jesus as a main character recur, they rise to a level of demanding deeper consideration. Beyond the possibility of the dream being initiatory, they may indicate a disturbance in the psyche, a raging conflict, or a neurosis—something is really stirring the muck deep down in the person, and they may require professional psychological help.

In one case, a woman went from dreaming that she was the Virgin Mary to thinking she really was Mary and giving off the energy of a holy figure. People responded to her vibe as if she was holy, and it reinforced her delusion.

But the bubble burst when she flipped to the opposite extreme, became hypersexual, and gave off a wicked vibe. The drastic flip is a symptom of Possession by an archetype.

Archetypes are powerfully energetic structures of the psyche composed of opposite polarities, and in this case, the opposites are known as the Madonna and the Whore, shadow expressions of the same archetype. Possession occurs in people who do not have the ego strength to withstand direct contact with an archetype, and it may be sparked by intensive spiritual and meditation practices and intense emotions and emotional conflict. The energy overfills them, the ego personally identifies with it (*Hey, I'm Jesus!*), and the person is taken over. The woman had done something terrible many years before the dreams started, and her secret guilt and shame ate at her, making her vulnerable to archetypal Possession.

Dreaming of being Jesus can lead to the same dangerous territory and risk of possession. It can show grandiosity or delusion, but let's be clear that the dream author could put you in that role for benign reasons, too; for example, to reflect the good you do for people and the sacrifices you make. Either way, it's wise to treat such dreams as if they come with a sign that warns "Danger: High Voltage!"

> **Dreaming of being Jesus can lead to the same dangerous territory and risk of possession. It can show grandiosity or delusion....**

"Jesus dreams" make a powerful impression and are easily confused as spiritual visitations. It's wise to first assume that the dreams are symbolic and personal to you. Walk through the interpretation process like you would with any dream. Decode the symbolism; analyze the story; look for personal parallels; and ponder the meaning of the experience, why you gave it to yourself, and what you may learn.

A man experienced a powerful dream where he's in a grassy field and sees thousands of people around him. Suddenly, Jesus enters the scene, and they all bow down. Jesus looks at him and sweeps his arms to indicate the mass of people. "To follow me, you must *carry* these," he says. The emphasis on "carry" strikes the dreamer as important, and now, he's upright. He looks over and sees an old man supporting himself on his shoulder. The look on the man's face asks, "Is it okay?" The dreamer decides yes, I will carry you. The dream came in response to the dreamer's many personal questions about what's asked of him as a follower of Jesus, and the answer is simple. When someone needs help, offer it freely. He doesn't even have to go looking to help—the people he can "carry" will come to him. Carrying implies the willingness to go to any length necessary.

A woman asked for a raise at work; her request was rejected, then she was told to give an answer the next morning as to whether she'd continue employment with the company. She liked her job but felt stung by the rejection, and that night, she asked for a dream to help her make the decision. She dreamed that she saw Jesus with long arms made of intense fire. With a sweep of his fiery arms, he proclaimed, "On to bigger things!" She took the message to mean that bigger things awaited her and she was safe to leave her job. She did so and soon found opportunities for more rewarding and enriching work.

Be mindful of the pressure to interpret a Jesus dream so that it conforms to expectations—the faithful and believers want it to confirm their faith and beliefs, and the opposite camp insists it's meaningless and confirms nothing. But it's your dream, and how you interpret it is your choice. "Dreams follow the mouth" is a Hebrew saying from Kabbalah that expresses the wisdom of interpreting a dream so that it leads to a good outcome because the interpretation of it—what comes from the mouth—is a self-fulfilling prophecy. And Jesus was a Hebrew!

See also: Armageddon, Entities, Ghosts/Poltergeists/Spirits, God, Suicide

LUCIFER

Great stories have antagonists. Try reading or writing a story with no antagonist, opposition, or contrary point of view—*boring!* As much as we say we like harmony and happy endings, we are drawn to disharmony and tragedy. Music that hits unexpected notes captures our ear, and for centuries, composers and musicians have cleverly used "the Devil's interval" to strike a dissonant note that stirs listeners with pleasure. Lucifer as an antagonist is to stories what the Devil's interval is to music, a character that creates excitement by doing, saying, and symbolizing the unexpected. Lucifer is the one we love to hate.

From a religious point of view, nothing is lovable about Lucifer. He is nothing but bad and trouble, but from the dream author's point of view, everything can be loved about an antagonist that juices up a story and is dangerous and contrarian.

People who have dreams featuring Lucifer tend to only see the spiritual bad guy who rules Hell and walks on Earth seeking the ruin of souls. They think about it literally, but instead, think figuratively like a storyteller, and in Lucifer, we have a symbol that embodies what we don't like or know about ourselves. That use of the meaning plays out in a dream where a woman

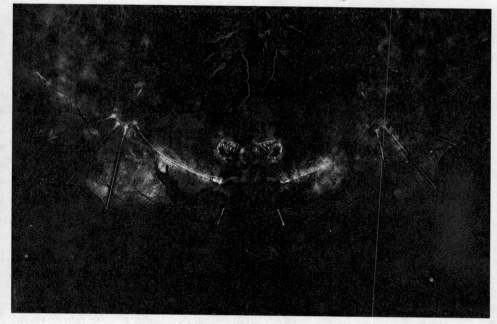

While Lucifer was actually the Bringer of Light, most people think of the figure as the Devil, an antagonist, but also at times in terms of sex, excitement, and enticing danger.

marries Lucifer in her apartment in front of her friends and family—a happy occasion. Lucifer, dressed in a tux, has red skin and horns, the prototypical devil image. As the evening winds down, the sexual tension winds up between the dreamer and her new husband. She wonders, *Hmm, what's he got down there? Will she be able handle intercourse?* It fills her with the excitement of not knowing what to expect.

The dream interpreter may wonder, *Hmm, what is she psychologically bonding with that Lucifer symbolizes?* Marriage is a bonding ceremony, so one way of interpreting the symbolism of marrying Lucifer is that it shows bonding in the dreamer's personality between herself and what Lucifer symbolizes. You may think it must be something dark or evil, but do you see that idea in the dream? No, and if Lucifer was a bad guy, he'd *act* like it or the dreamer would sense it. You might even think that the dream somehow involves the idea of kinky sexual quirks because of the dreamer's thoughts about intercourse—it doesn't get any kinkier than getting it on with Lucifer!

But those thoughts are in response to what she subconsciously knows about Lucifer's meaning as a symbol. When she looks him up and down and thinks about sex, she's really thinking about her excitement related to delving into the unknown. She has begun practicing divination and studying astrology, and it's leading her deeper into esotericism. Lucifer, believed by some to be the source behind that knowledge, is the ideal symbol, and marrying him is the ideal way of symbolically saying that she's deepening her commitment to the practices. It's changing her and her life, like marriage does. A new world is opening up for her and she doesn't know what's coming next, but the thought of it is as exciting as the anticipation of sex.

The dream takes place in her apartment because it conveys the idea of her daily life—her esoteric practices are a normal part of her routine. And her family and friends are in the scene because the dream uses them to express the idea that she can maintain her most important relationships while going through big changes in her personality. She is also integrating the personality changes into her "inner family and friends," the aspects of herself that already exist in harmony within her. She's building a relationship with what Lucifer represents about herself.

The dream builds atop esoteric and occult associations with Lucifer. Plus, the dreamer views him as a sympathetic character in human history, as "the light bringer" like Prometheus, who stole fire from the gods and gave it to humans because he felt sorry for them living in the cold dark. Similarly, Lucifer taught humans how to enlighten themselves through esoteric and occult practices, contrary to the jealous, Old Testament god who, to keep humans powerless and in the dark, forbade the practices.

Now we see personal empowerment as a layer of meaning to the dreamer's thoughts about intercourse with her new husband. The penis is a symbol of power and virility. When she anticipates what he's got *down there* and whether she can handle it, she's really wondering how far she can go in her empowerment.

A very different way of viewing Lucifer than the standard model, wouldn't you say? It illustrates the crucial importance of figuring out what your dream symbols mean personally. Dreams certainly can and do use common associations, but if that's the only lens you look through, you are bound to miss the meaning in many dreams.

In a dream like the one above that features a wedding, the dreamer is in the wedding party and waiting for the groom, Lucifer, to arrive. She's responsible for decorating the wedding cake. It's shaped like a ruined building, and the dreamer puts the icing on it, enacting the meaning of the metaphor "icing on the cake." It's popularly thought of as meaning the final step of a process, the thing that solidifies a person's thoughts, feelings, perceptions, and motivations—or think of it as "the last straw."

The last straw for the dreamer is what she perceives as the intolerance of religious bigots, especially toward gays and queers. By contrast, Lucifer is, in her view, accepting of everyone. A wedding is a celebration where diverse groups come together in harmony, and that's the idea the dream means by creating a wedding scene. The cake is made to look like a ruined building to symbolize the dreamer's changing belief structure—a building is a structure, after all. The belief structure of intolerance will be *eaten* by her new belief structure of acceptance and diversity, symbolized as Lucifer's wedding party.

> **Lucifer is, in her view, accepting of everyone. A wedding is a celebration where diverse groups come together in harmony, and that's the idea the dream means by creating a wedding scene.**

The above examples demonstrate the wide range of personal associations that dreams use to create the symbolism of Lucifer. Far from being dark dreams, they are enlightening and playful. On the flip side are dreams that play on the dark and bad associations: Lucifer the deceiver, the killer, the archenemy, the ruler of Hell, the nemesis of God, and the face of ultimate evil. Before giving examples of dreams that create symbolism and stories from those associations, be forewarned that the first one is super graphic. Here it is:

In the dream, a teenager is in bed, lying on his side with Satan—another name for Lucifer—behind him. Satan rapes him anally, then digs poop out of his rectum and smears it on his face. The dreamer returns the favor by rubbing poop in Satan's face. The awful situation driving this dream is the dreamer's flame war with a classmate. They say and do terrible things to each other and "rub it in each other's faces," a meaning enacted in the dream by rubbing poop in each other's faces. The dreamer is locked in a struggle with hate and vengeance, two popular associations with Satan, and rape is a dramatization of how he feels about it.

"Living hell" is the association one woman's dream uses to express her fear of getting pregnant. In the dream, she thinks her boyfriend crawls into bed with her, but it's really Satan, and by the time she realizes that, she's already in his clutches. She feels his erection enter her and can do nothing to stop it. But at the same time, it has a strange pull on her, and she doesn't want to stop—she enjoys it but is scared out of her mind that she'll get pregnant. And that's the truth the dream dramatizes. She enjoys sex with her boyfriend but is scared to death she'll get pregnant, making her life a living hell. When her boyfriend gets into bed with her, so does her fear, symbolized as Satan.

Pregnant with Lucifer's baby—it's among the most common themes that women experience in "Lucifer dreams," and fear of pregnancy is a common cause of them. It subjectively characterizes their thoughts and feelings about the prospect of pregnancy. The ante raises when they are pregnant and don't want to be, and it's like a parasite taking over their body. Lucifer is parasitic, feeding on the life of the host. Women who get pregnant when they don't want to be are prone to having dreams about being in the grip of something destructive and evil. Their life is no longer their own, taken over by an unstoppable power. Lucifer is a symbol that gives the dream author a rich story theme

Women dreaming of being impregnated by Lucifer are a common theme and could represent a fear of being pregnant and becoming a mother.

for speaking about things we can't control. And if a pregnant woman considers having an abortion but is torn by religious conflicts, oh, boy, do her dreams respond!

"Something bad has gotten into me" is another idea that being pregnant with Lucifer's baby conveys. Whatever the bad thing is, it has associations with Lucifer. For example, the desire for vengeance grows inside of a person in a bad way. Trauma and repressed emotions grow and take on a life of their own, like Lucifer's baby growing inside of them.

Dreaming about possession by Lucifer conveys similar ideas. At its simplest, it means that something bad has gotten into the person, and it must be awfully bad because Lucifer is the worst. But dreams exaggerate and dramatize, so it's not always a worst-case scenario. Psychosis, mental and emotional illness, spiritual darkness, and life-threatening diseases and conditions are the worst. But it may simply be a foul mood that possesses the person or a temptation—after all, Lucifer is the master tempter and the one in mythology who persuades humans to defy God and indulge in the pleasures of the flesh, and dreams love metaphors that express the paradoxes of life. Lucifer is, in a sense, the big middle finger raised at authority and the restrictions it imposes, especially religious authority.

It's a different story, though, if the dreamer reacts with happiness about the possession or is happy about being pregnant with Lucifer's baby. It may indicate that a benign or good association is the basis of the symbolism—for example, a powerful idea or feeling is brewing inside of the person; they are standing up for themselves; they are forming their own ideas about life, morality, and spirituality. But the association could be subjectively good and not objectively so, like when possession means that the person has given up a struggle against something dark, gaining relief from tension at the expense of losing the ego power to make their own decisions. The discussion in the Possession entry offers more insight about this subject.

Outside of religious circles, you don't find as many nightmares and dark dreams that use Lucifer in a classic or biblical way. But the story is very different for people on the path of righteousness and deep spiritual devotion! In their dreams, Lucifer and his minions use endless tricks, traps, ploys, and assaults to break down their convictions and lead them astray. The spiritual warfare of their daytime lives continues and even intensifies in their dreams.

Take, for instance, the dream a pastor had where he's alone inside the church he leads. Soon, his congregants will arrive for services, and he's terrified because he senses Lucifer's presence inside the church. He rebukes Lucifer and hears diabolical laughter in response. Following the sound to the altar, he sees a little girl in a white dress, the image of purity and innocence. But her eyes tell a different story with their coldness, and a righteous fury rises in him. He yells, "Be gone, Satan!" and the girl's mocking laughter fills the church. The volume of his voice increases. "This is God's house!"

Just then, he hears the first congregants enter the front doors of the church. Like lambs, they are easy targets for the wolf, he thinks. Lucifer senses his fear, delighting her. "I'll be back, priest. Or, maybe, I never left." The girl then vanishes, and the pastor quickly pastes a serene countenance over his troubled one so he can greet his flock.

> **Outside of religious circles, you don't find as many nightmares and dark dreams that use Lucifer in a classic or biblical way.**

When trouble enters a spiritual community, it can be like a thief in the night. And when church members and leaders dream about the trouble, they may encounter images of spiritual evil. The dream author may choose Lucifer over other characters to play the role when the trouble is especially insidious and diabolical. But in the above dream, the trouble is within the pastor, not his church.

The church setting symbolizes his role in life as the leader of a spiritual community, and the setting inside the church means *inside of himself*. The crux of his inner conflict is found in his belief that he must present a perfect image to his congregation—the image of purity, symbolized as Lucifer disguised as the little girl. He fears that failing to find and remove any fault or imperfection within himself will open the door to spiritual evil using him to get to his congregants, which the dream shows as the congregants entering the church while he's still trying to banish Lucifer. The little girl's statement that "maybe I never left" means that the pastor can't banish something that's part of himself. He can suppress it for a time, make it disappear temporarily, but not forever.

The dream is not saying that anything is evil about himself or his church. His fear of hidden evil in himself is the real source.

Fear—it's the source of many nightmares, and the dream author has countless ways of symbolizing it. When fear is the meaning behind Lucifer as a symbol, you feel it, and the dream's content reflects it. Work backward by thinking like a storyteller and figuring out why the dream chooses Lucifer as a symbol for fear. Fear of the unknown is a biggie—for all that we know about the mythology of Lucifer, most people can't say for sure whether or not it's a real entity. Tragedy is another fear; it strikes seemingly randomly, but we wonder if we've done something to deserve it—is it cosmic punishment? Dr. Carl Jung summed up the idea as "the uncalled-for God," a supernatural force that enters our lives unbidden and unwelcome. We love it when God is on our side and life is blessed and hate it when life goes terribly wrong.

Enter Lucifer, who revels in ruin. He is a character for dreams that reflect our sense of something unseen working against us. Where are the places within us where our own darkness and ignorance can lay traps and spoil our plans? Where is the trickster in the shadows, pointing its finger with a smirk that says, *Look inside of you, for I am here and you will deal with me, like it or not!*? Like the biblical Job, we may not recognize ourselves as the cause of our sorrows. And, like Job, try as we might to control our destiny, bad things still happen to good people, and we find ourselves on our knees and at the mercy of forces infinitely more powerful than us. Our dreams shine a light into those dark spaces.

> **Fear—it's the source of many nightmares, and the dream author has countless ways of symbolizing it.**

See also: Armageddon, Dark Magicians, Demons, Devils, Evil, Falling, Pennywise the Clown, Possession, Slenderman, Snakes

Epilogue

Steve Rogat wears button-down shirts and jeans instead of animal hides and bird feathers, but beneath the clothing, he's cut from the same cloth as the shamans who practice their craft in the jungles, forests, and deserts. He's from Long Island and talks like it, with a salty and playful sense of humor, and he's the person you turn to when no one else can help. It's how I ended up in his home office outside of Raleigh, North Carolina. The evil man from my nightmares had struck again, and here I was, pushing 40 years old—30 years after the original nightmare—still trying to save my soul.

Steve enters your life when the time is right. The stars align. Or you get a referral, which in my case came from someone I was dating who knew me well enough to sense that my troubles were more than a big ego and bad personal habits. Finding her bottle of fine whiskey is the last thing I remember from the night before we broke up. I woke up in the morning with a smashed toe and a soon-to-be ex-girlfriend next to me in bed. She knew Steve because she went to him when no one else could help her say goodbye to the spirit of her husband—he died in an accident and left unfinished business. I wasn't big on shamans at the time, but when she told me the story about her deceased husband and wrote down Steve's name and number, something clicked. The time had come to find out what really haunted me.

People think that a nightmare ends when you wake up and that whatever power or force it wields extends no further than the dream space. Not always true. Some nightmares are so energetic, they alter reality and the dreamer. Somehow, the evil man who first appeared in the black car chasing me down the roads of my childhood neighborhood reached out and zapped me with bad juju in ordinary waking life. Knowing all the theories about the causes of nightmares was little help. I could easily identify them in my life: addiction, conflict, "personal demons." But they weren't the cause; they were the result. Something pulled the strings from behind the scenes, and my dreams called it the Dark Master.

How do you defeat a Dark Master? You employ one who works for the Light. That's Steve.

I told him my story: the first nightmare at 9 years old; the discovery of a family feud as the cause behind it; the cycles of addiction and despondency and the recurring presence of the Dark Master in my nightmares; his presence in the shadows of my waking life; the nightmare where I tried to kill him and he just laughed. I also shared something I suspected about my ancestors. Long ago, in the Highlands of Scotland, they massacred a rival clan. It would explain a family feud with hatred so powerful that it carried down through the generations to me.

When I finished, Steve "went upstairs" to consult with his spirit guides. Then, he said, "Your ancestors were not involved in the Massacre of Glencoe, but generations ago—maybe six or seven, who knows for sure—one of your ancestors seduced and stole the husband of a woman in a rival family. That woman swore revenge and paid a sorcerer to curse the women of your family line to marry tragic men. The sorcerer in your nightmares is the one who cast the curse. He died, but as a spirit, he's bound to the power he abused. He's bound to you."

If I could say "WTF?!" 100 different ways, that moment was perfect.

"Before you were born, you chose to take on the mission of ending the curse," Steve said, answering my "Why me?" question before it was asked. "The first time you were conceived—I see that your mom was young and probably didn't know she was pregnant—your body was female. That attracted the curse to you—it's against the women in your family line. But that pregnancy ended early in miscarriage. A year or two later, your mom got pregnant again, and that body is the one you're in now."

I didn't know about all that stuff, but I could say for sure that generations of women in my family had married tragic men, and I hadn't said a peep about it to Steve. My maternal grandma married five men—some of them violently abusive and hopelessly addicted—and she outlived them all. Her mom followed the tragic pattern, and so did my mom in her first marriage (my father wasn't abusive, but he drank heavily). And my sister—my nightmares about a demon inside of her body suddenly made sense. She wasn't married yet, but mysterious illnesses and health conditions plagued her, and in an indescribable way, it felt like we sought the same answers in life.

Holy crap!

I was about to ask Steve what could be done about it when he did the mind-reading thing again and answered my unspoken question: "We send the sorcerer into the Light."

At that point, most people would probably be wondering what in the world they'd gotten themselves into, but it made perfect sense to me.

Steve offered me a stool, and I sat down. On his office wall, I saw a poster of the human body and its energy systems. On his shelves sat figurines and crystals and tools for bodywork and magic. He played a recording of shamanic drumming and asked me to relax. Then, he went to work by applying healing energy to places in my body where I'd experienced traumas and mysterious aches and pains. He settled on the spot between my shoulder blades, behind my heart, where I ached the worst. I felt him working it while shaking a rattle and chanting. After a while, he said, "Oh, boy, this is a tough one. It doesn't want to come out. Jason, this pain can end now, but you must want it to happen. Let go!"

Beneath the knots, something bad had lodged near my spine, and I was holding on to it the same way that a body holds on to a parasite instead of killing it. I mustered my energy and lent it to the task, but it sensed us coming and burrowed deeper. Finally, Steve got a firm hold, and we concentrated with all our might. A moment passed. And another. And another, stalemated in a battle of wills. I couldn't walk away without a resolution. Surely, my life would soon be over.

Then, with a huge sigh of relief, it was done. Later, Steve shared with me that he had removed a metaphysical knife, black as a Nazgul blade, from my back. It acted as a beacon for the Dark Master, in his realm, to find me in this physical realm and zap me subconsciously through my feelings. It gave him a pathway to my heart's energy field—and it's why I'd tried so many times to help myself, to live in the Light, only to gradually and insidiously slip back into darkness. I was a maestro at screwing up my life, but boy, did I have help!

Mind. Blown.

"Now we can get to the source," Steve said. "Follow my lead. We're going where the Dark Master lives. And stay alert—he's a liar and will try anything to stop us."

Steve cranked up the juice, and together, our minds left physical reality. I don't know if we went up or down or sideways, but we were no longer only in his office. I sensed being in two places at once, in ordinary reality and simultaneously beyond it. Soon, though, we hit a barrier that wouldn't give way; we opened the door only to find a brick wall. Years of sporadic meditation practice and visualization training helped me maintain my concentration, but strain and fatigue threatened to derail me. Doubt entered my mind. What if we shook the hornet's nest but couldn't finish the job?

Steve implored, "Look up—the funnel cloud. It's not after you—it wants *him*!"

For years, I'd had terrifying nightmares about a funnel cloud hunting me. And suddenly, it appeared; in my mind's eye, I saw myself inside it, surrounded by swirling, churning clouds of energy. I looked up. The freaking *Eye of Providence* stared down—not just an image but a living presence—and the truth split open the sky and thundered down: the funnel hunted the Dark Master, not me, and God had showed up during my hour of greatest need! I didn't tell Steve ahead of time about my tornado nightmares—he saw them as if they were his own. He is a master of the dream world, as shamans are trained to be.

I felt a channel open directly to the Dark Master. Suddenly, he appeared, in whatever reality he inhabited. He wanted me to hate him—to despise him! He sent pictures into my mind of the generations of my family he'd harmed and destroyed. He delighted in the torment we all suffered. So much pain.

I had every right to hate him. During the nightmare, when I found him in his fortress, when I stood over his coffin and tried to strangle the life out of him, I sensed what he'd done. It made me rage. And suddenly, I understood that you can't kill what's already dead—that's why in my nightmares, I found him in a coffin, and his body looked cadaverous. He was dead but somehow still alive.

This time, I came prepared with the training to think my way through it. My mentor, Larry Pesavento, discussed the *Star Wars* mythology with me many times during our sessions. Anger is Luke Skywalker's weakness, and the Dark Lord exploits it. But an antidote exists, and as I teetered on the edge of giving in to rage, I remembered what Larry taught me. He'd prepared me for this one crucial moment, as if he knew one day that I'd face it. This was the day.

I thought of all the people in my family who had suffered because of the Dark Master. I thought of my pain and the 30 years that I'd fought for my life—fought for my soul. Oh, I wanted to rage—to get my hands on that neck again and finish the job, but Jesus said to pray for your enemies. It activates a force that makes things right. I said:

"I forgive you. In the name of my family, I forgive you. Now—go into the Light!"

Energy surged from below me. With Steve's help, I channeled it up my spine and focused it above my head, where the Eye looked down. Then, a pyramid of light formed around my body, with the Eye at its peak. The suction pulled the Dark Master up, up, and away, into the Eye, and then, it was gone.

Steve clapped his hands once—the loudest clap I've ever heard. And it was done. I was free.

***

Is the Dark Master more than a nightmare figure? I've asked myself that question 10,000 times and promised in the Prologue that I'd answer it for you. I'm well acquainted with the therapeutic techniques for working with dream imagery and the theories and data about what causes nightmares. And now, after my sessions with Steve and a dozen years of exploration and practice, I know the places that shamans call "Other Realms" and the astral planes, but I prefer the term "imaginal." Imaginal means a place accessed through imagination, but it's not imaginary. Our physical eyes see outward, and our mind's eye sees inward. Both directions stretch for infinity, and both are equally real.

The Dark Master is real. That's how I had to understand him in order to have any chance of ridding him from my life. I don't know if Steve's narrative about a family curse is true in the strictest sense. Shamans work with our narratives to create a space for healing. The fruit of the tree is all that matters. In the imaginal realms, all of Creation is understood and *experienced* as a unified field of consciousness, and *everything* is an aspect of consciousness. Everything—including the Dark Master.

Behind every sorcerer is the same shadow manifestation of an archetype that convinces people to abuse the mind's powers. Dr. Carl Jung says that psyche and matter are opposite poles of a spectrum, and when you journey to the bottom of the psyche, you find yourself in matter, in physical reality. It's the premise of the ancient philosophy of panpsychism and a basis for the power we call magic.

But during my inner journeys, I heard hints that more existed to the story about what would make me the Dark Master's prize if he could claim me. Knowing it for myself, though, proved to be the hardest lesson of all. When I looked at him in my nightmares, I saw an "other," someone separate from me. But a fundamental lesson in dream psychology is that everything you encounter in your dreams somehow leads back to you. The hint that came to me through intuition—which is the counterpart to reason—is that I see myself in the Dark Master.

I am him, and he is me.

He may be a sorcerer bound to me and my ancestors through use of black magic, or maybe not. Doesn't matter—I had to lay claim to him and take responsibility if I was to ever resolve the division.

The Dark Master first appeared in my nightmare to claim my soul, and at the time, as a 9-year-old, I didn't know what the soul was but did know that it was the most fundamental thing about who I was. Take my soul away, and I no longer exist. Not only do I die, I lose my essence. I become him and no longer exist. That's the fundamental difference between ownership by taking responsibility and possession by denying it.

That last sentence is the crux of understanding nightmares.

And now, friends, we come to another crux, the terrible truth. I am complicit. If I had no darkness within me, the Dark Master would have nothing to work with—and since darkness is an aspect of the Cosmos, it's within us all. My nightmares about the Dark Master made it clear that I have a choice, and it's the most important one of my life. I could have been that man who serves the Dark Side—serves only himself—and it grants him the illusion of possessing power. Already, by the time I met the dream analyst in 7th grade, the allure pulled me in. The teacher who invited the analyst—thank you, Mr. Whitmore—caught me reading a book about witchcraft and chanting the spells in German. Just goofing off, I thought, but he sensed the darkness gathering around me. He may have saved me—saved my very soul—by intervening the best way he knew how: pointing me to my dreams and planting a seed that took decades to grow and mature.

The Dark Master entered my nightmares and stared me full in the face because if I was to go down that path and be that guy, I would do it consciously, knowing the stakes. No excuses, no pleading innocence. Him claiming my soul meant *my* choice to become a Dark Master. Even now, as I write these words, my ego grasps at the prospect of wielding power, of *being* power that most people have no clue exists.

But thankfully, I had my Yoda, my mentor Larry, who taught me the fundamental difference between the power of the Dark and the power of the Light. And I had my Obi-Wan, Steve, who taught me how to use my power responsibly. When you serve the Dark, you serve yourself and simultaneously lose yourself. When you serve the Light, The Force, it works through you but isn't you, and by knowing and living the difference, you preserve and expand yourself by knowing who, and *what*, you really are. The choice is laughably easy to make but gaining the right perspective to truly understand the choice is, for me at least, the hardest thing to overcome.

And thankfully, I also had my friends and loved ones, especially my mom, who brought out my good side and instilled in me the ethics and morality of sharing and caring. And my dad, who rode to the rescue more than once when my ship was sinking.

My nightmares were a blessing in disguise. They led me to seek healing and answers, which led me to study and explore dreams, which led me to my calling in life—and to my greatness. And I did it while saving my soul.

Index

Note: (ill. indicates photos and illustrations.

Index

Index